Contents

Wilbert R. Shenk

The practice of mission originated with the people of Israel in the intertestamental period. Jesus criticized the particular form this mission took over time—but he retained mission itself, transfiguring it and calling his disciples to continue his mission to the whole world. This is the normative model of mission for the disciple community.

Wilbert R. Shenk

The work of Jesus the Messiah embodies the *missio Dei*. This is normative for all mission and must determine the character, strategy, and stance of mission in our contemporary world. This allows for neither triumphalism nor defeatism. It calls for missionary witness that embraces the fullness of the gospel in response to the times in which we live.

David A. Shank

The missionary task is best understood through the work of Jesus the Servant Messiah, through whom God fulfills his redemptive mission to the whole world. The life, death, resurrection, and exaltation of Jesus inaugurate the messianic dynamic in its essential meaning. It is this work and revelation, the dynamic of God's saving love, that motivated the early church to follow the Messiah in continuing that mission.

The work of the Messiah is identified with the kingdom or reign of God. Messiah came to inaugurate God's new order in the midst of a world that remains unreconciled to God. Jesus the Messiah began his ministry by identifying with God's realm. His teaching, especially in the Sermon on the Mount, and his actions interpreted and applied the meaning of the kingdom.

The Holy Spirit continues the Messiah's work in the world between Pentecost and parousia, convicting of sin, converting the repentant, and creating the messianic community. The Spirit empowers the messianic community for witness and leads it in facing and overcoming the forces of evil.

The church is the called-out community. It consists of those who have responded to Messiah's invitation to join God's new order. As such, the church is the firstfruits of the new creation, an earnest of the final consummation. The church is also the instrument of witness and service in the world according to the pattern and spirit of the Messiah.

The Bible portrays a drama being played out in the world. The world represents those forces opposed to God. The mission is carried into the heart of this conflict. God loves the world and responds redemptively to it in the work of Jesus and the messianic community.

The Transfiguration of
MISSION

BIBLICAL
THEOLOGICAL
&HISTORICAL
FOUNDATIONS

Institute of Mennonite Studies (IMS)
Missionary Studies, No. 12

Edited by
WILBERT R. SHENK

HERALD PRESS
Scottdale, Pennsylvania
Waterloo, Ontario

Library of Congress Cataloging-in-Publication Data
The transfiguration of mission : biblical, theological, and historical
foundations / edited by Wilbert R. Shenk
    p. cm. — (Missionary studies : no. 12)
    Includes bibliographical references and index.
    ISBN 0-8361-3610-1
    1. Missions—Theory. I. Shenk, Wilbert R. II. Series.
BV2063.T73 1993   92-37009
266'.001—dc20   CIP

The paper used in this publication is recycled and meets the minimum requirements of American National Standard for Information Sciences—
Permanence of Paper for Printed Library Materials, ANSI Z39.48-1984.

THE TRANSFIGURATION OF MISSION
Copyright © 1993 by Herald Press, Scottdale, Pa. 15683
    Published simultaneously in Canada by Herald Press,
    Waterloo, Ont. N2L 6H7. All rights reserved
Library of Congress Catalog Number: 92-37009
International Standard Book Number: 0-8361-3610-1
Printed in the United States of America
Book design by Gwen M. Stamm

1 2 3 4 5 6 7 8 00 99 98 97 96 95 94 93

Preface

T HIS VOLUME is the fruit of several years of collaborative work. Indeed, its origins go back to 1975. When several of the present contributors first explored the potential of a fresh approach to the theology of mission from the standpoint of the messianic dynamic.

In 1989 four of these chapters were presented at the annual Overseas Missions Seminar, Mennonite Board of Missions, and in 1990 four more were presented at the same forum. In July 1990 the writers met for two days to work through the chapters before each writer prepared a final draft.

The project has been made possible through the financial support of Mennonite Board of Missions.

Introduction

Wilbert R. Shenk

A S W E C O M E to the end of the second millennium since Jesus the Messiah appeared on this earth, we hear intense criticism of the Christian mission, especially as it has been carried out over the past five centuries. It is well to recall that missionary action has always been subject to criticism and has frequently been the center of controversy.

Mission did not originate with Jesus the Messiah. A missionary tradition was established within Judaism before Jesus. The importance the rabbis placed on the proselyte is evident in the Talmud. The rabbis were enthusiastic about the prospect of winning proselytes from among the *goyim*, in fulfillment of the vision of the nations learning to worship Yahweh.[1]

In his criticism of the Pharisees, Jesus included a sharp attack on this proselytizing mission, "for you traverse sea and land to make a single proselyte, and when he becomes a proselyte, you make him twice as much a child of hell as yourselves" (Matt. 23:15, RSV). Jesus did not reject the mission. Rather he denounced the Pharisees for replicating in their converts the same legalism they themselves practiced (Matt. 23:2-7).

Such religion reinforced ethical behavior that ratified the status quo rather than transforming unjust sociopolitical structures and mores that had been roundly condemned by the prophets. Instead of calling people to true worship of God, they fixed attention on a religious system. There is a piety that is outwardly correct but lacking in godly compassion. At this point, Jesus' attack on the religious leaders is consistent with the prophetic tradition of the Old Testament. The true test of religion is whether the people of God practice justice and live righteously. This is measured concretely by the way the socially powerless—widow, orphan, and alien (Jer. 7:5-7; 22:3; Mic. 6:8)—are treated. Religion which does not result in justice and righteousness falls under the judgment of God.

Jesus the Messiah did not reject mission; he transfigured it. Soon after selecting his twelve associates, Jesus dispatched them on missions with the instruction to do what he had been doing. They were to announce that the kingdom of God was at hand and confront and repel evil powers—thus liberating the oppressed, healing the sick, and inviting all people to repent and turn toward God (Matt. 10:1, 7-8). The mission of the disciples was to be characterized by vulnerability and dependence on the people among whom they served (10:9-11). Jesus enlisted the disciples fully in his mission of introducing the reign of God.

Mission is always at risk of being distorted or misdirected. Over time the Jewish mission had become deformed; but this model of mission was to exert considerable influence on the understanding of mission of the earliest followers of Jesus. Within the original Christian community, a momentous struggle developed between the Judaizers and the party of Paul. The only kind of mission that made sense to the Judaizers was that modeled on the earlier Jewish mission. Paul struggled mightily against this understanding on grounds that it negated the gospel of Jesus the Messiah.

Down through the centuries, mission has continued to be at risk. We have already noted how Jesus condemned the making of proselytes. Starting in the fourth century C.E., methods based on coercion began to be used in gaining adherents. This particular deformation was a direct result of the alliance between church and state initiated by the Emperor Constantine.

Whenever the church has accommodated itself to the controls of culture, it has lost its sense of being in the stream of Messiah's mission. Such accommodation usually means that a particular worldview—such as modernity—rather than Messiah's message, has become dominant for the church in its mission.

In short, there is never a time when Messiah's mission is not at risk. The scene of mission is the world. In a changing world, the messianic community must continually discern the path of faithfulness.

In our quest for greater effectiveness in mission, we must avoid what has been called "the fallacy of misplaced concreteness." Is not the purpose of mission to extend the church, the body of Christ, in the world? Does not this call us to concentrate on the growth of the church?

The answer seems so obvious—but it is spurious. If we emphasize the church instead of focusing on Jesus Christ, we have misplaced our loyalty. This fallacy sets us up to proselytize, that is, merely to win more people to our side. Keeping attention fixed on Jesus the Messiah does not diminish the importance of the church; rather, it recognizes that the church must continually draw on its head for life and direction. The grand purpose of mission is that the world might encounter the living God revealed in Jesus the Messiah (cf. R. Allen, 1913: chap. 2).

Repeatedly throughout history, messianic resurgences have renewed the meaning of obedience to the mission of Jesus the Messiah for the disciple community and for the world. One thinks of movements such as the Lollards, the Waldensians, the Czech Brethren, the Anabaptists, the Moravian Brethren, the Pietists, and the Wesleyans. All arose on the margins of the church and were rejected by church leaders. These movements sought the renewal of the church through new encounter with the gospel and are responsible for fresh creativity in the church's ministry to the world. The Pietist-Wesleyan movements in the seventeenth and eighteenth centuries set in motion much of the missionary and philanthropic work that followed in the eighteenth and nineteenth centuries.

Today we are being prodded to "complete the evangelization of the world by the year 2000."[2] The very phrasing invokes shades of the Christendom tradition—a tradition established through the forced conversion of entire groups of peoples and held intact through the coercive powers of state and church controlling the whole of life. There is no disputing the urgent need for evangelization in this generation, but we must reject any implicit note of cultural triumphalism. We must not think it in our power to complete the task within a particular time frame or according to a particular methodology.

> This calls for a theology of mission that makes the mission of Jesus Messiah the *sine qua non* of the nature and purpose of the church. The theology of mission should be integral to the entire theological enterprise. This posits the normative relationship of church to world to be that of missionary witness as modeled by Jesus the Messiah.

In the twentieth century the Christian churches—and the missionary movement by extension—have been plagued by reductionisms that put limits on the scope of the gospel. This has resulted from the way Christians have reacted to the challenge of modernity, especially as expressed through modernism and fundamentalism. This has produced dichotomies that divide the gospel into component parts so that some groups emphasize proclamation (the Word) while others advocate witness through compassionate service (the deed).

Increasingly it has come to be acknowledged that both extremes, however earnestly and honestly held, diminish the scope and power of the gospel. But the practical effects of this earlier conflict continue to be felt, even in those churches which did not subscribe consciously to either extreme.

> An adequate theology of mission must be faithful to the fullness of the gospel. Only a theology based on the kingdom of God present and coming, led by God's Messiah, is capable of holding the whole together.

Western theology has weakened the force of the gospel message by drawing a distinction between evangelism and ethics. This has created a situation in which gospel, the basis of evangelization, has been emptied of its ethical content, while ethics are severed from the foundational message of the gospel. Thus the evangelist is expected to preach about Jesus Christ who will forgive sins and restore to right relationship with God; but Christian ethics have been dominated by the idea that the life and teachings of Jesus—especially as found in the Sermon on the Mount—cannot possibly have been intended as the basis for ethical guidance. This distinction reaches a particularly crucial point when questions of violence, unjust and oppressive systems, and warfare must be considered.

The missionary task is to invite men and women into a new kind of community, one in which even enemies can be reconciled. The mandate is to go to all nations. Thus the new community by definition consists of people drawn together under the leadership of the Suffering Messiah regardless of race or nationality, forging a new allegiance that supersedes all other loyalties. It is urgent that Christians reclaim the unity of evangel and ethics as we witness in a world divided by nationalism, classism, racism, and religious loyalties.

> The goal of mission is the establishment of God's new order in which righteousness, justice, and peace dwell. The gospel of peace is nothing less than the vision of shalom into which God invites all people. The gospel is not first of all a program but an invitation to new relationship within a new order of reality. Evangel and ethics are not opposites or even

separable parts but an identity which is the basis of both missionary witness and discipleship.

Various mission models have been employed over the past two millennia. All reflect the socioeconomic and political contexts in which they arose. The gospel inevitably will be carried in earthen vessels. But this history teaches us that each model has also been based on a particular understanding of the nature of the gospel. A Christendom gospel had no capacity for being self-critical of crusades and campaigns, for the church was viewed as intrinsically a part of the accepted sociopolitical order. Sects that understand the gospel to call for a radical withdrawal from the world weaken their authority to challenge a society by their negation of society. The model of mission established by Jesus the Messiah is the prototype for all faithful mission.

> Mission is a continuation of the narrative, begun with the calling out of Abraham, continued through the people of God in the Old Testament, transfigured by Jesus, and mandated to be extended by his messianic community under the leadership of the Holy Spirit throughout time to the ends of the earth.

Jesus the Messiah took an existing form of mission and transfigured it. Proselyting cannot be the means of transforming men and women into the likeness of Jesus himself. Proselyting represents to us human efforts that deform mission. Much of the criticism that has been made of missionary work, especially during the modern period, is directed against deformed mission practices. The argument put forward here is that mission in every generation is at risk because of the temptation to resort to methods and tactics that produce proselytes, on the one hand, or rely on various forms of coercion, on the other.

As we approach the beginning of the third millennium since Jesus the Messiah, and as we ask what the outline of the missionary task will be in the future, we believe we must turn again to the source of mission: the God who creates and redeems as revealed in the work of Jesus Messiah.

What will authentic mission modeled by Messiah mean for the community concerned to follow obediently its Messiah leader in a world of ever-widening chasms? What is authentic mission in a world with rifts widening between rich and poor, social classes and ethnic groups; a world of exhausted modernity and threatening technologies; a world driven by the relentless quest for power by all sorts of special interests; a world wanting to be reassured that there is an anchor but increasingly unable to have faith and hope?

Amid the extremisms of the day, the erosion of the past, and the uncertainties of the future, the messianic community is privileged to bear witness to the life-transforming power of the reign of God which alone can make "all things new."

Notes

1. Bernard J. Bamberger concludes, "We have seen that both in Palestine and Babylonia, throughout the entire space of time considered, despite the fall of the state, despite persecution, despite the rise of Christianity, the Rabbis wanted converts and got them—and held them. Their success in the face of such discouraging odds is the best proof of their missionary ardor, and of the warm welcome which proselytes received" (1968:291). Richard R. De Ridder devotes a chapter to "Jewish Proselytism" in his important study (1975:88-127). See also Braude (1940).

2. See the review of such plans in Barrett and Reapsome (1988).

References Cited

Allen, Roland
  1913 *Missionary Principles*. Grand Rapids, Mich.: Wm. B. Eerdmans, reprinted 1964.

Bamberger, Bernard J.
  1968 *Proselytism in the Talmudic Period*. New York: KTAV Publishing House (first ed. 1939).

Barrett, David B., and James W. Reapsome
  1988 *Seven Hundred Ways to Evangelize the World: The Rise of a Global Evangelization Movement*. Birmingham: New Hope Publishers.

Braude, William G.
  1940 *Jewish Proselyting in the First Five Centuries of the Common Era—The Age of the Tannaim and Amoraim*. Providence, R.I.: Brown University.

De Ridder, Richard R.
  1975 *Discipling the Nations*. Grand Rapids, Mich.: Baker Book House (reprinted 1971 ed.).

The Transfiguration of
MISSION

CHAPTER 1

The Relevance of a Messianic Missiology for Mission Today

Wilbert R. Shenk

IN THE SUCCEEDING CHAPTERS it will be argued that the faithful stance of the messianic community in the world is that of missionary witness. The basis for this stance is the work of Jesus the Messiah. The essential meaning of the messiahship of Jesus was that he was sent into the world in the name of the Father and in the power of the Spirit for the salvation of the world.

The mission of the triune God has been thrown into bold relief in Jesus the Messiah. Authentic discipleship, therefore, entails missionary encounter with the world. As the first epistle of John puts it, "as he is so are we in this world" (1 John 4:17b).[1] The disciple living in companionship with Jesus the Messiah must ineluctably be drawn into the passion of the triune God for the salvation of the world.

The Missiological Task

The term *missiology* has come into use in English rather recently. Although used in Europe much earlier, it was not accepted in Anglo-American circles until about 1960. Traditionally, the preferred terms were *philosophy of missions* or *science of missions*. The plural form *missions* was used almost exclusively until International Missionary Council discussions of the *missio Dei* in the 1950s established the point that the mission of the triune God is prior to all else.[2] There is only one mission; the countless missions on which Christians have been sent over the course of nearly two millenia are but responses to that one decisive *mission*. Failure to grasp this point opens the way to a false sense of self-responsibility and autonomy. The authority for all missionary action is the *missio Dei*. Our efforts and actions must be submitted to the priority of God's missional purpose.

The Function of Missiology

Mission denotes action: being sent with a commission to perform a certain task, acting in the name of a superior, carrying out an important mandate, serving as ambassador on behalf of one's leader. It is not a specifically religious term. It is used by military, government, business, and many other secular groups.

Missiology is the formal study of the Christian mission, including the biblical and theological foundation of mission; the history of the course taken by the missions; analysis of the contemporary context; and a discernment of social, political, economic, and religious trends that will influence the direction of mission in the future. In other words, to do its work properly, missiology must keep four aspects continually in view: the normative, the historical, the present, and the future. In this book we are concerned largely with the first aspect, but that concern arises from a particular historical and theological awareness.

The Historical Context

As writers we are keenly aware of being products of the twentieth century. Further, our roots are in Europe and North America—the so-called West—the center of several centuries of pervasive and relentless intellectual, industrial, political, and social development which has spread round the world, unleashing the forces of modernity. On the one hand, this powerful expansive movement has led to imperial extension by the West into much of the rest of the world. On the other hand, it helped generate two world wars fought by the leading industrial and political powers, not to mention numerous other military conflicts. The twentieth century has been a period of unrelieved tension and of fast-paced change on many fronts. Powerful ideologies with messianic pretensions have overshadowed and imposed themselves on this century. The Cold War, 1945-1989, cast a pall over much of the last half of the twentieth century.

Missions and Christendom

Although the end of Christendom as a historical reality cannot be dated precisely, its imminent collapse has been remarked by careful observers over the past century. Christendom originated in the fourth century when the successors to Emperor Constantine gave to Christianity official standing and outlawed its rivals.[3] This change of status fundamentally altered the position of the church in society. From being a marginal, socially inferior, and economically weak group, the church became one of the dominant institutions in society. It acquired immense wealth and political power linked with a strong sense of *territoriality*. From being an oppressed minority, the church now became an oppressor, enabled by its alliance with the political and military authorities to coerce the unwilling to become "believers." Without this fundamental change in the identity of the church there could have been no Christendom.

Within recent centuries, however, two phenomena have contributed to the collapse of Christendom. The first was the Enlightenment. From the late seventeenth century onward, it set in motion intellectual and political forces that undermined the privileged position of the church in the West. The Enlightenment had released into Western culture dynamic forces marked by abounding confidence in the capacity of human reason to overcome all obstacles to progress.[4] This movement held the whole world and all aspects of life within its purview. Along the way many old structures and systems came under heavy bombardment from Enlightenment forces and were eventually destroyed.

Religion was a special target. The Enlightenment movement was confident of its destiny to ensure the progress of the whole human race. Modern missions were born in this environment. In some respects missions were a counteraction to the Enlightenment, especially in their attempt to extend the influence of the Christian faith. In other respects modern missions were carriers of Enlightenment values throughout the world: the superiority of Western culture, the spirit of progress, and the rationalistic view of life. In the West the authority of religion declined steadily from the nineteenth century onward.

The second phenomenon which contributed directly to the collapse of Christendom was the modern mission movement which patiently and persistently pursued an initiative without precedent in the history of the church. Aided by advances in transportation and communication—direct fruits of scientific knowledge—missions followed a vision of reaching the whole world with the Christian message. The movement has had as its goal the extension of the body of Christ to every tribe and nation throughout the world. This action decisively breached the boundaries of historic Christendom.

Symbolically, modern missions may be dated from 1792 when the English Baptist cobbler-preacher, William Carey, published *An Enquiry into the Obligation of Christians to Use Means for the Conversion of the Heathens* and, prodded by Carey and his sympathizers, the Baptists founded a missionary society that same year. Over the next thirty years, many other groups in Great Britain, Europe, and North America would emulate this step. This set a pattern that continued to be followed by one group after another throughout the next two hundred years.

Two centuries later we can say, quite simply, that this movement has changed the face of the Christian church worldwide. In 1800, seven years after the Carey family had arrived in India, an estimated 86 percent of all Christians in the world were white Europeans. By 2000 at least 60 percent of all Christians will be found in Asia, Africa, and Latin America. While this unprecedented movement outward was going on, the church in the West—the heartland of Christendom for nearly 1,500 years—was losing strength spiritually and numerically. The implications of this historical shift are still not widely understood and appreciated by Christians in the West. Its meaning will become inescapably clearer as we move into the twenty-first century.

The modern mission movement has come in for its share of criticism, particularly from two sources—those within the family of faith who are members of churches which are themselves the fruit of missions, and those beyond the Christian family.

The first group asserts that the church in the West, including Western missions, has compromised them and the Christian message by an uncritical hand-in-glove alliance with Western political, economic, and military power. In other words, the Christendom version of the Christian faith has proved to be nonexportable and is a historical embarrassment.

The other class of critics, largely unsympathetic to the Christian faith and its mission—and not without considerable hypocrisy—scores missions for cultural and religious imperialism. In this regard missions, lacking critical distance from their sending cultures, were only continuing to play the role assigned by Christendom.

As we look back on some three centuries of the modern project which has reshaped the world so decisively, we are increasingly aware of how ambiguous "modernity" and "progress" have proved to be.

Modernity introduced influences that have penetrated every facet of human existence. Yet the Enlightenment, in spite of the enormous benefits it has brought to humankind, has been found impotent to deliver human beings from their morally crippling ego-centeredness. Every system or artifact human beings devise, regardless of all it promises to contribute to human welfare, is marked by human fallibility and is subject to manipulation for selfish ends. For example, capitalism, the dynamic economic engine which has provided the motive power for the modern period, has at its core and as a basic premise the pursuit of self-interest (i.e., the profit motive).

Modernization has forced the restructuring of traditional societies, shattering their network of social supports and controls. Life in the modern world demands mobility and individualization but results in anomie. The nuclear family has been placed under constant strain and the individual carries a heavy load while feeling alienated. Those who cannot cope and compete fall victim; those who serve the system by submitting to its dictates are rewarded.

The modern mission movement could not escape dealing with this Enlightenment worldview, whose influence pervaded all aspects of human endeavor in the West and spread inexorably throughout the world. In every age the church has had to contend with competitor claimants. Part of the censure of modern missions is that they, at worst, were confused as to which authority they were representing, or, at the least, left people around them confused. Did not they uncritically follow the flag of empire while protesting their allegiance to the cross? The dark shadow of Christendom considerably complicated the missionary's task by making it difficult to see the situation fully; but in the long run, Christendom itself could not survive in the crucible of mission.

The Situation at the End of the Twentieth Century

Historical overhang. Although the modern mission movement hastened the breakup of Christendom, we are left with the residue of that long history in terms of how we understand the church and its mission. Furthermore, with regard to ecclesiology, we have been poorly served by the theological guild which, particularly in the nineteenth century—the very period of the rise of modern missions—paid little attention to the nature and calling of the church (cf. Berkhof, 1979).[5]

Christendom as a system was predicated on coercion. Many of the tribes of Europe were "converted" to Christianity under duress. For this reason alone it is gratuitous to speak, as some now do, of the "reevangelization" of Europe or the West. Those who were the object of this "first evangelization" found themselves forcibly subjugated by a religiopolitical coalition.[6]

This is the antithesis of being evangelized. Once in the church, people were held in check by a range of sanctions. Baptism was a highly political act. The state collaborated with the church in maintaining this so-called Christian society, for it was in the interest of each to ensure that the entire population be citizens/members. In 1949 historian Herbert Butterfield celebrated the fact that for the first time in fifteen centuries in the West we might assume that no one needed to call themselves Christian because compelled to do so by government (1949:135).[7]

One implication of this religiopolitical arrangement was that there was no place for mission to the West, for the whole society was "Christian" by fiat. The church as a missionary presence in society was unthinkable, an anomaly to a corpus Christianum. Thus the church of Christendom was a church stripped of its missionary consciousness, prostituted by connivance between state and church hierarchy.[8]

But missionary impulses could not be suppressed altogether; semiautonomous monastic orders were allowed to engage in missionary work, pacifying those tribes and clans not yet incorporated fully into Christendom. From the fifteenth century, when several popes issued bulls authorizing the Portuguese and Spanish crowns to send expeditions of conquest of the rest of the world—with the stipulation that missionaries be included in the contingents—mission was understood to be an activity directed to peoples beyond the pale of Christendom.

This accounts for the way Christendom reformulated the church's understanding of mission; but there is yet another dimension to it. Stephen Neill (1968: esp. 71-75) has analyzed the way this religiopolitical reality worked itself out in official church statements where the nature of the church is defined. Once the church has surrendered its mission to its society, all that remains is a static and institutional understanding of the church. It is this static ecclesiology which became the foundation for the churches of the Reformation. Here we cite the relevant articles.

> **Augsburg Confession (1530):** Moreover, they teach that one holy Church is to remain in perpetuity. The Church is the congregation of the saints in which the Gospel is purely taught, and the sacraments are rightly administered.

Thirty-Nine Articles of Religion on the Church (XIX): The visible Church of Christ is a congregation of faithful men, in which the pure Word of God is preached, and the Sacraments be duly administered according to Christ's ordinance in all those things that of necessity are requisite to the same.

Heidelberg Catechism (1563): That out of the whole human race, from the beginning to the end of the world, the Son of God by his Spirit and word gathers, defends and preserves for himself unto everlasting life, an elect community in the unity of the true faith, and that I am, and forever shall remain, a living member of the same.

A Roman Catholic statement from late in the same century as these Lutheran, Anglican, and Reformed statements is that by Cardinal Bellarmine:

The Church is a company of men, bound together by the profession of the same Christian faith and the fellowship of the same sacraments, under the governance of legitimate pastors, and in particular of the one Vicar of Christ upon earth, the Bishop of Rome.

In one crucial respect these speak with one voice: All emphasize the *being* rather than the *function* of the church. At no point do they indicate the church is other than the means of preserving proper order and a fortress within which the faithful—or "elect community" (in a phrase from Heidelberg)—are protected and preserved. These authoritative declarations do little to help the church realize its calling to be the instrument of the Messiah's continuing mission to the world. Indeed, they betray no sense of responsibility to do so. The focus is decidedly inward; the emphasis is on control.

We have already examined the historical matrix which formed the mentality of which these documents are a fruit. Theological formulations are always conditioned by the time and place in which they are produced, whether that be in the sixteenth century or the twentieth.[9] But we must also recognize how far-reaching is the influence of such statements. The basic habits of thought reflected in these sixteenth-century statements have continued to be influential right up to the present. Free and Nonconformist churches were equally shaped by this mentality. Only in exceptional cases, such as that of the first generations of the Moravian Brethren in the eighteenth century, did anything approaching a genuinely missionary ecclesiology see the light of day.

By and large mission has remained peripheral to the vision most

Christians have of what the church is and ought to do in spite of the modern mission movement. It should come as no surprise that with the collapse of the structures of Christendom, on the one hand, and a failure to recover a missionary ecclesiology, on the other, the church in the West is a church in serious decline.

The period since 1945. In the years following World War II, a frequent theme in mission studies was "the crisis of missions." The crisis was genuine. The world system was forcibly reorganized in response to the global struggle between the two dominant systems—the capitalist led by the United States and the communist championed by the Soviet Union. This led to an arms race of unprecedented proportions between the superpowers which has consumed staggering amounts of precious resources at a time when the world's poor were sinking ever deeper into their poverty.

The rich nations became involved in development aid to the less developed countries, but by 1970 the "revolution of rising expectations" of the 1950s was judged largely to have failed. So-called development aid was viewed by the West primarily as a tool of foreign policy and as an opportunity to develop markets for domestic exports. By the 1980s the great ideological struggle was a spent force. In 1988 British Prime Minister Margaret Thatcher, an ideological conservative, on a visit to Washington, D.C., took stock of the rapid changes occurring in the USSR and Eastern Europe and declared "the Cold War is over."[10]

Not only was the Cold War over; the communist bloc was on the verge of breakup. In the months following, one country after the other went through economic and political upheaval. It remains far from clear what the new patterns will be. But the challenge raised by the seventeenth-century Enlightenment to feudalism and totalitarianism continues to inspire peoples the world over to struggle against all forms of tyranny.

To summarize, the period since 1945 has been a time of ideological struggle, rapid economic growth followed by stagnation for the rich nations, growing frustration and despair on the part of the poor, the collapse of most political systems based on Marxist ideology, and the world system in flux. The Christian mission has felt directly the impact of these instabilities and stresses in the world sociopolitical system. The "crisis of missions" is not over.

New centers emerge. With the loosening of the grip of the USSR and United States over their respective blocs, new centers, especially of economic power, began to emerge. The economies of Japan and

Germany increasingly outperformed that of the United States. The Soviet bloc as a whole sank into economic difficulty and this hastened the breakup of the bloc in the late 1980s. Militarily, the United States emerged as the dominant world power, but that power was no longer the singular instrument of political and economic policy.

This shift to new centers is even more evident in terms of the Christian movement. In many countries in the West, both formal membership and active participation in the church has been declining for several decades. By 1990 somewhat more than half of all Christians were to be found in Asia, Africa, and Latin America. Although these newer churches typically lacked economic, political, or social power, nonetheless they felt an increasing self-confidence. This shift was marked by an important conceptual shift.

The key *missiological* development in the past two decades has been from indigenization to contextualization. This has at least two implications. First, it signals a new determination on the part of the churches outside the West to assume responsibility for working out their theological and ecclesial identity in terms of their own historical and cultural context, rather than attempting to do this via the Western experience using Western theological constructs.

Second, it means these churches are determined to pursue their own agenda in mission to the world. The first development has already produced a series of new theologies reflecting the cultures and experiences of Christians in diverse places. The second development is beginning to give rise to new initiatives in mission on the part of churches in Asia, Africa, and Latin America. All of this has important implications for the future of the Christian movement.

The Messiahship of Jesus—Foundation of Mission

Attempts to develop a theology of mission over the past century have been characterized by a wide variety of approaches. First one idea has been emphasized and then another. Theologies of mission have been written emphasizing culture, anthropology, kingdom of God, Jesus Christ, Holy Spirit, eschatology, the mission of God, and the church. If mission studies have been marked by uncertainty as to the proper basis for mission, academic theology has been largely oblivious to mission both as a proper theological theme and as the organizing principle for the life of the church. There has been a veritable flood of scholarship in the twentieth century concerned with Christology, but it is Christology largely devoid of mission to the world.[11] It is scholarship detached from life.

Varieties of Mission

Each mission bearing the name "Christian" is an effort organized to achieve a certain goal. The tendency is to reduce the scope of the gospel by making it coextensive with a particular mission. But this can only lead to a narrowing of the scope of mission. Every human undertaking is bound to be incomplete. But vigilance must be maintained against the temptation to present any particular program or experience as a full measure of the gospel.[12] Three types illustrate incomplete or inadequate approaches to mission.

Cultural missions. This type encompasses a range of responses to human needs based largely on cultural resources. Human needs in one culture are responded to with the resources of another culture. It has had a long and honored place in the classical missions' repertoire—education, medicine, agriculture, community development, emergency relief, and social-service missions. Over time it came to be recognized that healing, educating, and improving the quality of life of a people could not be done successfully only with materials and techniques imported from another culture. The people being served had to be active participants in the process. Enlightenment worldview and values, Western wealth, and more elaborate technology became significant barriers to the effectiveness of missions conceived largely in cultural terms. This worldview and value system continually came into conflict with the worldview and values of the other culture. Missions operating at this level did not take people and culture with sufficient seriousness.

Spiritual missions. This variety has been a dominant one in the nineteenth and twentieth centuries. It has emphasized the Jesus of personal piety and spiritual salvation. It is both a reaction to the Enlightenment and a reflector of it. It reacted against the emphasis on the potential of humans to solve all problems through the application of rational thought because this seemed to deny the importance of God and the transcendent. The result was a concentration on the soul and salvation in the future life.

But coupled with this has been an emphasis on technique and method. In some circles evangelism has become synonymous with certain methods and techniques—i.e., evangelistic meetings, evangelistic methods, evangelistic literature. This variety has found it difficult to enter deeply and empathetically into another culture since culture is viewed through hostile eyes, is treated as transitory and therefore not of primary worth, and is believed to be in opposition to the spiritual.

Yet even those who operate out of this framework ultimately cannot avoid becoming involved in the practical and immediate issues of the people among whom they serve. In the face of calamity where human life is at risk, simple decency and compassion will override dogma. The missionary cannot refuse to respond. Thus the missionary is left in the uncomfortable position of coming under censure from a theological vision for which there is no precedent in the ministry of Jesus the Messiah or in the experience of the early church and which is unresponsive to the needs of the people to whom one is called to witness of "good news."

Post-Christian mission. A third variety is being put forward with vigor at the present time. The proposal itself is not new. Rather it recurs like the tide, ebbing and flowing. Earlier in the twentieth century, it had such prestigious sponsors as Ernst Troeltsch, William Ernest Hocking, and Arnold J. Toynbee. Since the 1960s it has been given new impetus by Wilfred Cantwell Smith, Stanley Samartha, Paul Knitter, and John Hick. It might seem that it is inappropriate to label it "mission" at all because of its censure of Christian mission, as this has been conceived in the past, and its insistence that Christians not call adherents of other faiths to embrace Jesus Christ as Savior and Lord. But it has exhibited an "evangelical" zeal for attacking Christian mission and offering a program of its own.[13]

The argument proceeds from the observation that we live in a new historical situation inasmuch as religious and cultural pluralism has become a dominant feature in many countries—but especially in the West—in a way never known before. Given our modern insight into the nature of religious reality, we must insist that there are many paths to God, with no one religious tradition enjoying a privileged position. In this view the church's historic understanding of Jesus Christ as unique Savior and Lord poses an especially troublesome stumbling block to achieving rapprochement among the religious traditions—which is held to be the priority goal.

Those who identify with this position agree on a few basic premises but are not of one mind as to what the content of the alternative view ought to be. In place of a Christocentric framework, we are urged to adopt, among other proposals, a "reality-centric" (Hick) or "soteriocentric" (Knitter) basis.[14] Proponents of such alternatives insist that all religions are united in their quest for God as Transcendence. To affirm that we come to know God only through Jesus Christ is presumptuous. In the pluralist-relativist view, we cannot speak of truth claims as mediated to us in Jesus Christ as being uniquely, and therefore universally, valid. The revelation of God in Jesus Christ may be efficacious for those who have lived under the influence of Christianity; but it is arrogant of Christians to believe they ought to invite people of other religious and cultural traditions to come to Jesus as their Messiah.

Several observations may be made with regard to this proposal. In the first place, pluralists effectively argue for a return to a religious vision based on tribal/ethnic loyalty and historical accident. Following the logic of this position, if I am born in India, only Hinduism is the appropriate faith; but if I am born in Italy, I am fated to be a Roman Catholic. (In cultures that are increasingly secular, what compelling reason is to be offered for proposing a faith other than that of secularism?) Second, in this view religions are static; there seems to be no place for religious innovation which has been one of the constant features of human experience. Finally, with considerable self-assurance, it is asserted that, in any case, all religions ultimately are headed toward the same goal—"salvation."

This lack of logical rigor is seen, for example, in the work of John Hick who does not hesitate to posit that all religions, whether it is recognized or not, are pathways to a single ultimate Reality.[15] If one holds to the pluralist-relativist position consistently, one should not, of course, prescribe such a position for anyone else. Indeed, the consistent relativist-pluralist has no logical grounds to be concerned with the question of what others believe, nor can there be incentive to engage in a mission which seeks to bring about religious change or conversion.

No missions of outreach, in the normal understanding of that term, have been organized on the basis of the pluralist position. It is a "mission" of reaction to and critique of mainstream Christian convictions, which it seeks to revise.

Messianic Mission

Of the three varieties of mission described in the previous section, two are inadequate and one is irreconcilable with mission. Such reductionisms must be resisted, for they do not enable us to grasp the fullness of God's intention and provision "for us and our salvation." Our conviction is that God's saving mission is disclosed to us most fully in Jesus the Messiah (see Brunk, 1990). It is in the sending of the Son that we are finally enabled to see God the Father. God's purposes in creation, having been temporarily thwarted by the Fall, are being accomplished in redemption. In Jesus the Messiah, God assumes a face and a name. "The Word became flesh and dwelt among us" (John 1:14) means that God has established a new means of access so that the communion and harmony of Eden may be realized. It is the particularity of the incarnation that establishes the universal validity of Jesus Christ.[16]

In the introduction to this volume, reference was made to the criticism Jesus leveled at the Jewish proselytizing mission. It was emphasized that Jesus did not condemn and reject the mission; rather, he transfigured it. That is to say, Jesus filled it with dynamic new meaning and immediately enlisted his disciple community in carrying out his mission. Instead of sending his disciples out to win converts who would pattern themselves after a law code, Jesus authorized the disciples to invite people into a life transformed through reconciliation with God, a relationship which meant liberation from the bondages in which they had been held. Rather than resorting to coercive tactics to win converts, Jesus told his disciples not to impose themselves on anyone (Matt. 10:14). Their appeal was to be based on God's gracious action on behalf of all people in sending the Messiah: "Freely you have received, freely give" (10:8 NIV).

The mission of Jesus the Messiah was to liberate people from the sin of ego-centeredness and set them free to serve God and others. Modernity promised through "enlightenment" to free people to enjoy "Life, Liberty, and the pursuit of Happiness"—in the words of one famous Enlightenment document (*Declaration*, 1776). But such ideologies have failed and will continue to fail, because they are not radical enough; these cannot get to the root cause of the human predicament.[17] Each one merely rearranges the furniture in the old human house rather than constructing a new edifice with appropriate new furnishings.

The Bible draws a clear line between human efforts to achieve salvation, which are always inadequate, and that which God alone can do. Paul wrestles with this theme repeatedly. In Romans he carefully adduces all the relevant evidence. He recognizes the light of truth or conscience that is in every human being regardless of whether they are Jew or otherwise. Yet that alone is insufficient. He concludes that sin is a universal reality even as God's provision in Jesus Christ is universally available (Rom. 3:21-25). At the heart of biblical faith is surrender of the self into the hands of God, an act modeled supremely by Jesus the Messiah during his passion (Luke 22:42). It is in surrendering to God's will that the way is opened to enter into the fullness of God's gracious provision.

The work of Jesus the Messiah both provides the basis for human salvation and defines the continuing mission of salvation in which the whole messianic community is called to participate. Because they personally had tasted of that salvation, the disciples are qualified to bear witness to the world (1 John 1:1-3). They knew what it had meant to live in bondage to sin; they could testify of life liberated from the power of sin and death.

A Relevant Missiology

In this chapter we have investigated theological, historical, and missiological reasons why we must actively seek *The Transfiguration of Mission*. We have briefly sketched out some of the main features of the church and mission that have determined the church's response to the world for some 1,500 years, especially the complicity of the church in the wielding of political and economic power and the consequences this has had for the nature and mission of the church itself. It is important that the church be delivered of those patterns of mind and practice that are less than faithful to the gospel. But the church must set its face to the future; that is where the frontiers of mission lie.

A *relevant* missiology will be one that brings the fullness of biblical revelation in Jesus the Messiah to bear on the mission task as it is unfolding before us. The burden of this work has been to ask what this implies for faithful discipleship.

The frontiers of mission in the twentieth-first century will be markedly different from those of the past two hundred years. We will have moved even further away from the legacy of Christendom. The church, more widely dispersed than ever before, will be in a minority position in most countries with the specter of persecution always hovering over some part of the messianic community somewhere. But there will be important continuities as well. New messianic pretenders, not a few of which are antagonistic to the Christian faith, can be expected to continue appearing on the stage, to make their bids for human allegiance. Masses of people will continue to live without any clear awareness of God's love as revealed in Jesus the Messiah.

A relevant missiology will be one that helps the church embrace its mission fully through a clear discernment of the times, together with a vision of what a dynamic missionary response requires. The church must maintain an awareness that faithfulness, both to its own nature and to its responsibility to the world, requires a stance of missionary encounter.

This stance calls the messianic community, dispersed throughout the world, to give unswerving loyalty to Jesus the Messiah. This is not an escape from responsibility for the world because the world can never be freed from the gods and idols of power—nationalism, materialism, militarism, classism, self-centeredness—apart from God's intervention. This, indeed, is the highest form of loyalty the messianic community exercises toward the world: pointing beyond the present imperfect order to a "new heaven and new earth" (Rev. 21:1).

It is no small encouragement that representatives of other ecclesiastical traditions, including Stephen Neill cited above, have been grappling with the future shape of the church precisely in the West, the historic heartland of Christendom. The task is made all the more urgent by the sifting and shrinking of the church in the West. A representative voice in this regard is Karl Rahner who discerned this to be a "transitional" period in history. He foresaw a "church made up of those who have struggled against their environment in order to reach a personally clear and explicitly responsible decision of faith" (Rahner, 1983:24).[18] He saw this as the *sine qua non* of the church of the future. It must be a church with a defined sense of mission to its society.

Chapter by chapter we will seek to build up a model of mission, taking our cues from the norm given to us in God's Messiah. This norm holds together all the elements necessary to the *missio Dei*. Such elements include the following: *Jesus the Messiah*, God's anointed one, in whom God's reign is inaugurated in the world and through whom that reign will be fully established; who makes peace by the blood of the cross, reconciles former enemies, and forms of them the messianic community. *The Holy Spirit*, who continues the mission of the Messiah in the world during this the missionary age. *The messianic community*, the instrument of Messiah's mission in whose life the reign of God is actualized through its living out of the messianic ethic—overcoming the sins of the "isms" which have destroyed fellowship and thus life itself. *The eschatological framework of mission*, which keeps present and future together by allowing the power of the eschaton to shape the life of the messianic community now while they, in hope, anticipate the glorious consummation of all things. All this is of the essence of evangelical faith, and evangelical faith cannot but be expressed in response to what God has done in Jesus the Messiah. This, we submit, is the norm for mission.

Does this messianic model suggest a particular strategy for the next stage of mission? One searches the Scriptures in vain for any discussion or description of mission strategy. But there is a consistent thread running throughout the story of "calling and sending," beginning with Abraham and continuing with Jesus and the early church. It is to be seen most fully in Jesus. In Jesus the Messiah, God takes on human form, identifying fully with the objects of his love. God works through the Committed One or community to achieve the divine plan.

Yet standing over the incarnation there is always the cross and atonement. The incarnation signifies total vulnerability and expendability, including the risk of crucifixion. The fundamental missionary stance is that of the servant. The strategy is the incarnation. The sign marking the way of mission is the cross. Yet the movement of mission is God's triumphal procession through history which is gathering into God's family "those who are being saved." This is a movement free both of the gloating of triumphalism and the despair of defeatism because it is led by the Martyr-Messiah whose message is the gospel of peace, the Lamb who conquers by love alone.[19]

A relevant missiology will be based on the work of Jesus the Messiah. It will always be *missiology enroute*. It is not a set of timeless axioms waiting to be applied in all situations. Rather it will be a dynamic missiology to the degree it is continually tested and applied as the messianic community witnesses to the world of its own experience of being transformed through encounter with the Messiah.

Notes

1. Scripture references in this chapter are from the Revised Standard Version unless noted otherwise.

2. George F. Vicedom traces and expounds this theme in *The Mission of God* (1965), translated from *Missio Dei: Einfuhrung in eine Theologie der Mission* (1958).

3. Special appreciation is expressed to Alan Kreider for reading this chapter in first draft and helping to clarify several points, especially with regard to the history of Christendom, a theme he is researching in relation to its continuing relevance for the mission of the church.

4. In his history of the Enlightenment, Peter Gay begins his second volume with these words: "In the century of the Enlightenment, educated Europeans awoke to a new sense of life. They experienced an expansive sense of power over nature and themselves: the pitiless cycles of epidemics, famines, risky life and early death, devastating war and uneasy peace—the treadmill of human existence—seemed to be yielding at last to the application of critical intelligence" (1973:3). This was an intoxicating vision.

5. Berkhof observes that ecclesiology has been essentially static for centuries. He urges the study of ecclesiology, indeed all of theology, from the standpoint of the church's relation to the world (1979:411).

6. This is an excellent example of how history typically is written by the conqueror rather than the conquered. Where can one find an account of what it meant for the tribes of Europe to be overrun militarily, culturally, and religiously told from their viewpoint? These peoples could not have heard "good news," for they were conquered and forced to submit to Christendom. It is nothing short of travesty to term this process of "Christianization" as evangelization. It would be far more honest and constructive to

quit pretending that for vast numbers of people there ever was a *first* evangelization. This would open the way to ask whether the present blight on the church has any connections with this historical background. If so, what does this tell us about evangelization in the future? We must stop treating the gospel ideologically as a mandate for conquest. It is precisely this historical awareness that has caused significant reaction among Europeans to Pope John Paul II's call in 1985 for the "reevangelization" of Europe. The Pope's appeal has come across to many as a renewed attempt to restore Christendom. See Rene Luneau (1989). This consists of eighteen chapters by leading French Catholic intellectuals.

7. Butterfield (1949) emphasizes the new opportunity before the church because of the removal of coercion. He himself was a product of the British Nonconformist tradition which had struggled long against this very thing. However, four decades later we observe that the decline of the church in the West has not been stanched simply by the removal of this historical offense. The church has yet to respond repentantly but with missionary intention.

8. The force of this assumption is made plain by the following statement by Richard Hooker, the formative theological influence in the Church of England in the sixteenth century: "We hold, that seeing there is not any man of the Church of England but the same man is also a member of the commonwealth; nor any man a member of the commonwealth which is not also of the Church of England . . . no person appertaining to the one can be denied to be also of the other" (*Laws of Ecclesiastical Polity*, Book 8, Chapter 1, Section 2; cited in Staples, 1980). Thanks is expressed to Roelf Kuitse for bringing this to my attention.

9. Neill illustrates the importance of historical context tellingly—commenting on the foregoing doctrinal statements: "The reader of John Calvin feels himself never very far away from that small, vigorous, and not always orderly republic of perhaps 10,000 inhabitants, over which the eye of John Calvin and his fellow-pastors could observantly rove, and all the inhabitants of which could be gathered together to hear the exposition of godly doctrine from Calvin's pulpit. The English phrases call up a vision of the typical English village of not more than 400 inhabitants, where all are baptized Christians, compelled to live more or less Christian lives under the brooding eye of parson and squire. In such a context 'evangelization' has hardly any meaning, since all are in some sense already Christian, and need no more than to be safeguarded against error in religion and viciousness in life" (1968:75).

10. It was an earlier British prime minister, Winston Churchill, who on a visit to the United States in 1947 announced that an "Iron Curtain" had fallen, dividing the world into blocs, a phrase that became the potent symbol of the Cold War.

11. Christopher Rowland (1985) observes that considerable scholarship has concentrated on Christology as the central theme of primitive Christianity but neglects a corollary theme as important as eschatology (p. xvi). This has a serious distorting effect. The same point can be made about mission. The whole of the New Testament was written in the thick of missionary engagement, but modern scholarship has managed to suppress this contextual/historical dimension. Martin Kähler argued that theology in this perspective should be a "companion of the Christian mission . . . not a luxury of the world-dominating church [but] . . . rather, a product of the emergency situation within the church militant" (cited by David J. Bosch, 1982:27).

12. It is an instructive, if not altogether edifying, exercise to take a directory of Christian mission and service agencies, such as the *Mission Handbook* (Roberts and Siewart, 1989), and peruse the names of agencies with an eye to theological, ideological, or circumstantial basis for their founding.

13. See Gavin D'Costa, "The New Missionary: John Hick and Religious Plurality," *International Bulletin of Missionary Research*, 15:2 (April 1991), pp. 66-69.

14. The most accessible exposition of this position is the volume edited by John Hick and Paul F. Knitter (1987). One of the contributors, Raimundo Panikkar, has subsequently sought to distance himself from the position the editors espouse. See his let-

ter to the editor, *International Bulletin of Missionary Research* (1989:80). That Panikkar does not wish to be "thrown into the same bag" is clear enough; but his position remains opaque even to the alert reader. See also, Paul F. Knitter (1985) and John Hick (1973). The Hick-Knitter project has been answered by a group of fourteen scholars in Gavin D'Costa (1990).

15. In a careful critique of Hick's position, Julius Lipner (1991), Divinity School, Cambridge University, said, in summary: Hick's position provides basis neither for dialogue nor mission. Hick ignores the profound and important differences between religions in his rush to fit the data into his schema. Lipner demonstrated the logical inconsistency running through Hick's writings because of his dogmatic insistence that all religions share a common faith in a Transcendent Reality. For a comprehensive study of Hick's position, see Gavin D'Costa, *John Hick's Theology of Religions: A Critical Evaluation* (Lanham, Maryland: University Press of America, 1987).

16. There are various universalisms. Each universalism has its counterpart particularism. It is thus not a contradiction to speak of both the particularity of the incarnation and the universal significance of Jesus Christ.

17. It is to the credit of communist theorists/leaders such as Mao Tse-tung that they recognized the need for a "new human being" if their utopian vision of society was to be achieved. That the Marx-inspired movement has largely failed is due not to lack of keen insight but rather to their dogged insistence that the human being is capable of achieving this essential *newness* through rational historical effort. The Christian notion of conversion is the truly radical answer to human sinfulness.

18. Cf. Karl Rahner (1983:19-34). See also Rahner (1967:77-101), Jürgen Moltmann (1977:7-11, 314-36), George A. Lindbeck (1971:226-43), and Paul Peachey (1992).

19. See the moving discussion by Kenneth Cragg (1989) of suffering love. Cragg challenges Christians to reclaim the original essence of the faith.

References Cited

Berkhof, Hendrikus
  1979 "The New Community," *Christian Faith: An Introduction to the Study of the Faith*. Sierd Woudstra, trans.; Grand Rapids, Mich.: Eerdmans.

Bosch, David J.
  1982 "Theological Education in Missionary Perspective," *Missiology*, X:1 (January).

Brunk, George R. III
  1990 "The Exclusiveness of Jesus Christ," *Jesus Christ and the Mission of the Church: Contemporary Anabaptist Perspectives*. Erland Waltner, ed.; Newton, Kans.: Faith and Life Press.

Butterfield, Herbert
  1949 *Christianity and History*. London: G. Bell and Sons.

Carey, William
  1792 *An Enquiry into the Obligations of Christians to Use Means for the Conversion of the Heathens*, new facsimile edition (1961). London: The Carey Kingsgate Press Limited.

Cragg, Kenneth
  1989 *What Decided Christianity*. Worthing, West Sussex: Churchman Publishing Co.

D'Costa, Gavin, ed.
  1987 *John Hick's Theology of Religions: A Critical Evaluation.* Lanham, Md.: University Press of America.
  1990 *Christian Uniqueness Reconsidered: The Myth of a Pluralistic Theology of Religions.* Maryknoll, N.Y.: Orbis Books.
  1991 "The New Missionary: John Hick and Religious Plurality," *International Bulletin of Missionary Research,* 15:2 (April).

Declaration of Independence
  1776 Drafted by Thomas Jefferson; adopted July 4, 1776, by the Second Continental Congress, Philadelphia, Pa.

Gay, Peter
  1973 *The Enlightenment—an Interpretation,* vol. 2: *The Science of Freedom.* London: Wildwood House.

Hick, John
  1973 *God and the Universe of Faith.* London: Collins.

Hick, John, and Paul F. Knitter, eds.
  1987 *The Myth of Christian Uniqueness: Toward a Pluralistic Theology of Religions.* Maryknoll, N.Y.: Orbis Books.

Knitter, Paul F.
  1985 *No Other Name? A Critical Survey of Christian Attitudes Toward the World Religions.* Maryknoll, N.Y.: Orbis Books.

Lindbeck, George A.
  1971 "The Sectarian Future of the Church," *The God Experience.* Joseph P. Whelan, S.J., ed.; New York: Newman Press.

Lipner, Julius
  1991 "In Quest of Religious Dialogue," Edward Cadbury Lectures, Birmingham University.

Luneau, Rene, ed.
  1989 *Le reve de Compostelle, Vers le restauration d'une Europe chretienne?* Paris: Centurion.

Moltmann, Jürgen
  1977 *The Church in the Power of the Spirit.* New York: Harper & Row.

Neill, Stephen
  1968 Lecture 2: "The Missionary Dimension," *The Church and Christian Union.* London: Oxford University Press.

Panikkar, Raimundo
  1989 Letter to the editor, *International Bulletin of Missionary Research,* 13:2 (April).

Peachey, Paul
  1992 "The 'Free Church?': A Time Whose Idea Has Not Come," *Anabaptism Revisited: Essays on Anabaptist/Mennonite Studies in Honor of C. J. Dyck.* Walter Klaassen, ed.; Scottdale, Pa.: Herald Press.

Rahner, Karl
  1967 *The Christian of the Future.* New York: Herder and Herder.
  1983 *The Shape of the Church to Come.* New York: Crossroad (first published, 1974).

Roberts, W. Dayton, and John A. Siewert, eds.
  1989   *Mission Handbook: USA/Canada Protestant Ministries   Overseas*, four-
         teenth edition. Monrovia, Calif.: MARC.
Rowland, Christopher
  1985   *Christian Origins—From Messianic Movement to Christian Religion*. Min-
         neapolis: Augsburg.
Staples, P.
  1980   "Zending en evangelisatie vanwege de 'Church of England,' "
         Wereld en Zending XX.
Vicedom, George R.
  1965   *The Mission of God: An Introduction to a Theology of Mission*. Gilbert A.
         Theile and Dennis Hilgendorf, trans.; St. Louis, Mo.: Concordia Pub-
         lishing House. Originally *Missio Dei: Einfuhrung in eine Theologie der
         Mission* Munchen: Chr. Kaiser Verlag (1958).

CHAPTER 2

Jesus the Messiah: Messianic Foundation of Mission

David A. Shank

C H R I S T O L O G Y is traditionally the study of the doctrine of Jesus Christ as it has been pursued in the life of the churches of Christ since the crucifixion and resurrection of Jesus of Nazareth. It covers the rich expressions of apostolic understandings as well as the post-apostolic developments leading up to the so-called ecumenical creeds, including the perceptions that these eliminated. It includes high scholastic developments, the fivefold Reformation and their scholastic Protestant outgrowths; it involves the modern critical developments of the nineteenth and twentieth centuries' scholarship on "lives of Jesus" as well as contemporary post-dogmatic approaches.

Today, at least for churches originating in the West, Christology involves not only the critical studies of the canonical texts of the New Testament—especially the four Gospels. It also includes an effort to translate the results of these studies into Western understandings that have been shaped by the thought and technology of modern sciences—physical, biological, historical, psychological, sociological, anthropological, religious. Nothing is more noticeable today than the great variety of understandings and interpretations that constitute christological thought in the churches, including those well beyond the West, to say nothing of references to the past. The diversity is understandable and justifiable from a biblical point of view,[1] as well as from the highly diverse human, cultural, and worldview contexts from which that material comes. This chapter sketches a framework for the Christology inherent to the mission and life of the churches of Jesus Christ throughout the world today.

Professor Andrew Walls presents an excellent periodization of the history of the churches "based on the dominant cultures with which Christianity has been associated at various times" (1985:58). Nevertheless, he says, "there is no simple 'Christian civilization' but an endless process of translation into various languages and cultures and subcultures within them" (:58). His schema is as follows:

Jewish phase	ca. 30-70
Hellenistic-Roman phase	
(includes Eastern Orthodoxy)	ca. 70-500
Barbarian phase	ca. 500-1100
Western phase	ca. 1100-1600
Phase of expanding Europe	ca. 1500-1920
Southern phase	since 1920

With this historical framework before us, three observations are significant for our christological reflection at this juncture in Christian mission.

1. The foundations of understanding and interpretation, including the canonical writings of the churches, are grounded in the first forty years—the Jewish phase.

2. Up until about 1920 the Christian scene, from the standpoint of culture and civilization, has been dominated and conditioned by the Hellenistic-Roman phase. It was initially extended into the phase of "barbarian" syncretization, then into the Western phase with its European expansion until the post-World War I period. During this latter period, the Greek-Latin filters for understanding Christ and his work dominated the scene through the colonial and missionary expansion of Christianity.

3. In the current Southern phase, a result of Christian mission, churches in non-Western cultures read and interpret the Scriptures and understand Jesus Christ from their own cultural/civilizational perspectives alongside that of Western christological reflection from A.D. 70 to 1920.

For centuries the dominant and imposed Christology in the churches, evolving within the Greek language and cultural ethos, was discussed almost exclusively in the Greek mode. "Christ" is, of course, the English transliteration of the Greek *Christos*; but beyond that the

Greek-Latin categories of reason, law, spirit and matter, nature and substance, and person could practically drown out other dimensions and perceptions.

To illustrate, if one speaks of a "Messiah doctrine" today, it has a different feel to it than speaking of "Christology," which literally means the same thing. "Messiah" implies a specific historical personality who poses as effective redeemer and liberator in a given context of oppressive alienation. Yet the term "Christ" in the Greek tradition often ignored the holistic Hebrew dynamics, with their social, economic, and political implications for faith, all of which are inherent in the language of "messiah."

Kenneth Cragg makes this point quite forcefully and his word needs to be taken seriously (Cragg 1968:57-58). In reality, by A.D. 500 the good news of Jesus the Messiah had spread into various Mediterranean cultures with Scriptures existing not only in Greek but also in Syriac, Coptic, Latin, Ethiopic, Armenian, Gothic, and Slavonic. Yet the dynamics of imperial unity, first invited by the Donatist controversy, co-opted the "Christ" and ultimately commanded a uniform Greek-Latin understanding—cutting off traditional Hebrew roots—of the Hebrew Jesus of Nazareth, first confessed by Jewish apostles as Israel's Messiah for the world. This engendered a knowledge/life dualism which led to a separation of faith and life.

In the 1500 years since the crystallization of the Orthodox and Roman Catholic creeds within Constantinian imperial Christianity, Christology has majored in the static and ahistorical dimensions of divine-human relationship and mediation. Except for the heterodox, sectarian, millennial, and monastic traditions, much less concern and attention has been given to the human, temporal dimensions of the divine-human relationship of Messiah Jesus. Hence a vacuous neglect of their implications for mediation between the future and the present as well as between people, peoples, and institutions in the present. However, allowing for some important exceptions, this accent has shifted significantly in the West under the pressures of the Hegelian and Marxist preoccupations with the dynamics of history, the demise of the Constantinian synthesis, and the contemporary apocalypse of the technological cul-de-sac as demonstrated in World War II and subsequent wars. Indeed, the horrors of the Holocaust within Hitlerian messianism forced Western Christianity into a new encounter with Judaism and a rediscovery of its own Hebraic roots. All of this has implications for christological reflection at a time when there is a Western consensual reaching-out for a more humane way into a more humane future.

On the one hand, the logical Western problem-solving approach is that of squarely facing the human problem, looking for a way out, and then concocting a "christology" as an ideology of salvation. There is, on the other hand, the quite different approach of grasping the fundamental roots of apostolic messianic understandings during that beginning forty-year formative period, taking them seriously as foundations for faith, and then facing the world, its problems, and the future in that light. One suspects that the two approaches may have some parallels and similar accents, yet crucial differences may be as important as that between Messiah and anti-Messiah, even as such came to be experienced by Anabaptists in the beginnings of the unraveling of the great sacral construction of Constantinian Christendom.

Despite the later Greco-Latin cultural imperium, it is clear that the early churches in Judea were Jewish with Hebrew language and thought patterns, albeit deeply affected by the culture of exile and the contemporary Hellenist influences. There remained an essential, non-ethnic, non-parochial, and non-negotiable foundation of Hebrew thought. A divine/human dialectic and travail is engaged in fulfilling history,[2] with the beginning of a new realization of God's good will and blessing for Israel and all the nations with the fulfillment of a universal messianic hope through Jesus of Nazareth.

But the early Greek-inspired shift from the "horizontal," temporal, historical mediation of the future to a largely "vertical," ontological mediation downplayed the earthly accents and the social, economic, and political preoccupations of the biblical Messiah's work of salvation, redemption, and restoration. Instead it favored the divine/heavenly (spiritual, eternal, immortal) preoccupations and accents of the Greek cultural ethos. This shifted the holistic thrust of the biblical message and gospel of the Messiah to accentuate spiritual good news about the eternal heavenly hereafter. The old covenant was seen to be earthly and temporal and filled with "types" of spiritual realities of the new covenant which fulfilled them. The exodus/liberation of Israel was a typological forecast of inner spiritual salvation from the earth and sin to heaven's promised land through the heavenly Savior. And in that journey the church of Christendom during more than a millennium was indeed recognized and charged with the spiritual side of the empire.

Happily, in some circles in the West a theological thrust oriented to the kingdom of God has served to pull together the earthly and the heavenly, the material and the spiritual, in a more nearly holistic understanding of messianic mission. But the flywheel of the past has often limited effects on the Christology of the same circles.[3] On the other hand, the various liberation theologies (Latin American, black, feminist) have emerged as a theological mainstream starting with the particular oppression—social, economic, political, sexist, racist—along with a materialistic dialectic as the instrument of analysis and strategy. Then, accenting certain elements of biblical concern from within the prophetic and messianic tradition, these theologies have brought to the fore the exodus, the political dimensions of Jesus' mission, and his identity with the marginal ("God's option for the poor," as made explicit by liberation theology), thus challenging the whole Western church's notion of salvation and Christian mission.[4] But this is clearly a thrust different from that of the vigorous Pietism and Evangelicalism of the eighteenth and nineteenth centuries which had an aggressive sociopolitical agenda, so well illustrated by the anti-slavery campaigns or the Blumhardts of Bad Boll, Germany.[5]

In this current context, does the so-called sectarian tradition, perennially outside the theological mainstream, have anything to offer on Christology in view of mission? With the openness in the West and the new approaches in the non-Western cultures despite the major Western influence through missionary activity, it is perhaps not inappropriate to look again—from the sixteenth century's left-wing perspective—at the early christological accents of the first messianic communities centered on Jesus of Nazareth. This tradition emerged out of the rejection of the Constantinian synthesis and, like the messianic communities within the Roman Empire, bore with the Jews and Muslims a major brunt of the triumphant temporal power—Christendom structured on a spiritual, heavenly Christology. In any case the intention in this study is to underscore elements from the first forty foundational years of messialogical thought as well as from the Anabaptist tradition of the sixteenth century as part of a catalytic brew within which locally accented christologies may ferment.

Given the cultural pluralism of the churches in the world today, a variety of christologies is quite understandable and almost unavoidable, regardless of the main traditions in which the mission-planted churches have been immersed. This has been heightened by the World Council of Churches' encouragement and support of theological "contextualization" worldwide—the context as a starting point for theology. In Evangelical circles it is well illustrated by Vinay Samuel and Christopher Sugden in *Sharing Jesus in the Two-Thirds World* (1984); for conciliar and Catholic circles, *The Bulletin of African Theology* is the best illustration. The concern raised by the present chapter is related to the question of whether there are traditionally neglected *sine qua non* dimensions of christology which ought not be ignored in any of the current diverse formulations.

One of the lesser but more noticeable elements in this study will be the use of "Messiah" rather than "Christ." Meanings associated with "Christ"—often with anti-Jewish overtones in those years between A.D. 70 and 1920—shift not only the original intent but also the impact. Thus this text will use Messiah, messianist, messianic, messianism, messianity, and for "christology," messialogy. The implications, however, if taken to their inherent conclusions, are important.

The first is that using these terms frees and encourages Christians/Messianists outside the West to do their own messialogical reflection with a knowledge of the ways in which one's cultural history can encapsulate and domesticate Jesus and the apostolic faith to its own detriment as well as to that of others.

Second, use of these terms enhances the validity of plural accents in Christology, in the West as in the rest of the world, while recognizing an essential framework within which the divergences are fully and correctly honored and valued.

Third, for Western churches caught up in the fruits of the secular reaction to Western hellenized Christology, it is important for them to see themselves again from within the framework of the essential apostolic messianism, rather than to judge and critique the latter from the latest evolved perspective of modern Western consciousness with the domestication and parochialism that that involves.

Finally, in a time when the religious pluralism of the world continues to challenge the truth of God in Jesus the Messiah, particularly in religious circles with atrophied Christian roots, it may be helpful to restate the essential content of messialogical thought with its parameters.

The present writing is from a perspective which has emerged from within the history of that Anabaptist messianic community which knew the intense suffering, persecution, and martyrdom of nonresistant powerlessness at the hands of the sacral Christendom it challenged and experienced as anti-Christ in the name of Christ. Although that community inherited from the Christology of the Western creeds an authoritative mediating Christ, the Jesus in the Gospels—as taught by his apostles in the New Testament writings—had more authority than the creeds and their formulations.

The community thus had a strong commitment to the normative importance of Jesus' life-patterns and teachings on forgiveness, love, and service for all human life and institutions. Baptism was a covenant with Jesus Christ in the mutuality of life together in the assembly of his followers. There was a clear vision of eschatological triumph which called forth a childlike obedience like that of Jesus, despite humiliation and suffering. The Holy Spirit was experienced as freedom, capacity, and mission for a human transformation which challenged the cultural canons of the day.

Such a tradition, so "at home" in the Scriptures and so much "enroute" in the world, is intuitively suspicious, not only of the world pressures which oppose the life of God in Jesus the Messiah, but also of passing theological and christological fads which emerge from within the religious life of that world. Yet, in these efforts of one more Westerner to suggest for world mission an essential understanding of Messiah, it is only honest to admit also that if in this essay he cannot avoid reading the Scriptures from a Western perspective, it is one that in its infancy at least challenged Western Christianity . . . unto death.

So it is correct to call this perspective "neo-Anabaptist"; but this has its own requirements. First of all, it must be biblical. Second, it must allow biblical understandings to critique the current ones (whatever those might be) rather than to project those back into the biblical understandings, admittedly a difficult task. Third, its conclusions are taken as a position on which to stand independently of its "effectiveness" or its "relevancy"; it does not need to be justified before the world to whom it witnesses, since it only seeks to be justified by God.

First Thessalonians: The Earliest Clues

One good point at which clearly to peg early understandings about Jesus is the oldest and first New Testament canonical writing, the missionary letter written by apostles Paul, Silas, and Timothy to the new *ekklesia*/gathering of believers and disciples in Thessalonica, a principal metropolis of Macedonia. Written about A.D. 51-52, scarcely more than twenty years after Jesus' death and resurrection, the letter came from a group headed by one who some seventeen years earlier had officially headed a violent persecution of the new movement within Israel. While on a mission to the nations/Gentiles, Paul was accompanied by both an official representative and a leading brother of the original Jerusalem *ekklesia*/gathering, along with Luke, his personal physician, and a young Greek, Timothy, born of a Jewish mother. Paul was fully qualified by more than fifteen years of service in the new movement and fully authorized by the mother assembly in Jerusalem for taking it into areas where it was yet largely unknown.

From the story written by Luke some 20 to 30 years after the mission to Thessalonica (Acts 17:1-9), we are told that it was a relatively brief mission because of open opposition. Paul argued from the Jewish Scriptures in the synagogue for three Sabbaths, proving that it was necessary for the Messiah to suffer and to rise from the dead and saying, "This Jesus, whom I proclaim to you, is the [Messiah]" (17:3).[6] As a result some Jews believed in Jesus as the Messiah and attached themselves to the apostolic team, suffering the jealousy of fellow-Jews who openly opposed the movement. The apostolic team was accused of "turn[ing] the world upside down" (17:6) and "acting against the decrees of Caesar, saying that there is another king, Jesus" (17:7). Even if the accusation had been false, the political overtones of the messianic message are evident in that if there were none, the dead Jesus could represent no threat, either to Jews accused of rebellion or to the local authorities under Roman rule.

In addition to the Jews who believed, there were a great many pious Greeks and not a few of the leading women, possibly also from among the Greek population. These were the highly divergent religious and social roots of a new *ekklesia*, itself a word also for a Greek political formation. A new messianic gathering, or assembly, had emerged as a consequence of a messianic proclamation by a team endowed with a messianic consciousness, naming Jesus of Nazareth the present acting transcendent Messiah/King with universal authority—higher than the head of the Roman Empire.

The Messianic Content of 1 Thessalonians

Titles. The salutation and the final greetings of the letter are like a parenthesis, opening with "To the [ekklesia] of the Thessalonians in God the Father and the Lord Jesus [the Messiah]": "Grace to you and peace" (1 Thess. 1:1) and closing with an anticipation that "the God of peace himself [will] sanctify . . . wholly" (5:23) the believers in view of "the coming of our Lord Jesus [the Messiah] . . . The grace of our Lord Jesus [the Messiah] be with you" (5:24-28). In those two parameters God is confessed as relationally intimate (Father)—something unusual for the Jews of the time—and as effecting a reign as "God of peace,"[7] while the man Jesus is confessed as Messiah and Lord. Both are in intimate association as the effective source of essential manifestations of God's reign. In this brief letter "[Messiah] Jesus" appears two times, "[the Messiah]" is found three times, "Lord Jesus [the Messiah]" is found five times. "Jesus" is used three times; "the/our Lord Jesus," six times; "the Lord," thirteen times; "[God's] Son," only once.

Confession and proclamation of faith. "Lord Jesus the Messiah" is here much more than a name or a title; it is in fact a double confession of faith: "Jesus is the Messiah," and "The Messiah Jesus is Lord." It is the full confessional identification of Jesus of Nazareth with the promised and awaited Messiah of Israel's prophets and with God and his purposes. "Messiah" appears ten times in 1 Thessalonians; "Lord (*kurios*)" appears twenty-four times. Indeed, "Jesus is Lord" rapidly became the most-used confession in the new Hellenistic assemblies, but it must be seen as an apostolic usage meaning "Jesus [the Messiah] is Lord" (see Neufeld, 1963:141). Indeed, two decades after his crucifixion and resurrection, "Jesus" within the movement was already wholly identified with the title and function of Messiah.

The only Scriptures at Thessalonica, beyond this authoritative apostolic letter, were those of the synagogue, but they were now interpreted in the light of what the letter calls "gospel" (1 Thess. 1:5), "gospel of God" (2:2, 8-9), "gospel of [the Messiah]" (3:2), "the word" (1:6), "the word of God" (2:13), or "the word of the Lord" (1:8; 4:15). This can surely be summarized by this primary confession that we have seen, but there are other suggestions of brief formulas of proclamation and confession of faith:

> you turned to God from idols, to serve a living and true God, and . . . wait for his Son from heaven, whom he raised from the dead, Jesus who delivers us from the wrath to come (1:9-10).

> For since we believe that Jesus died and rose again, even so, through Jesus, God will bring with him those who have fallen asleep (4:14).

> [according to] the word of the Lord, . . . the Lord himself will descend from heaven. . . . And the dead in [the Messiah] shall rise first; then we who are alive, who are left, shall be caught up together with them in the clouds . . . and so we shall always be with the Lord (4:15-17).

> God has not destined us for wrath, but to obtain salvation through our Lord Jesus [the Messiah], who died for us that whether we wake or sleep we might live with him (5:9-10).

One cannot but be struck by the core of faith: Messiah's dying and rising again is to effect already a human salvation, which is to be wholly fulfilled in his endtime appearance (parousia: 1 Thess. 2:19; 3:13; 4:15; 5:23) and final gathering of the faithful, of which the Thessalonian gathering from among Israel and the nations (Jews and Gentiles) is already a part.

Self-described apostolic impact. If there was clarity of conviction and proclamation in power in the Holy Spirit (1 Thess. 1:5) by the apostolic team, as indicated above, there was also, from their point of view, an equally vital collective demonstration of the gospel in their lives (2:4-10) which made them, with Jesus, worthy of emulation (1:6). The apostolic team was itself clearly a validation of the message and an integral part of its impact.

Salvation in the Thessalonian *ekklesia*/gathering. As cited above, salvation already known was that of "turn[ing] to God from idols, to serve a living and true God, and to wait for his Son . . . Jesus who [now] delivers us from the wrath to come" (1 Thess. 1:9-10). The letter speaks of "your work of faith and labor of love and steadfastness of hope in our Lord Jesus [the Messiah]" (1:3). As indicated, they had become "imitators" of Messiah's apostles and Jesus himself, receiving the word "in much affliction, with joy inspired by the Holy Spirit . . . and became an example" to other believers in the area (1:6-7). They "became imitators of the churches of God in [the Messiah] Jesus which are in Judea" (2:14), knowing with them the suffering implicit in their calling with Messiah (3:3). Finally, the "word of the Lord sounded forth from you . . . your faith in God has gone forth everywhere" (1:8).

The salvation outworking anticipated by the apostles in the assembly included leading "a life worthy of God, who calls you into his own kingdom and glory" (1 Thess. 2:12); steadfastness in affliction (3:3); "instructions we gave you through the Lord Jesus" how to live and please God (4:2ff.). The manifestation of mutuality is already at work in love (eight uses of *agape* or derivatives) as taught by God (4:9), but it is anticipated in mutual comfort (4:18), mutual encouragement and mutual edification (5:11), mutuality of peace (5:13), mutual kindness and refusal of repaying evil for evil (5:15), and patience for everyone (5:14). There is to be respect and love for their leaders and concern for the idle, the faint, and the weak. Self-control regarding sexual practice and personal life is to be received through faith, love, and hope of salvation (5:8). But beyond the confines of the gathering itself, love (3:12) and kindness (doing good) is for all, with no resisting of evil with evil (5:15). They are to live with bodies disciplined, by working with their own hands, being self-supporting, quietly minding their own affairs, and thus commending the respect of outsiders. And all this while their faith is going forth everywhere (1:8) and in the face of great opposition (2:2).

Résumé of Messianic Understanding

Within the letter is a fourfold understanding of "the Lord Jesus, the Messiah." First, Jesus suffered in the line of the prophets (1 Thess. 2:15) when he lived a pattern of life that is imitated (1:6), having given clear instructions on how to live and please God (1:5) and a clear word of eschatological promise (4:15), which all ended in his death at the hands of fellow Jews.

Second, Jesus rose from the dead, and he now sends out apostles with the good news of his messiahship: he died and rose again and is coming to fulfill salvation of a gathered humanity in the midst of coming judgment (wrath). The Holy Spirit through the apostles creates assemblies of the great messianic ingathering which learn from the apostles, Jesus, and each other. Called into the kingdom and glory of God by the Messiah, they suffer opposition and the temptation to turn aside; but they live in the grace and peace given by him and the Father, kept by their faith, love, and hope in him, whose full ingathering they await. They become notorious sharers of their faith and the gospel they received. They are to work out their salvation in their gathering/assembly/*ekklesia*/church in a common life of love and mutuality, refusing evil for evil. In the larger society, in spite of opposition and affliction, they are to show love and kindness to all, refusing to render evil for evil, in line with instructions from Jesus through the apostles.

Third, the coming "day of the Lord" (1 Thess. 5:2) is to begin with the unannounced "coming" (1 Thess. 1:10; 2:19; 3:13; 4:15; 5:23) of God's Son Jesus to command both the resurrection of the faithful who lived and died in the Messiah and the final gathering together with them of the transformed living faithful.

Finally, the ultimate salvation of all from the coming wrath is to be fulfilled in an ongoing life with the Lord, Jesus the Messiah, in the reign of God without end.

An Early Transcendent Messiah-Understanding

If little is given in 1 Thessalonians about Jesus' life, it is apparent that much of the description of the Thessalonian *ekklesia*/gathering cited above is a result of such sharing during the mission. Most important, clearly the life, teachings, death, and hope of Jesus are the historical foundation of all the rest, even though the "coming of Messiah" for the final ingathering has now become the focal point of orientation for the time since Jesus' death and resurrection. But most of the letter concentrates upon that present time of Messiah and his church: time of the Holy Spirit, time of grace and peace, time of service—like Jesus—to the true and living God, with its testing through opposition and suffering, its work of faith and witness, its mutuality in faith, love, and hope.

The fourfold messianic understanding portrays a picture of human history under the reign of God with culminating events fulfilled and articulated by the life, death, resurrection, present ministry, and coming of the Messiah Jesus as he gathers together God's people (for the moment in smaller scattered gatherings) in view of the salvation of humanity into the service of God. There is the event of Jesus' life, teaching, sufferings, and death; there is the event of the resurrection; there is the event of exaltation lived in fellowship with the apostolic gathering sent out on the mission of assembling disciples; there is the eschatological event-to-come of the full ingathering of the people of God with the appearing of Messiah.

The close relationship of God as Father with Jesus the Son/Messiah is further enhanced by the repeated, almost regular, use of *kurios*/Lord for the Messiah. This was the word used in the Septuagint for Yahweh in his sovereignty, since the Greek usage itself accented such sovereignty in divinities and those rulers seen to be divine; it clearly stressed the kingly sovereignty of the Messiah Jesus in relation to that of God's kingdom (cf. 1 Thess. 2:12). To the extent that the Messiah is so associated with God's sovereignty, one can speak of an early transcendent Messiah-understanding (i.e., Christology), even though the concern is that of the mission and function of the Messiah and not the precise nature of the association or relationship. But there can be no doubt that Jesus the Messiah is fulfilling his kingship from a position of transcendence in God.

The fact that all within the letter hinges upon singleness of faith in that messianic transcendence of Jesus and his finalizing mission in human history is further underlined by the absence of language and ideas so prominent in later canonical writings: fellowship, eternal life, justification, redemption, adoption, regeneration, sacrifice, justice/righteousness, atonement, reconciliation, blood, election, and no mention of baptism or the Lord's Supper. Indeed all of these will be used later to explain, interpret, expound, or explicate and apply the simple message: Jesus, whom you imitate with joy in the midst of severe suffering, suffered and died for you and is risen and exalted as Messiah/King to give you the call of God into his kingdom and glory, delivering you from sin and the coming wrath, as you live in the Holy Spirit with faith, love, and the hope of life with him forever, when he will appear in the midst of all his gathered people; your gathering in

Thessalonica is a manifestation of his messiahship, as you stand firm in him and follow his instructions.

The message is one of redemption more universal than that to the Jews in Palestine living under Roman oppression. But since Paul possibly had no contact with Jesus before his death and resurrection, one can rightfully ask whether this was his own interpretation and understanding which he projected back upon the Jesus story. Or was it Jesus' own self-understanding as he communicated it to the twelve who fully authorized the mission to the Gentiles as led by Paul? In any case there is no doubt about the character of the movement as messianic. Is it the one intended by Messiah himself? This is the question that naturally throws us back to the Gospels, written later, and perhaps even reflecting some of this understanding. We should nevertheless observe that Paul had indeed worked closely at Antioch with Mark, one of the Jerusalem church's recognized ministers of the oral tradition about Jesus and his mission. And Luke was indeed Paul's close friend and companion.

But before looking at the Gospels, we should first recall the general context of Jesus' and Paul's messianism.

The Context of Jesus' Messianism and Service

The Covenants of God

The ongoing creative work of God and its redemptive fulfillment, as seen within the unique perspective of Israel's inspired writers, can be briefly summarized in the progressive covenantal self-commitments by which God is tied and bound, within creation, to humanity and its condition. The successive covenants are God's sovereign and compassionate acts of grace and faithfulness to all of human creation, even when they are given to and through Israel; to them Israel and humanity are expectantly invited to respond by choosing to serve God, according to this self-revelation.

1. After chaos, there is from God both **good creation and blessing** for the primeval couple made in the divine image, in view of dominion over the earth for God.

2. With the disastrous consequences of the primal apostasy in its wish for absolute autonomy and freedom "as God," there is given the **promise of a posterity** that will crush the primeval seducer, liar, bringer-of-death-and-alienation.[8]

3. After the corruption and violence which ensued, followed by flood and destruction, there is the universal **covenant of providence**

for the emerging and expanding nations, with a clear limitation of vengeance/violence within the human family—made in God's image indeed, yet now with an evil-inclined heart from childhood, and so recognized by God.

4. After the nations' collective heaven-grasping with its Babel confusion and dispersion, a **covenant of call (election) with blessing** is promised to Abraham and Sara and their posterity in view of blessing for all of the nations (*pars per omnes*).

5. After Israel's experience of God's liberation from pharaonic oppression and slavery, without their own use of violence,[9] God makes a kingly **covenant of law** of priestly service to and for the nations.

6. With Israel's constant disobedience and abandon of God's covenant and kingship, God grants Israel a "king like the nations" with a later **royal covenant** of Father/Son love for an heir ("anointed"/Maschiach/Messiah/Christ) of King David. The reign of blessing and peace (shalom) over God's people would know no end.

Henceforth, the people of Israel, the kingdom of Israel, and the Messiah from within Israel's Davidic dynasty are seen to be inseparable because all result from God's covenantal commitment and are tied to the faithfulness of God to the covenant. But Israel gives extreme neglect to the divine intention that this promise, these actions, and fidelity of God are in view of the blessing and peace (shalom) of salvation for all of the nations' service to the Creator and creation.

The movement in history has been from creation to humanity, followed by alienation from God and his purposes; from salvaged but alienated humanity to Abraham and Israel, for all of humanity; from unfaithful Israel to a faithful remnant, for all Israel; from the remnant to the one "Anointed"—the Messiah. According to the prophets, when Messiah comes, he is for the remnant, the remnant is for all of Israel, Israel is for all of humanity, and humanity is for all of the earth as creation.[10] Henceforth, Israel in the midst of foreign oppression, exile, dispersion, and the return of many to Zion is constantly confronted with the bitter facts of that yet-unrealized messianic fulfillment.

With the hellenization of the Near East, the Syrian persecution of Israel in their own land, and later control by Egyptian overlords, an unsuccessful Hasmonean (non-Davidic) dynasty's confusion invited in the Roman Empire with an ultimate military occupation and forced integration into the empire. Smoldering hopes for a national liberator—the Messiah—were constantly stirred and fanned through the presence of Roman imperial rule, taxes, military legions, and imposition of a pagan culture and lifestyle.

The Messianic Problem

The central issue of hope in God's covenanted promise, with its questions, debates, and reflection in Israel, is what one can call "the messianic problem." The problem can be summarized briefly in three questions: When shall Messiah be revealed to Israel? Who is Messiah? How shall Messiah's reign come into existence and be carried out in the face of pagan imperial domination of Rome, disputing Jewish vested interests, and contradictory religious parties?

These were the troubling unanswered questions for the circles in Israel, by then purified of idolatry and deeply chastened by its history of being dominated, oppressed, and continually harassed by the occupying foreign power and its Jewish collaborators.

The Socioreligious Particularity of Jesus of Nazareth

In this context Jesus of Nazareth appeared in Israel's life, with his baptism by John the Baptist, and in the history of the nations, when he "suffered under Pontius Pilate." His unique stance which took place within a socioreligious/political context has been well described as "quadrilateral."[11]

1. Jesus was not a part of—nor identified with—the Jewish Sadducean religious and social establishment, nor with priests and scribes, nor with the Sanhedrin rulers who had determined a *modus vivendi* with Rome. On the contrary he expected and proclaimed radical change and transformation in view of the coming kingdom of God, the prophesied and awaited final consummation of God's purpose for humanity in creation. Could he be the Messiah?

2. But neither was Jesus a part of the revolutionary Zealots with their armed resistance in view of restoring King David's theocratic kingdom of Israel. They believed firmly in the God-sent plenipotentiary liberator/Messiah who would forcibly remove pagan domination. While Jesus did not have a takeover program for social or political action, he was clearly in touch with Zealots. Yet he called for a revolutionary turnaround, or repentance (*metanoia*), in light of the kingdom of God; he acted in the light of its presence in himself for those about him, for Israel's salvation, in view of the full consummation of God's purpose for humanity.

Thus Jesus rejected the pressures of his being acclaimed the Zealots' national Messiah and called for a renunciation of violent force: not resisting the evildoer but offering goodness, blessing, and prayer for those who hate, curse, and persecute. He was more revolutionary than the Zealots. He represented "a decidedly non-violent revolution . . .

emerging from man's most innermost and secret nature, from the personal center, from the heart of man into society . . . a conversion away from all forms of selfishness toward God and his fellow man" (Küng, 1978:191). Society, in Israel and the nations, had to be transformed through transformation of people's inner being (cf. Mark 7:20ff.). Could this be the manner and strategy of Messiah?

3. Was Jesus then for social withdrawal? There was just such a movement in his time, a kind of Jewish communal reality, the Essenes, about which we know more as a result of the Qumran manuscripts found in the late 1940s. If there was any connection between their ritual baths, understandings, and hopes and those of Jesus, it was quite possibly indirectly through John the Baptist. However, Jesus was not isolated from the social world of his day but was in the very midst of it, rejecting the notion of cutting one's self off from the "sons of darkness" as did the Essenes. Could this be the way for the Messiah to be recognized? He was not a fanatical ascetic as they were, since he was free to reinterpret certain traditional practices of the Law, defending his disciples for not fasting and even facing the charges of being a glutton and a drinker. Indeed Jesus' alternative was not for an elite in separated communities, but for all persons everywhere. He was in touch with people from all walks of society, including non-Israelites.

4. Both the violent Zealots and the communitarian Essenes had attempted radical responses to the unfaithful and accommodating socioreligious establishment they faced. Both accepted the rule of God as they understood it and were ready to assume its full consequences in a life-or-death commitment, yet with opposing strategies. However, if unlike them, one did not accept a break "at the roots," what other possibility was there? It was the way of the "devout" or "pious"—cheerfully, inconsistently working out diplomatic adjustments and attempted harmonizations of God's Law, yet quite obviously involving moral compromise: the way of the Pharisees. Their hope for a restoration of Israel through Law by keeping with its external, legal, and ritual preoccupations was clearly not the approach of Jesus. He was not a pious legalist, and he opposed self-righteousness; yet he did not ignore the Law of God. On the contrary, he called for a higher understanding and deeper commitment to it in its source in the Creator-Redeemer God, whom he called "Father" with a very provocative familiarity! But since he freely broke the detailed, stringent Sabbath laws which had developed with interpretations of creation's story, how could this be the Messiah?

The description of these current options leads us to a fuller examination of Jesus' own self-understanding, from the traditions in the Gospels.

Messianism in the Gospel Tradition: Conceptual Elements of Jesus' Messianism

The earliest "Christian" confession in the midst of Israel—"Jesus is the Messiah"—was a response to at least four major strands of thought within Israel's life: (1) the universal reign of God, believed in (prayers were adressed to the "King of the universe") but clearly not (yet) wholly realized; (2) Israel's calling—and betrayal—of its holy priestly mediation of God's mercy and justice to the nations, as it had been experienced in the exodus from Egypt; (3) the prophetic denunciations of the ruling elites' political, social, and economic oppression which accompanied their apostasy from Yahweh; (4) the promised restoration of Israel and its world mission through the royal covenant with David and his dynasty in the *Maschiach*, the God-anointed one, the Messiah (the Christ).

For these strands to come together, focused in one personality incarnating them all, required the merging of several prophetic images and titles: (1) the "son of David/son of God" fulfillment of the royal covenant; (2) the "son of man" of Daniel 7:13ff., the heaven-borne restorer of universal dominion under God; (3) the "servant of Yahweh," the Spirit-anointed messenger of God who calls Israel and her elite back to God in a new covenant, then takes the message of redemption to all nations in view of a universal redeemed community with God in its midst; (4) the "suffering servant" who incarnates mediation in a life and death that transcends the failed sacerdotal and sacrificial system in Israel. We review each of them to see how in the gospel tradition their contents fill out the messianic image in Jesus of Nazareth that we have already seen in the letter to the Thessalonians.

The Messiah

The open identification of Jesus and the Messiah, so central to the Thessalonian epistle, should in one sense come as quite a surprise since it is quite clear from the text of the Gospel of Mark with its many stories, that there was a great deal of reluctance on Jesus' part to use the title and language of "messiah." Quite specifically following Peter's confession, the twelve are warned not to tell anyone (Mark 8:30). This fact has been called "the messianic secret"[12] in scholarly circles from which the following conclusions can be summarized:

Jesus never spoke openly of himself as "the Messiah." At the same time, everything that he said and did had messianic significance, particularly the proclamation of the Kingdom of God as being decisive for the present and the future and his interpretation of his ministry as an effective sign of the kingdom, already present. He thus awakened messianic expectations and encountered faith which believed him to be the Messiah. Yet he seems to have done everything possible to discourage the propagation of that title as applied to himself (my summary of Tuckett, 1983).

How shall we explain this fact? On the basis of contemporary Jewish writings and history, we know that the messianic expectations generally centered upon a strong and mighty national leader who as a powerful military instrument of God's righteous cause would violently defeat and dominate the Roman oppressor, recreate national independence, and restore the Davidic kingdom to its former glory, all as a vindication of Yahweh before the nations who did not accept his kingship.[13]

Jesus, in his life and ministry, was permanently being confronted with that conception. This becomes clearest when Peter, in response to Jesus' question about his identity, openly confessed Jesus' messiahship but just as openly refused Jesus' own clear understanding of his ministry, rejection, betrayal, suffering, and crucifixion (Mark 8:27-38). For Jesus, that refusal was satanic; it was clearly the crucial issue that he had faced and dealt with in the desert temptations following his baptism/presentation to Israel.[14]

The words of the prophets in Israel had made it clear that Messiah would bring the kind of redemption and blessing that would overcome social ills, economic injustice, and political oppression; this was inherent to the mission of Messiah. He was to bring his people back to God and the Law and bring God's full salvation to his people and to the nations. Thus the content of the messianic mission was not in question; what was at issue was the nature of that mission. How would Messiah fulfill his God-anointed mission to Israel and the nations? Was there another option besides that of narrow nationalism, violent repression, and domination from the summit of human hierarchy by forcing and imposing the kingdom with human power and prowess in the name of Yahweh?

Jesus' answer to that question has ever since been a part of the concern for understanding the specificity of Jesus' messianism, as well as the nature of redemption he brings and the salvation he fulfills. Unfortunately, Western Christianity, with the dualism so characteristic of Greek thought, has at this very point generally misconstrued the issue as one of "political messiah versus religious messiah," heavenly kingdom versus earthly kingdom. The great biblical scholar Oscar Cullmann is one of the best recent representatives of such thought, constantly distinguishing between the political messiah of Judaism and his own understanding of what he called the "spiritual messiahship" of Jesus. "Jesus knows that the specific ideas relating to the Jewish Messiah are of a political nature, and nothing is more foreign to his conception of his calling" (Cullmann, 1963:120).

The elimination of the political, social, and economic concerns from Jesus' understanding of his messiahship simply vitiates the holistic restoration and salvation thrust of Israel's prophets "when predicting the sufferings of [Messiah] and the subsequent glory" (1 Pet. 1:11b) as "indicated by the Spirit of [Messiah] within them" (1 Pet. 1:11a). Perhaps the most striking illustration is the typical interpretation of Jesus' word to Pilate, "My kingship is not of this world; if my kingship were of this world, my servants would fight, that I might not be handed over to the Jews; but my kingship is not from the world" (John 18:36). In the Western spiritualist tradition, the word has been construed to mean a dominion "not on earth" rather than as a reference to a non-"worldly" (seen as not conformed to God's will) ethos or quality of dominion. However, Jesus' own insistence is upon being "in the world" and is contrasted with being "of the world" and not with being "out of the world" (John 17).

The issue is the nature and quality of the mission of Messiah, who is political by definition.[15] The issue is not one of whether political, social, or economic concerns are included in Messiah's agenda, but rather of how they are to be dealt with. And here we must turn to other dimensions of Jesus' understanding.

Son of God

As was already indicated, "son of God" is a royal title, but it was applied first of all to Israel itself when the "first-born sons" of Pharaoh and Egypt were lost in order to save Yahweh's "first-born son," Israel (Exod. 4:22-23). Later in the time of Israel's kingship ("like the nations" and only permitted by God), the term was applied to the king in Israel as a title (cf. Ps. 2:7) for one who fully represents all of Israel and who yet receives authority and unction/anointing as God's representative, ruling for God.

Especially did that title become meaningful as a future hope because of the Davidic covenant earlier referred to and given through the prophet Nathan: "I will establish the throne of his kingdom forever. I will be his father, and he shall be my son. . . . your kingdom shall be made sure for ever before me; your throne shall be established for ever" (2 Sam. 7:13-16ff.; cf. 1 Chron. 17:11-15ff.). The Chronicles text adds, "I will not take my steadfast love from him" (1 Chron. 17:13). The Davidic covenant was foundational to the Jewish kingdom's identity, and in times of exile and non-Davidic rulers, it was foremost in Israel's thought.[16] Later, particularly in the Greek context, "Son of God" became one of the most-used titles for Jesus except for "Lord" and "Christ," but it had lost its messianic functional impact.

What seems most important is that beginning with this Jewish royal understanding and title, Jesus demonstrated the messianic Father/Son unique relationship and intimacy in a way which makes it a reality that moved well beyond the scope of nationalist preoccupations but not beyond the political ones. Indeed, that intimacy and sense of uniqueness would ultimately be associated with the later Greek emphasis on the divinely "substantial" Son of God. Yet this sense of uniqueness and intimacy does not eliminate the messianic dimension but gives it a scope in God that reaches well beyond Israel to a fuller universal messianism and dominion. "Son of God" must not be extracted from that messianic meaning and context.

In the last week before his death, Jesus himself tried to make the Jerusalem leaders more sensitive to this reality during his open discussion about Psalm 110:2. "How can the scribes say that the Christ [Messiah] is the son of David? David himself, inspired by the Holy Spirit, declared, 'The Lord said to my Lord, Sit at my right hand, till I put thy enemies under thy feet.' David himself calls him Lord; so how is he his son?" (Mark 12:35-37). Indeed, how can the Davidic dynasty have a scion who is higher than the founder of the national dynasty? Yet does not David himself recognize it to be true? This very real transcendent political preoccupation was in Jesus' consciousness just a couple of days prior to his crucifixion . . . and resurrection. Was he not calling Israel to readiness for that answer so soon to come?

Son of Man

It is most significant that Jesus clearly preferred to give himself the title "Son of man." We find it fifteen times in Mark's earliest written presentation of the oral tradition. Indeed it is found some sixty-nine times in the synoptics and a dozen times in the Gospel of John, with practically no other use of the title in the New Testament writings (see Acts 7:56; Rev. 1:13). However, despite that fact, as one recent christological study notes in dismissing its importance, "it has never played a major role in the theological definition of Christ's person" because it is "associated with—if not synonymous with—the title 'Son of God' (Mark 14:62 and parallels)."[17] Eclipsed in that manner by many theologians, its meaning—so significant for Jesus—has nevertheless appeared to have had a significant continuity in the thought of Paul, which we have already seen (1 Thess. 4:15) in his understanding of the yet-to-come eschatological ministry of the Messiah Jesus, to which we will later return.

It is not possible here to develop the ancient Jewish and non-Jewish roots of the title which was quite current in some circles in Jesus' time.[18] Suffice it to say that it referred to a "heavenly" or "ideal" man, representing on the one hand the beginning of humanity with Adam's dominion and on the other hand the "endtimes" (*eschaton*) when such dominion would again appear with humanity under God. Both deal with the representative human, "man" called to be faithful to his divine destiny to be the image of God (Cullmann, 1963:151). In Daniel 7 he appears in the eschatological context "with the clouds of heaven" (7:13) and is presented to the Ancient of Days; dominion, kingdom, and glory was given him "that all peoples, nations and languages should serve him" (7:14) in an "everlasting dominion, which shall not pass away, and his kingdom one that shall not be destroyed" (7:14). The expression is interpreted as being a personal representation of the collective "saints of the Most High"; it did not escape integration into the self-understanding of one who proclaimed the kingdom of God as present in his words and ministry.

The use of the title by Jesus must have carried some ambiguity, however, for in Job and the Psalms the expression is often used to refer to humankind generally, and peculiarly to human frailty in responsibility before the eternal Creator-God (cf. Ps. 8:4). Further, in the writings of Ezekiel, the term is found over eighty times in reference to the prophet. In the opening vision, seeing himself only as a "child of man" in the face of the glory of the transcendent God, the prophet falls on his face (Ezek. 1:28); called to his feet, he is given the Spirit with strength to proclaim the message of God (2:1ff.). Thus he becomes a messenger of God's word of judgment and salvation to a rebellious people. Not as a "son of Israel" to Israel, but as a "son of man" (son of universal humanity) to Israel and all the nations, the prophet is called to judge both Israel and its enemies in view of their salvation.

In the early part of Jesus' ministry, the title he used could easily have been understood as open acknowledgment of such a prophetic ministry and was recognized as such (cf. Matt. 16:13; Mark 6:15; John

6:14). And Jesus could also use it for himself in the sense of frailty and humiliation. The very question to Peter, "Who do men say that the Son of man is?" (Matt. 16:13), indicates the ambivalence of the term, for if it had clearly meant the transcendent, eschatological king, there would have been no reason to raise the question. But there can be no doubt that following Peter's confession, such an orientation became unambiguous.

Henceforth, Jesus' use of the title referred to the eschatological "man" in his exaltation, thus accenting the more his betrayal, rejection, suffering, and death. It is the judicial dimension of the Son of man in his exaltation that is most often underlined in Jesus' words and understandings. Matthew 25, with the judgment between sheep and goats, is the most striking; here the nations are judged in relationship to their responses to the needs of "these my brethren" (Matt. 25:40). We see it again in Matthew 24:29-31 where the tribes of the earth will mourn as "his elect" are gathered under the authority of the Son of man; in Luke 17:22-37 the "days of the Son of man" are compared to those of the flood in the time of Noah and the judgment of Sodom and Gomorrah. Most striking, of course, is Jesus' startling response to the high priest: "You will see the Son of man sitting at the right hand of Power, and coming with the clouds of heaven" in answer to the question, "Are you the [Messiah]?" (Mark 14:61-62).

Here is open acknowledgment by Jesus that he is not only the "son of David"/Messiah of Jewish national concern, but also the "Son of man"/Messiah of present-day and ultimate eschatological significance. It is indeed the image of Daniel 7 on the one hand, yet tied clearly to the righteous ruler of Psalm 110 who executes judgment and high priestly mediation among the nations with obviously more universal authority than the seat of the high priest of Jerusalem before whom he appears. The combination illustrates Jesus' consciousness of a coming magistracy to be exercised prior to the fulfillment of God's universal eschatological reign—a political function and mission obviously greater than that of the simple messiahship of national Israel and its imperial interests, of which he is accused.

What is unique in this understanding of the "Son of man" is the earthly humiliation of this ideal, heavenly man—the image of God—in an earthly testing, as a prerequisite to the exaltation of universal magistracy. Indeed, the Son of man to whom judgment is to be given is not an ideal man in the heavenly world; he is rather one who on earth, in the flesh, in the world struggles and agonizes in his human calling of righteousness and love to be faithful to his identity and destiny as the true and faithful image of the Father-Creator of humanity who sends him.

The testing of the cross is that which must happen as an ultimate test of that faithfulness: only he is worthy of exercising eschatological judgment who has suffered in death the loss of his freedom, precisely because of his free and faithful obedience in love, while continuing to love and forgive his enemies, respecting even their freedom to kill him. It is this "image of God" which was demonstrated by Jesus the Son of man before the coming day was over. On the one hand, it was the fullest human response to God's covenant of grace and faithfulness; while on the other hand, it became the new covenant of God to all of humanity (*uno per omnes*).

The ideal or prototypical and representative humanity as image of God, with its fulfillment in an ultimate humiliation due to human faithfulness to God as a condition of glory, are inherent in Jesus' appropriation of the title, Son of man, and his understanding of its ultimate eschatological importance. That orientation and its tension in which he lived is well-depicted in a later commentary which had recognized that representative role so well: "looking to Jesus . . . , who for the joy that was set before him endured the cross, despising the shame, and is seated at the right hand of the throne of God. Consider him who endured from sinners such hostility against himself, so that you may not grow weary or fainthearted" (Heb. 12:2-3; cf. 2:6-10.).

Servant of Yahweh and the Suffering Servant

The servant (*ebed*) in the Servant Songs of Isaiah (42:1-4; 49:1-9; 50:4-11; 52:13—53:12) is in the Septuagint translated as *pais* which can in turn be translated either as "servant" or as "child" (as in Acts 4:27, 30, KJV).

It is important to note that in Jesus' time this "servant of Yahweh" was identified either with the coming Messiah or corporate Israel. This identification was both in the Qumran writings and in the Targum of Isaiah, but all of the traces of suffering and humiliation had been removed from that understanding, as being incompatible with Messiah and his mission. What was significant for Israel was that he was the anointed one—the one to whom God's Spirit is given (Isa. 42:1), that is, the *Maschiach*, the Messiah—who is to "bring forth justice to the nations" (42:1), persevering in his universal mission "till he has established justice in the earth" (42:4). This is, of course, an eminently political function given as the basic calling, mission, and purpose of the servant, the context of all of his activity—as well as in the collection of Servant Songs. In his person, the servant is a "covenant to the people [Israel], a light to the nations" (42:6) as the bringer of God's justice.

If, from the womb, the servant of Yahweh was chosen to bring about the restoration of Israel, his ultimate mission through Israel was to be that light so "that my salvation may reach to the end of the earth" (Isa. 49:5-6). Contrary to Judaism's understandings, it is as the servant of rulers (49:7) that he will attract the homage of rulers! Prior to the song of Isaiah 52:13ff., the task of the servant is given as that of bringing good tidings (gospel) of peace, goodness, and salvation—of proclaiming to Jerusalem, "Your God reigns" (52:7) (kingdom of God). Through the redemption of Jerusalem "before the eyes of all the nations," all the ends of the earth will see the salvation from Israel's God (52:7-10). All of this had clear import and significance for Judaism in Jesus' time.

Thus, from the perspective of the texts themselves, it would appear that Cullmann overstates the case when he insists that "the principal function of the servant of God is found in his sufferings and his substitutionary death" (Cullmann, 1963:55). Rather, it is in the context of this principal (political) function of bringing justice to the ends of the earth through Israel—and only in the perspective of this mission—that the servant becomes despised (Isa. 49:7), smitten, and spat upon (50:6), becoming indeed the suffering one, wounded, bruised, chastised, oppressed, afflicted as an offering for sin. But even after the self-giving unto death, the mission is not terminated, even though the death itself becomes also a means of justice—"make[ing] many to be accounted righteous" (53:11). Indeed, as the song of Isaiah 52:13 begins, "He shall be exalted and lifted up, and shall be very high."

The mission of the servant is the restoration of Israel by preaching the peace of the reign of God, in view of the establishment of justice among all the nations. Thus the servant's "sufferings and substitutionary death" to which Cullmann refers are first of all the consequences of a prophetic preaching mission of persuasion for justice and peace, with only God to justify him before those who reject and oppose that mission (Isa. 50:7ff.) in which he "poured out his soul to death" (53:12).

It was just such a reception, at the hands of those opposed to God's reign, which was unacceptable and impossible for the Messiah as understood by Judaism. But the vicarious suffering and death were also a function of the servant as "offering for sin" (53:10), "for the transgression of my people" (53:8), "[bearing] the sin of many . . .

[with] . . . intercession for the transgressors" (53:12); their first consequence was a posterity that would also be made righteous. The servant's place as one who is great and who divides the spoils of victory is
also a consequence of his first of all giving his life in that mission faithfully unto death. His exaltation is a consequence of his faithfulness despite rejection, suffering, and death.

In the perspective of the whole—both that unacceptable to the Judaism of Jesus' time and that marginalized by Cullmann in our
time—the Messiah is a prophet-king who is God's chosen servant for
justice to Israel first, and thus through Israel is servant to the nations.
In that mission he suffers and dies at their hands, thus fulfilling a
priestly service of reconciliation as the one who representatively suffers and dies for all. But the mission continues: the servant "shall pros-
per, he shall be exalted and lifted up, and shall be very high" (Isa.
52:13) . . . "till he has established justice in the earth" (42:4), for that is
the mission.

Independently of current Jewish understandings, Jesus fully assumed the *ebed*-Messiah alternative, including the suffering unto
death, starting with the Spirit-empowering at his baptism by John.
There the servant-king messianic commission is explicit (Mark 1:11
and parallels, in the light of Ps. 2:7 and Isa. 42:1), and in the Gospel of
John the "lamb" of God of Isaiah 53:7 is also made explicit in the language of the Baptist. Thus, as already indicated, Jesus knew himself to
be the chosen Messiah of Israel for the nations, with the high calling of
reestablishing peace through justice through the appeal and persuasion of the proclaimed Word of God by a faithful servant—without
self-defense, violence, or deceit (Isa. 53:9). Jesus said it clearly in one
very important logion in Mark's Gospel: "For the Son of man also
came not to be served but to serve, and to give his life as a ransom for
many" (Mark 10:45). The declaration is made in the context of contrasting Gentile ("the nations") lordship, rule, and authority with that
of Israel's calling as the faithful covenant partner in the kingdom of
God, of which Jesus was the supreme instance.

This manner of ministry was dramatically represented and symbolized in Jesus' washing the feet of the disciples at the Last Supper:
"an example, that you also should do as I have done" (John 13:15).
Here again the reference is to a political style—a servant-Messiah: "the
leader [should be] as one who serves. . . . I am among you as one who
serves" (Luke 22:26-28). The high point of Jesus' ministry, the paschal
celebration in view of the coming final sufferings and death, is specifically set forth in explicit servant language and action. The references

to death "for many" (as in Isa. 53:12) in Mark 14:24 and parallels in that context confirm this self-understanding as "suffering servant."

It is not strange, of course, that this would be confirmed in other Gospel writings.[19] The Gospel of Mark, and especially the passion narrative, has been seen by scholars to have been written in the light of the "servant" messialogy as it was known and expressed in the oral tradition which emerged from Jesus' own self-understanding (cf. Cullmann, 1963:63). This appears as well in the earliest reported preaching in Jerusalem where the servant (or "child") theme is accented in the context of Peter's ministry (Acts 3:13, 26; 4:25, 30). Indeed, the "righteous one" of Isaiah 53:11 was clearly a part of the current language of the early days (Acts 3:14; 7:52; 22:14). Significantly, both remain important in the much later epistle of Peter, where the "servant" (1 Pet. 2:21ff.) and "the righteous one" (3:16-18) is appealed to as the example for the disciples' daily way of life as well as the way to God.

One also recalls the important application of Isaiah's suffering servant to Jesus in the ministry of Philip to the Ethiopian minister of Queen Candace (Acts 8:32ff.). The very early *homologia* that Paul exploited in his exhortation to the Philippians (Phil. 2:1-11) describes Jesus' earthly ministry as the "form of a servant" (v. 7; cf. "form of God," v. 6), who as man, "humbled himself and became obedient unto death" (v. 8). And most significantly, the apostle exposes it as the mind-set of the Messiah Jesus to be appropriated by his disciples (v. 5). Finally, this is also most obviously reflected in the apostles' early self-designation as "servants" in juxtaposition with Jesus' servanthood (Acts 4:29) or as the usual way of describing themselves and their associates (Rom. 1:1; 1 Cor. 4:1; 7:22; Gal. 1:10; Phil. 1:1; 2 Pet. 1:1; Jude 1:1).

The evidence indicates that probably the earliest messianic understanding of the post-resurrection community, informed by the risen Jesus (as reported by Luke 24:26f. and 45f.), was that which experienced and knew Jesus as *ebed Yahweh* and the Servant-Messiah (Cullmann, 1963:79). Although the language—and understandings—were eventually to become marginal in the Greek contexts which eclipsed those of Judaism, even there they nevertheless retained some importance both for liturgy (see Didache 9:2; 10:2; 1 Clement 59:3; 61:3) and for life-pattern (e.g., 1 Clement 16) as in 1 Peter.

One could, of course, ask why this servant Christology which was so important both in Jesus' consciousness and in the early life (Andrew Walls' "Jewish phase") of the church was later to lose vital significance. Was the servant/slave language culturally unacceptable for the context of the Greek world? Was it seen as inappropriate ideology for the empire? Here we simply stress its singular importance, for this is in fact the essential revolutionary turnaround in the disciple-community's messianic consciousness. This is the itinerary from Peter's confession of Jesus as Messiah, through his sword-carrying and sword-wielding defense of Jesus in the garden, to the authoritative apostolic word which gives the Messiah Jesus' nonresistant suffering in doing good as the supreme example to be followed in the vocation of his disciples (1 Pet. 2:21ff.).

This servant Christology was present also in the oldest document, addressed to the Thessalonians, by one who made exactly the same conversion as Peter and was ultimately preaching and practicing that same servanthood. But in our earlier examination of that epistle this concept was not then seen so clearly, nor was its significance and its source well understood.

> To the church . . . in God the Father and the Lord Jesus [the Messiah]: Grace to you and peace. . . . You became imitators of us and of the Lord, for you received the word in much affliction . . . so that you became an example. . . . The word of the Lord sounded forth from you. . . . You turned to God from idols, to serve a living and true God. . . . We exhorted each one of you and encouraged you and charged you to lead a life worthy of God, who calls you into his own kingdom and glory. . . . You . . . became imitators of the churches of God in [the Messiah] Jesus, . . . for you suffered the same things. . . . We live, if you stand fast in the Lord. . . . May the Lord make you increase and abound in love to one another and to all men, as we do to you. . . . For you know what instructions we gave you through the Lord Jesus. . . . Be at peace among yourselves. . . . See that none of you repays evil for evil, but always seek to do good to one another and to all. . . . May the God of peace himself sanctify you wholly. . . . The grace of our Lord Jesus [the Messiah] be with you (1 Thess. 1:1—5:28).

There are, of course, deep roots for this servanthood in the vicarate given to the human couple as God's servant in and over creation and in God's liberating Israel from Egypt ("that they may serve me").[20] This is clearly repeated in their God-given mediating vocation as "kingdom of priests" (Exod. 19:4-6) in the midst of the nations. Through *torah* and the prophets we know of a created humanity and a redeemed Israel for the service of God in and over earthly creation; but where is that servanthood and service visibly realized? It is promised by the word of God through the prophet Isaiah as a specific characteristic of God's anointed, the Messiah, the one for the many; it was self-consciously fulfilled by Jesus of Nazareth.[21] But even as it was unacceptable to official Judaism, it was also not congenial to the later dominant Greek mentality nor to the barbarians among whom their Christianity spread and extended itself worldwide.

Yet then and now, inside and outside of Israel, Jesus' fulfillment remains a permanent provocation and corrective to current and popular misunderstandings of messianism, giving a new and definitive meaning to the title: the Messiah, the Christ. But thus appropriated, it in no way whatsoever eliminates the full dynamics of messianic hope and fulfillment for humanity restored in community; there goodness and blessing, love/mercy and righteousness, create peace through the anointing by Jesus the Anointed One/Messiah and give evidence of God's salvation, holy presence, and reign in the midst of and for the nations which know no such hope.

Servant Elements of Jesus' Messianism

The Relationship to God as "Father"

There seems to be little doubt that the book of Deuteronomy had considerable influence in Jesus' personal training. The accent therein upon Israel's covenant response of service to God is repeated over and over again (cf. Deut. 6:13; 10:12, 20; 11:13; 13:4). And it is to this basic call to Israel that Jesus turned in the inaugural desert confrontation and temptation: "Away from me, Satan! For it is written: 'Worship the Lord your God, and serve him only' " (Matt. 4:10, NIV; cf. Luke 4:7-8).

The way Jesus understood that service to God is, however, not according to the types of slave to master, of subject to royalty, or even of creature to Creator. It is rather in an intimate parent-to-child-to-parent relationship of mutual love (cf. Deut. 6:5, quoted in Mark 12:33) and trust in which a common identity and destiny prompts in the one a willful, active, and obedient reflection of the life, character, purpose, and will of the other whose shared identity is thus totally disclosed. The idea of obedient sonship was not a new one for Israel (Tinsley, 1960); it only lacked full embodiment. That was promised, as we have seen, in the royal posterity of David—the Messiah, when he would come.

Without question, Jesus impressed those about him with the fact that he lived his inherited sonship in Israel in a unique way, as he spoke of and to Abba with an intensity and familiarity previously unknown.[22] It became public at least at the time of his baptism by John, when that affinity was confirmed with the word (Ps. 2:7; Isa. 42:1) to the *ebed* of Yahweh: "You are my Son [*ebed, pais*], whom I love; with you I am well pleased" (Mark 1:11, NIV). This central dynamic relationship expressed itself in an ethos of God's presence—the Holy Spirit—which for others henceforth characterized his life and service (cf. Newman, 1987). And this life core of anointed/messianic sonship was seen by Jesus also as a future reality and measure of judgment, beyond the crucifixion to the time of the *eschaton* when "the Son of man is to come with his angels in the glory of his father" (Matt. 16:27). Jesus' sonship was acknowledged by his apostles as an exposed "exegesis" of God (cf. John 1:18), fully identified with the eternal (John 8:58: "before Abraham was, I am") creating Word (John 1:1f.) and wisdom (1 Cor. 1:30) of God.[23]

The Relationship to Israel

Jesus' basic messianic approach. Jesus began his public ministry within the stream opened up by John the Baptist's ministry in which he called all Israel to repentance and righteousness of obedient faith in view of the kingdom of God (Luke 3:8; Matt. 3:9). Jesus, in accenting the kingdom of God and its justice, followed with that same call to all Israel in a way that has sometimes astonished. For it can even appear that he strictly limited his ministry and that of his missioners to "the lost sheep of . . . Israel" (e.g., Matt. 10:6; 15:24), even when he allowed for Samaritan or Gentile exceptions. In any case it has been well shown that his constitution of the twelve was an eschatological witness and a prophetic sign to the "twelve tribes of Israel," as illustration or demonstration of his intent to reassemble, to regather, to reconstitute, and to restore the people of God that all Israel was called to be.[24] How poignant that becomes in the Matthean-cited plaint: "O Jerusalem, Jerusalem, you who kill the prophets and stone those sent to you, how often I have longed to gather your children together, as a hen gathers her chicks under her wings, but you were not willing" (Matt. 23:37, NIV).

It is quite clearly the particular strategy of beginning again radically with the message and reality of God's reign at the grassroots (as yeast or seed) with the gathered remnant as the base in order to gather all of Israel. Yet Israel's salvation is ultimately in view of and the means of the Gentile nations' salvation (John 11:51f.; see Jeremias, 1958). It was in Israel first that God's messianic sonship needed to be recognized, sanctioned, and heeded. But it was a clear political strategy, in view of the assembling group (Hebrew: *qahal*; Greek: *ekklesia*; English: assembly/church) of God's faithful people for their calling in the midst of and for the nations. Jesus was clearly not totally misunderstood when he was crucified as the "King of the Jews."

The little apocalypse of the Gospels indicates both Jesus' sense of foreboding concerning the future of Jerusalem and his deepest desire to arrest that doom, even as Jonah in Nineveh (Matt. 12:41f.). Indeed, more than a half millenium earlier Jerusalem's destruction and Israel's exile under Babylon were seen to be precipitated (Jer. 34:17ff.) by its overt disobedience in reneging on the Jubilee covenant of justice and liberty which the Law of God had prescribed (cf. Lev. 25) as a sign of God's justice and mercy in the Passover and exodus.

Thus at the very beginning of his ministry in Nazareth, Jesus, following King Zedekiah, began with a royal call to that practice of economic justice and liberty (Luke 4:16ff.) in fulfillment of the Isaianic servant's vocation (Isa. 61:1f.; 58:6) and in view of Israel's salvation; it nearly led to his death. Nor did Israel as a whole heed the call, although the exception is clearly observable in a Zacchaeus (cf. Luke 1:9) who repented and in obedient faith received the salvation offered only days before Jesus' death at the hands of those who refused it. But his proclamation of jubilee makes it clear that Jesus in his preaching of the kingdom and the call to repentance and obedient faith was concerned about the total human welfare (shalom) of Israel: "Would that even today you knew the things that make for peace! . . . They will not leave one stone upon another in you; because you did not know the time of your visitation" (Luke 19:42-44; see Trocmé, 1973).

The messianic ways and means. In observing the ways and means with which Jesus carried out his messianic sonship and God-revealing service, we may often find grounds for the later development of particular, local, contextual Christologies, each of which makes a contribution to a fuller understanding.[25]

The manner or ways of Jesus' servanthood cannot be separated from his identity; these were the ways of the son. "Father"-oriented communion/prayer was a fundamental characteristic which has inspired mystical Christologies. His freedom in obedience to the Father has inspired Christologies of freedom. His victory over Satan in the desert, in later temptations with Peter's confession or in the garden, over evil spirits, and on the cross have contributed to Christologies of *Christus victor.* Jesus' gathering of a disciple-community has inspired strategies of congregation-planting. When the compassion of his freedom became a contestation of the established powers, he fully assumed the consequences of their hostility; it has inspired Christologies of contestation or revolution. He accepted suffering as inherent to his calling of doing and fulfilling God's justice, with forgiveness of enemies and the refusal of violence against them; it has inspired pacifist Christologies.

Jesus' total openness to persons of all social classes inspires Christologies of relationship and personhood. His rejection of power has contributed to kenotic Christologies. Since all of his filial service to God was seen as love (*agape*) for others including the enemy, it has inspired Christologies of love and the "man for others." Indeed, such love humanly fulfilled God's law without diminishing its intent; hence, Christologies of fullfillment. One cannot but be impressed with Jesus' preoccupation with service to the marginal: the poor, inspiring a Christology oriented to "God's option for the poor"; women, inspiring a feminist Christology ("Jesus was a feminist"); publicans and harlots, with a "Christ for the outsiders"; his "set at liberty those who are oppressed" (Luke 4:18), inspiring a Christology of liberation. All of them together indicate the way of the Son, the Messiah. Each is one part of the way.

The means—or techniques—of Jesus' servanthood reveal the many methods of articulating his messiahship with the various manifestations of alienation in the people among whom he moved and served. Beginning with his proclamation of the kingdom and the call to repentance, Jesus the preacher inspires a kerygmatic conversionist Christology, or a kingdom Christology. Thereupon follows his personal call to follow him, inspiring ethical Christologies of master-disciple, discipling, discipleship; Jesus can become a human model to follow. His response to the sick and lame; the blind, deaf, and the leper is one of healing and wholeness; it is not strange that Christologies of healing and care for the sick should develop from this dimension of his ministry. Where he meets those who are demon-possessed and totally alienated from others, he confronts and casts out evil spirits, manifesting the victorious power of the kingdom of God; given the context, such has often inspired Christologies of exorcism and power confrontation.

As a recognized rabbi/teacher among his fellow Jews, Jesus taught, often effectively with parables, as he reinterpreted the Law of God and the prophets, often in the light of his own work. He did not hesitate to confront prophetically the oppressive legalism and religious formalism and exploitation of his time. Both of these latter expressions have provided inspiration for prophetic and teaching Christologies of the Word. Jesus openly entered the domain seen as that of the divine and gave the priestly proclamation of forgiveness of sins; this has inspired Christologies of mediation of grace. His blessing and promises of blessing have certainly been exploited in Christologies of prosperity.

These summaries can perhaps be more fully completed with others. But all of these ways and means of Jesus' life, action, and service were expressions of his obedient sonship and a servant exegesis-revelation of the "Father"; he saw them to be in fact the very signs of his God-sent messianity. "Go and tell John what you hear and see: the blind receive their sight and the lame walk, lepers are cleansed and the deaf hear, and the dead are raised up, and the poor have good news preached to them. And blessed is he who takes no offense at me" (Matt. 11:4-6). What is important here is the recognition of all of these dimensions of Jesus' life and service as a fuller revealing of the Father by the Son. Each was a true—even as it was a partial—revealing of the Father.

Each partial understanding needs to be understood and critiqued in the light of the fuller one. Yet it was all implicit in the Jewish apostles' gospel ministry and life together in Thessalonica, when they lived and preached Jesus the Messiah two decades after his death and two decades prior to the destruction of Jerusalem which he had tried to save. They were indeed taking up the servant mission of Israel to the nations (cf. Acts 13:46f.) as they participated in the messianic end-time gathering of the peoples into the universal *ekklesia* of God.

It is not at all clear that all those who experienced personally that revelation of God and those signs of divine sonship, messianity, and the kingdom of God received them as such. Neither is it clear that they came—without offense—to faith in Jesus as the Messiah, the Son of God. Nor is it clear that through Jesus they all came to know God as "Father," living out the child-stance of obedient trust and love which would reflect God's life and reign, even as Jesus had taught and done. Nor is it clear that they all (only about 120 persons were in the Jerusalem circle in the days after Jesus' resurrection ministry) identified with Jesus' new community in Israel. But ways and means into that possibility had been present—as a revealing of the Father—for those who would "hear and see." Indeed each means had been a potential path into the "way" of Jesus' divine sonship and messianity, and thence to the Father who was thus made known for the salvation of Israel, itself the chosen instrument (the "kingdom of priests") of such ways and means of making God known for the blessing and salvation of the nations.

The Suffering Servanthood of Jesus' Messianism

The disproportionate amount of space given to the betrayal, trials, sufferings, and crucifixion of Jesus in the four Gospel accounts has focused particular attention on that death and its meaning, not only for the ordinary reader but also for theologians. Classical theology referred to this as the passive obedience of Jesus: that which he endured in his acceptance of death, and which happened to him; he was crucified by others (passive mode). Not enough attention was given to the active obedience of Jesus: that which he freely took on as task and calling, which he fully assumed, and which led to his death ("became obedient unto death" Phil. 2:8; "by the obedience of one shall many be made righteous" Rom. 5:19, KJV).

What has been correctly stressed much more in Western Christianity in recent years is Jesus' inaugural presentation in Nazareth in which he publicly proclaimed and defined his messianic mission: "The Spirit of the Lord is upon me, because he has anointed me to preach good news to the poor. He has sent me to proclaim release to the captives and recovering of sight to the blind, to set at liberty those who are oppressed, to proclaim the acceptable year of the Lord" (Luke 4:18-19). The immediate reaction to that proclamation, with the death intent, indicates that Jesus' death was first of all the consequence of his Spirit-anointed mission of righteousness and freedom for the peace of Israel, in view of the nations.[26]

"It is written" indeed that the servant of God would suffer and die, but we have already seen in Isaiah's songs that it was due to the servant's fully assuming the task of bringing forth "to the nations" the justice of obedience to God. And this meant that all of the forces of oppression and injustice in their disobedience to God would pit themselves against such a mission; it was the taking on of God's struggle with disobedient and sinful humanity as of old, as well as his covenant commitment to it. It was Jesus' active and faithful filial obedience in that mission that brought on the opposition which inflicted suffering and ultimately his death; it was "written," given his mission and its context of disobedient humanity, both in Israel and among the nations. At any point Jesus could have turned away from that mission and avoided the wrathful outworking of that disobedience in violent opposition and its consequences; but his calling was to absorb that injustice and persevere, to assume the consequences and persevere, vicariously to take upon himself that wrath.[27]

In his freedom of obedience to the Father's steadfast love, Jesus would also in steadfast love (*agape*) respect the freedom of others to reject his appeal by word and life for repentance. Yet in love he totally respected such refusal and offered forgiveness, even when it meant his own death. He was indeed "obedient unto death, even death on a cross," as the oldest Christian hymn says it (Phil. 2:8) and as the Isaiah song had indicated (cf. Isa. 50:4-9). As the Son of man (the one for all), he had offered to the Father the "living sacrifice" of his free and total obedience. As the Servant/Son he had freely sacrificed his own free life in death and thus revealed the Father and the extent and fullness of his love.

Even more, he had paid the price of forgiveness and atonement in fully assuming and absorbing the wrathful disobedience and injustice of humanity alienated from God; "the Lord has laid on him the iniquity of us all" (Isa. 53:6).[28] God's work as Creator-Father of humanity was fulfilled ("it is finished") in the human servant Jesus, the fully obedient child—the Messiah: son of Israel's David, Son of God, but also the Son of man—the one-for-all and once-for-all paradigm for humanity. Both his life and his death were essential to his unique work of justice for peace.[29]

Thus in addition to the Gospels' description of that God-purposed humanity, the space and attention given to Jesus' sufferings, crucifixion, and death served to underline once for all the fundamental and unique nature of Jesus' messianism when compared to other messianic pretenders during the last times (Mark 13:22). It further displays the events in Jesus' pouring out his life in self-giving as a full revelation of the sacrificial love of God, with free access to that love —and the new humanity in God—through the forgiveness offered in Messiah who lived and died in such manner. Messiah Jesus is God's new covenant solidarity with humanity for the elimination of all its alienation and its restoration.

The Vindication of the Servant-Messiah: The Resurrection

If there was any doubt that Jesus was the Messiah—and his death had totally reinforced those doubts—the disciples' experience of Jesus' resurrection from the dead not only finally erased them but absolutely confirmed that he was the Messiah, victorious over the powers that opposed him with death. The steadfast love that had conquered the temptations from disciples and the powers was totally vindicated. It had fully borne unto death the betrayals and the assault of the powers' injustice and sin without becoming like them or wiping them out. And now Jesus' resurrection vindicated that triumph of love and the sacrificial obedience of sonship. When humanity does its worst and kills the Son who reflects the image of God, Jesus' resurrection becomes the triumph of divine love and life. On the other side of death, Jesus explained the Scriptures to the disciples, showing them that "the [Messiah had to] suffer these things and enter into his glory" (Luke 24:26).

Jesus' messianity of servanthood in sonship newly revealed God as well as a new Israel and a new humanity. The obedience of *agape*/love unto death defined the nature of the messianic mission, and the bearing of sin with the forgiveness of the cross fulfilled the way into the new humanity. The resurrection confirmed this for the disciple witnesses and assured them of the risen Messiah's ongoing mission and magistracy in view of the restoration and salvation of all Israel and all the nations. Moreover, they were themselves commissioned by the risen Jesus for this mission with him through the preaching of the good news of his messiahship, his mission of governance, and his coming for its fulfillment. Starting from the new alternative human space of their Jerusalem assembly, they were assured of the presence of the Holy Spirit in their own relationships and mission as children of God through faith/fellowship in the Messiah, the Son of God.

Christological Understanding
The implications of the servant theme for our christological reflection and understanding are important. Understanding must include the messianic means, yet not be limited to any of them, since it must move beyond them to the heart of Jesus' messianity—the *agape* servanthood of faithful filial obedience as the mark and manifestation of God's reign and purpose in the midst of the people in God's service. The Messiah/King is freely and wholly in the service of God at the same time that he is freely and wholly in the service of God's people. He lives his sonship with God, fully trusting in the Father and his steadfast love unto death; he lives his kingship with the people as a fully obedient reflection of the Father and his steadfast love unto death. He is indeed a mediator-king, a priestly king.

In that mediation, the history and destiny of Messiah's people are inextricably bound to two factors. They are bound, on the one hand, to his fidelity in loving trust in the Father and his faithfulness in obedience to the Father's steadfast love; but they are also bound to their own measure of faithfulness in identification with him, as the mark and manifestation of God's reign and purpose. Jesus' obedience to the cross is the demonstration and historical guarantee and non-retractability of that fidelity ("The death he died he died to sin, once for all" Rom. 6:10), and his resurrection/exaltation is the guarantee of its living continuity ("the life he lives he lives to God" 6:10). That human fulfillment in God—as son of David and Son of man—becomes the non-variable determinant of Israel's and all the nations' history and destiny.

And this was the essence of Paul's messianism as he preached it at Thessalonica. At Athens only a few weeks later, he proclaimed it clearly: "In the past God overlooked such ignorance, but now he commands all people everywhere to repent. For he has set a day when he will judge the world with justice by the man he has appointed. He has given proof of this to all men by raising him from the dead" (Acts 17:30-31, NIV). Because of the unique character of this Messiah-event for all of human history, every people and each person is invited to turn forward in identification and solidarity with him and his community which lives in expectation of its fulfillment. It is that community's strength or weakness of identity/relationship to the servant-Messiah Jesus which ultimately becomes the major variable determinant in its history and destiny. But it is that unique, crucial, and nonretractable role for all human history and its fulfillment in God which is the non-negotiable dimension of Jesus' servant messianism.

The Mission of the Servant-Messiah as Lord

Whatever its strength or weakness, the identification with Jesus the Messiah by the community that bears his name is indeed that which testifies to the ongoing character of the Messiah-event. It is an event in continuity, still in process, in fulfillment within the times of the Messiah until he comes. Exalted in God's glory, Jesus is henceforth the mediator of access to the Father-child-Father relationship in God he so fully demonstrated, having personally fleshed out God's eternal Word and wisdom.

The apostolic witness to that ongoing event and mission comprehends several important dimensions of mediation.

1. The Anointed One becomes the Anointing One, the mediator of the fullness of the Holy Spirit. Hence, the interpersonal presence of God in the relationship between the community of Messiah and the Father, as between its disciple(s) of Messiah and the Father, is experienced also as the same interpersonal *ekklesia*-edifying power and dynamic known in Jesus: "you shall receive power when the Holy Spirit

has come upon you; and you shall be my witnesses" (Acts 1:8). In the Pentecost event, the *ekklesia*/community that was gathered together by the Messiah received the same endowment that Jesus had received in his sonship, the endowment he had promised. The church was henceforth identified with him in his messianic mission as the messianic community, potentially in the fullness of the Spirit and now universally so.

2. The Sent One becomes the Sending One, not just to all the cities of Israel; now the mission is universalized with the exaltation/glorification of the Messiah exalted in God. The followers are sent out; the disciples become apostles. The focus of mission is now "to all nations," "all the world," "all creation," "to the ends of the earth" (Acts 1:8; *et al.*). "Repent and be baptized . . . in the name of Jesus [the Messiah] for the forgiveness of your sins" (Acts 2:38) is to be proclaimed as the key to access to God the divine parent, and it is the covenant of adoption into the family of the gathered *ekklesia*, now fully identified with Messiah as the community of the Holy Spirit (love, joy, justice, and peace) in the midst of the many nations with their divergent cultures and politics.

3. Jesus's gracious, priestly proclamation of divine "Fatherly" forgiveness and acceptance was localized in the days of his flesh. Now those gifts are universally accessible (even if not known) in a universal intercessory mission, since "when he had made purification for sins, he sat down at the right hand of the Majesty on high" (Heb. 1:3). In his obedient life, Jesus perfectly fulfilled the will and intention of God for humanity. "And by that will [unto death], we [his church identified with him] have been made holy through the sacrifice of the body of Jesus [the Messiah] once for all" (Heb. 10:10, NIV). Thus his *ekklesia* is the unique witness to a new universal reality-as-possibility of sure confidence in the still-invisible but more fully revealed liberating God, "Father." There is access into "the Most Holy Place by the blood [i.e., his life freely poured out in sacrifical love unto death] of Jesus, by a new and living way opened for us through the curtain, that is, his body" (Heb. 10:19-20, NIV).

4. The humiliated Jesus has become the exalted Messiah with dominion over and in the world. Victorious in life over the powers of the world in his obedience unto death (cf. Col. 2:15), with continuity and confirmation of that life in his resurrection from the dead, he pursues that same triumph through his church (cf. the "Saul, why do you persecute me?" Acts 9:4) with reigning glory "at the right hand of God . . . until his enemies should be made a stool for his feet" (Heb. 10:12-

13). The messianic riddle of the cross-bound Jesus to the ruling Sadducees ("David . . . calls him Lord; so how is he his son?" Luke 20:44) is answered by that triumph and in that of the free obedient service of his oft-humiliated community which is called to live "in love, as [the Messiah] loved" (Eph. 5:1), to "follow in his steps" (1 Pet. 2:21), and to "walk in the same way in which he walked" (1 John 2:6).[30]

That apostolic consensus of faith is thus openly proclaimed in the earliest reported public confession of the church (Acts 2:34ff.) and is found in different authors' writings (1 Cor. 15:25; Rom. 8:34; Eph. 1:20; Col. 3:1; 1 Pet. 3:21; Heb. 10:12f.; 12:2f.; Rev. 5:5f.). In the perspective of that faith, the destruction of Jerusalem (Rev. 11:2, 8) and the future doom of Rome and all it typifies (Rev. 18) are (*sans* repentance) sealed and fulfilled in virtue of the triumphant freedom of the "Lamb who was slain" (Rev. 5:12; cf. Isa. 53:7). The Faithful and the True One, whose name is the Word of God, pursues prophetic war with the nations with the sharp sword that comes out of his mouth (Rev. 19:11-16); it is the ongoing combat of the call to repentance and the freedom of obedient faith that the servant in Isaiah 40—66 was to fulfill "till he has established justice in the earth" (Isa. 42:4).

5. In his universal magistracy and dominion over the world, Jesus the Messiah saves, restores, and heads a universal human community of many local assemblies. The free obedient servanthood to God and humanity in Jesus the Messiah, the Son of God, has become the divine measure and criterion of human freedom and historical fulfillment (Rev. 7:9-17; 22:3ff.) of this universal community of humanity (Rev. 5:9ff.). With and through his community of the Spirit, he is working out his purposes that everyone everywhere shall be given that offer and space of salvation to become together—in time and eternity, on the earth and beyond—all that God the Creator intended. "Behold, the dwelling of God is with men. He will dwell with them, and they shall be his people, and God himself will be with them [and be their God]. . . . I make all things new" (Rev. 21:3-5).

6. Yet in ways that are strange beyond our understanding, the Messiah in his faithful fulfillment of his agape mission sorrowfully respects the freedom of those who reject his love. As when he wept over Jerusalem in its refusal of his rule (Luke 19:41), his magisterial triumph must clearly bear all of those marks as he actively bears the outworking of wrath in all of human history, even as he once bore it on the cross. There can be no doubt of great suffering in the midst of triumph especially when the community of those who openly bear Messiah's name turns aside and betrays him, or turns away and abandons

him in the way he is (Heb. 6:6), thus emptying the good news of the cross (1 Cor. 1:17) and distorting the perception of God whom he had revealed by his combat in life and death. "As it is written, 'The name of God is blasphemed among the Gentiles because of you' " (Rom. 2:24; cf. Isa. 52:5).

Again, strangely yet realistically, Jesus foresaw such when he proclaimed the good news of the kingdom of God and allegorically saw it as seed falling into different soils: along the beaten path, upon rocks, among thorns, and only a small portion in productive earth (Matt. 13:1-23).

7. Though the apostolic writers bear witness to Israel's, Jesus', and their own faith in cosmic restoration through Messiah, which is made explicit in his triumph over death and victory over the powers, little attention could be given in this study to this dimension which is nevertheless fully shared in faith. Except for some discussion of the sovereignty of Jesus, we have given little comment about the Creator's ways and means in this regard. Another chapter deals more specifically with eschatology. Here we offer only this witness to the conviction that a most significant part in future developments must come also through the humanity which has been at fault in its alienation from God in his self-revelation: i.e., his Wisdom, his Word, and his Messiah.

But ultimately what comes must be through that community gathered and restored by Messiah and with which he is fully identified. It knows itself to be in, with, and under him, the servant Son of God, who wills to do the Father's saving will in and for creation in the Father's way and time. In that he fully revealed the purposes of God which yet await ultimate fulfillment.

Mission Now: God's Purpose Revealed and Fulfilled

It is quite obvious that it is impossible to deduce from the reading of the letter to the Thessalonians all that we have seen above. Yet all of this, gleaned from the tradition of the Gospels and occasional references to the broader apostolic witness, is wholly consonant with—if not implicit in—that early apostolic document. It appears urgent to this writer that the human-, community-, and history-fulfilling (i.e., sociopolitical) features of the mission of Jesus the servant-Messiah be seen as essential dimensions of an adequate Christology.

But foundational to those dimensions of apostolic understanding are the Son of man and servant embodiments of messianism, so fundamental to Jesus' own understanding of his identity and mission, and yet traditionally so neglected by the dominant theological traditions.[31] Without them, the distortions which Christian world mission in the Constantinian mode has offered to history are inevitable; they are analogous to Peter's messianic confession which Messiah Jesus rejected as not being the "things of God, but the things of men" (Matt. 16:23, NIV).[32]

Finally, there is something extremely ironic in the fact that Jesus who came to liberate Israel in view of the nations' salvation never openly attacked what the Jews perceived to be the enemy and source of their oppression, the pagan Roman Empire. Yet everything that Jesus incarnated was opposed to the alienating powers there at work. His political strategy of grassroots building of messianic communities ultimately overcame the power of the empire. But it is also ironic that at one level that victory should lead to a human change of strategy and the nature of those communities. The homeopathic cure of human servitude through servanthood of and for God shifted to that of human power.[33]

Indeed the extension of time, in the patience of God, with human and material development well beyond that anticipated by the twelve and Paul, oblivious to the expanses and potential of earth and its peoples with the leaven of the messianic good news, raises again and again questions about the ongoing mission of the *ekklesia* within the societies of the world where wheat and tares grow together. Yet in, with, and under the Servant Messiah Jesus, at least the die is cast: "For no other foundation can any one lay than that which is laid, which is Jesus [the Messiah]" (1 Cor. 3:11). Indeed, it was no accident that Anabaptist communities found it important to celebrate the washing of each other's feet in conjunction with the Lord's Supper, as described in John 13. The disciples' experience of the "full extent of his love" (John 13:1, NIV) was when the Lord and Master had washed their feet, setting for them an example of practical earthy servanthood as a parable of his life and death.[34]

When using the personal analogy in speaking of God and the *missio Dei*, one might well refer to the coherency of being, agency, and purpose. The purposive Creator-God of peace, the loving Parent who sent and inspired the Child-Servant Jesus and whose image he fully reflected, may best be undertstood as Being. The Holy Spirit may best be understood as Agency, effecting that historical purposiveness in all creation (more fully in Abraham's Israel with prophets, priests, and kings; and bodily in Mary's Jesus,[35] son of David, fully anointed Messiah, prophetic and priestly King) as well as the new restored community he gathers. But the purpose itself is only clearly revealed and understood in the human obedience of Jesus, God's faithful, suffering Servant Son, embodying God in his Wisdom and Word and perfectly fulfilling his saving work in the gathering of a universal people who share his service of love.

Whether the foundation and parameters indicated by this study will be heeded in continuing theological reflection about Jesus the Messiah one cannot know. It can only be noted again that now is a propitious time in God's mission and world for them to be appropriated.

Notes

1. There is the pluralism of names and titles and their meanings (e.g., John 1). There is the pluralism of time-events within the biblical telling of one Christ-event: preexistence, conception, birth/presentation, temple-at-12, baptism/endowment with Spirit, temptation, ministry, suffering, death, burial/descent into hell, resurrection, ascension, Spirit baptizing at Pentecost, sitting at the right hand, parousia; each has its potential for theological interpretation and accent. For example, "descended into hell," based on limited biblical evidence, had great importance for first-generation Gentile Christians; today it is nonexistent in many evangelical statements of faith. Each event of the total Messiah-event has lent itself to new and different insights as cultural, social, political changes offer different prisms for reading Scripture. As we shall see, even the pluralism within the ministry of Jesus opens up different christological perspectives: evangelist, healer, exorcist, prophet, teacher, man of protest. In a society where healing is traditionally controlled by "spirit powers," the healing ministry of Jesus opens up to a Christology quite different from that in the usual Western context. Then there is the pluralism of images for faith-appropriation of God in Christ: be born again, drink water of life, bear the yoke. Even the biblical language descriptive of Christ's work is pluralist: redemption, justification, adoption, regeneration, election, reconciliation; each has known its own theological and christological formulation. The argument of this chapter is that the foundational messianic dimension must be seen as the context for any and all of the varieties; the diverse approaches—to be valid—must at the least be within a nonnegotiable messianic context.

2. The best biblical scholarship indicates the uniqueness of Israel's faith as over against that of other sacral nations of the time.

3. "There is no reasonable doubt that Jesus rejected the ideas of political messiahship. His teaching regarding his mission was not cast in this mold. He eschewed the idea of violence and advocated an approach which would obviously have been a political non-starter (as in Hengel, 1971). No political revolutionary could ever have exhorted people to love their enemies. The Sermon on the Mount is intelligible as a spiritual directive, but makes nonsense as a political manifesto" (Guthrie, 1981:241).

4. "Salvation Today" was the theme of the conference of the Commission on World Mission and Evangelism held in Bangkok, Thailand, in 1973.

5. The Blumhardts of Bad Boll, Germany, were the forerunners to the Christocentric theology of Barth and Brunner and the founders of the Evangelical Academies of the German Protestant Church.

6. Scripture references, unless noted otherwise, are from the Revised Standard Version. I have replaced "Christ" with "Messiah" for reasons given earlier in my text.

7. This expression, "God of peace," appeared only once in pre-Christian litera-

ture (Testament of Dan 5:2) but is repeated by Paul (Rom. 15:33; 16:20; 1 Cor. 14:33; 2 Cor. 13:11; Phil. 4:9) and is found in Hebrews 13:20, reflecting both a new and important usage. See Klassen (1990:144); he also cites it as a "redefinition of God in a community where it was all too easy to visualize God as a God of war" (p. 153).

8. No African myth, says the African theologian John Mbiti, offers a solution to the ever-present primeval loss (Mbiti, 1969:99).

9. This oft-neglected part of the story has been best exposed by Millard Lind in *Yahweh Is a Warrior* (1980).

10. The simple naive reading of the Bible and the significance of the theological narrative of Creation, Fall, redemption, and consummation as hermeneutical keys are both objects of theological reflection and the epistemological means by which that reflection is controlled, as has been incisively formulated by Henry Van der Goot in *Interpreting the Bible in Theology and Church* (1984).

11. This is an adaptation from *Hans Küng, On Being a Christian* (1978: 177ff., cf. 211).

12. Christopher Tuckett (1983) brings together in a helpful volume, *The Messianic Secret*, recent scholarly thinking on the question.

13. The ideal, which dealt mostly with questions of race, land, and boundaries, was the "restoration of national independence and the installation of a new kingdom of Israel called to become a political and religious center of a society of nations bowed beneath the yoke of Yahweh and his people" (Coppens, 1968:176; my translation).

14. "Jesus believed himself to be the Messiah, but his conception of the messianic role was an unexpected and unpopular one. Because the title had such different connotations for Jesus and for those who heard him, he never used it of himself or unequivocally welcomed its application to him by others; and when his actions or words seemed to encourage the to him false conception of messiahship, he tried to prevent it by commands to silence. Nevertheless he did not deny his right to the title, but attempted to re-educate his hearers to the significance of it for him. And the claims he made to messiahship and messianic authority were of a parabolic sort whose significance was there, plain for all to see whose eyes were not blinded and whose ears were not clogged by misconceptions" (Dunn, 1983:128).

15. John H. Yoder has effectively pointed out that there is a political stance of Jesus with a remarkable consistency between the earthly and transcendent Messiah (1972).

16. It is very difficult to accept some scholars' rejection of the connection between Messiah and Son of God, particularly when there are important and crucial synoptic texts that make the connection explicit. The question of the high priest to Jesus, "Are you the [Messiah], the Son of the Blessed?" (Mark 14:61) and Peter's confession in the Matthean eye-witness account, "You are the [Messiah], the Son of the living God" (Matt. 16:16) must be accounted for along with some important textual readings of John 6:69.

17. See C. Norman Kraus' discussion (1987:93, n. 15). In fact both "son of the blessed" and "son of man" are titles which each give different content to Jesus' unique understanding of his messiahship.

18. See Cullmann, (1963:151ff.) and particularly Rudolph Otto: "The phrase ['the figure that you saw in human form' (cf. Dan. 7:13 'one like a son of man')] bore such emphasis in circles of readers familiar with this [Book of Enoch] and similar books, that when mention was made of 'the man', with association of judgment, the coming world, the right hand of God, the coming with or on the clouds of heaven, the words 'Son of Man' had the force of a title; and when an eschatological preacher spoke of the coming of the Son of Man and of his judgment it was known what he meant, viz., the king in the coming world" (Otto, 1938:226; see also pp. 176-218).

19. Matthew 8:16 (cf. Isa. 53:4); Matthew 12:18-21 (cf. Isa. 42:1ff.); John 12:38 (cf. Isa. 53:1).

20. Strangely, liberation theology, based also on the exodus as founding event,

generally gives scant attention to this closure in God's service, so integral to the pentateuchal account (cf. Exod. 4:23; 5:1; 7:16; 8:1, 20; 9:1, 13; 10:3, 7f.).

21. See Deuteronomy 6:13; 10:12, 20; 11:13; 13:4; *passim* from one of the sources most cited by Jesus. For this consciousness of literal fulfillment, see Luke 22:37 where his asking for swords is to fulfill the word of Isaiah 53:12: "he . . . was numbered with the transgressors."

22. "No Jew would have dared to address God in the manner Jesus did it always. . . . This term *abba* is an *ipsissima vox* of Jesus and contains *in nuce* his message and claims to have been sent from the Father" (Jeremias, 1964:20). With reference to the current discussions of patriarchy, and God as Father, see John W. Miller (1989).

23. The wisdom theme follows that of Proverbs 3:19 and 8:22-31. Jesus spoke of wisdom in Matthew 11:19 and 12:42; Paul used the theme in 1 Corinthians 1:18—2:16.

24. See the important gathering theme in Ezekiel 34—39 with Messiah fulfilling that role as king (37:24ff.). See also Gerhard Lohfink (1984) and John E. Toews (1989).

25. This composite Christology can be seen much in the same way as the "body and its members" image which Paul used in 1 Corinthians 12, when writing of the different spiritual gifts in the life of the church.

26. See the section, "Jesus removes the idea of vengeance [on the Gentiles] from the eschatological expectation" (Jeremias, 1958:41-46).

27. The prophetic word for the violent rebellion to God absorbed by Israel was "Assyria, the rod of my anger," (Isa. 10:5). See also "The Wrath of God in the Old and New Testaments" (Hershberger, 1969:17-20).

28. For a fuller discussion of "Vicarious Suffering" and nine other major biblical images used in New Testament understandings of the death of Jesus, see John Driver (1986:esp. pp. 87-100).

29. "This chapter is unique in the history of religion, and expresses an experience which is wholly irrational and not elucidated by any theory. A group of disciples experience atonement and sanctification in the humble voluntary suffering of their master in obedience to God" (Otto, 1938:261).

30. See "The Kingship of Christ in the Bible" (Visser t'Hooft, 1948). Unfortunately the generally good exposition of the theme does not tie it, as does the New Testament, to the earthly life of Jesus as paradigm for the glory of the church in its members. Hence, the constant risk of distorted triumphalism.

31. One contemporary Western mainline Protestant systematic theologian had given noticeable attention to this in his earlier writings before he renounced his own "deductive" methodology; but in that he also recognized its distinctiveness as rooted in the sixteenth-century Anabaptist critique of Western Christianity. See Gordon D. Kaufman's *Systematic Theology: A Historicist Perspective* (1968). Note the following sections: God's being as "servant" is revealed in the historic Jesus ("God's Coming into History," pp. 167-75); Jesus' servanthood is described (not negatively) as "technically developed in the so-called adoptionist christology" (p. 195) with a suggestion, nevertheless, for understanding the metaphysical claim about the unity of God and Christ, while rejecting "Messiah" as explicatory of the meaning of Jesus, implying (for him) "that one must become a Jew in certain respects before one can become a Christian" (p. 192, n.2; cf. pp. 190-97); the "nonresistance of God" as revealed by Jesus is seen as "divine perfection" and "the only way he can maintain the full integrity of those creatures to whom he has granted genuine freedom" and is expression of both power and love (pp. 219-21). See also the excellent pastoral chapter on "Servant God" in *Compassion* (McNeill, et al., 1983).

32. More recently, the "powerlessness of God" has taken on some importance in theological reflection in the West as self-directed criticism of the distorted "triumphalism" of Western Christianity. Here we have attempted to indicate that the weakness has been in a failure to recognize the suffering servant as Servant-Lord with his servant people, and in the zealots' omnipotent Lord who elevates servants through whatever means are necessary to make them lords. This chapter was written in 1990 be-

fore the appearance in English of Jürgen Moltmann's recent *The Way of Jesus Christ: Christology in Messianic Dimensions* (1990) where the basic preoccupation of this chapter is dealt with more completely.

33. This has been most helpfully demonstrated in a thorough analysis of the patristic literature by Jean-Michel Hornus in an adaptation of his doctoral thesis and translated from the French as *It Is Not Lawful for Me to Fight* (1980).

34. Avery Dulles in his useful *Models of the Church* (1974) also discusses one modern servanthood model of the church and concludes with: "The modern notion of the 'servant church' therefore seems to lack any direct foundation in the Bible. Yet it may not be out of place to speak of an 'indirect foundation.' The so-called Servant Songs in Isaiah are applicable to the Church as well as to Christ" (1974:93). The apparent contradiction is due to the model he critiques, in which the church in conciliar circles was seen to be strictly governed by the "agenda of the world," submitting to the world-defined needs as servant to master. The critique is fully justified. Indeed, that was the thrust of paragraph 7 of the introduction to this chapter. It is most unfortunate that Dulles does not follow through with the full implications of the applicability of the Servant Songs to the church via Jesus' self-identity and the church's solidarity with him. It is indeed direct biblical foundation, that of the pre-Pauline churches, to which Paul refers: "Your attitude should be the same as that of [Messiah] Jesus . . . taking the very nature of a servant" (Phil. 2:5-7, NIV).

35. This messianic activity and sign (cf. Isa. 7:14; Matt. 1:23) in the midst of entropy is seen by apostolic faith to be the first visible expression of servant messianism. The human embodiment in Jesus of the image of the self-revealing Father is seen to be the equivalent of the slave's mark of a pierced ear (cf. Psa. 40:6-8; Heb. 10:5ff.). It is the full acceptance of the created human role of obedient and faithful servant in creation (Phil. 2:7). Apparently only the full implications of the resurrection made the sign retrospectively understandable (cf. the "How can this be?" Luke 1:34, NRSV): all God's work, from God, initiated by God.

References Cited

The Bulletin of African Theology
        Scholarly quarterly, Kinshasa, Zaire: Association of African Theologians.

Coppens, J.
    1968   *Messianisme Royal.* Paris: Le Cerf.

Cragg, Kenneth
    1968   *Christianity in World Perspective.* New York: Oxford University Press.

Cullmann, Oscar
    1963   *The Christology of the New Testament.* Shirley C. Guthrie and Charles A. M. Hall, trans.; Philadelphia: Westminster.

Driver, John
    1986   *Understanding the Atonement for the Mission of the Church.* Scottdale, Pa.: Herald Press.

Dulles, Avery
    1974   *Models of the Church.* Garden City, N.Y.: Doubleday.

Dunn, James D. G.
    1983   "The Messianic Secret in Mark," *The Messianic Secret.* Christopher Tuckett, ed.; Philadelphia: Fortress Press.

Guthrie, Donald
    1981   *New Testament Theology.* Downers Grove, Ill.: InterVarsity Press.

Hengel, Martin
1971 *Was Jesus a Revolutionist?* William Klassen, trans.; Philadelphia: Fortress Press.
Hershberger, Guy F.
1969 "The Wrath of God in the Old and New Testaments," *War, Peace and Nonresistance* (rev. ed.). Scottdale, Pa.: Herald Press.
Hornus, Jean-Michel
1980 *It Is Not Lawful for Me to Fight: Early Christian Attitudes Toward War, Violence, and the State.* Alan Kreider and Oliver Coburn, trans.; Scottdale, Pa.: Herald Press.
Jeremias, Joachim
1958 *Jesus' Promise to the Nations.* London: SCM Press.
1964 *The Lord's Prayer.* John Reumann, trans.; Philadelphia: Fortress Press.
Kaufman, Gordon D.
1968 *Systematic Theology: A Historicist Perspective.* New York: Charles Scribner's Sons.
Klassen, William
1990 "The Voice of the People in the Biblical Story of Faithfulness," *The Church as Theological Community.* Harry Huebner, ed.; Winnipeg: Canadian Mennonite Bible College Publications.
Kraus, C. Norman
1987 *Jesus Christ, Our Lord: Christology from a Disciple's Perspective.* Scottdale, Pa.: Herald Press.
Küng, Hans
1978 *On Being a Christian.* New York: Wallaby Pocket Books.
Lind, Millard
1980 *Yahweh Is a Warrior: The Theology of Warfare in Ancient Israel.* Scottdale, Pa.: Herald Press.
Lohfink, Gerhard
1984 *Jesus and Community: The Social Dimension of Christian Faith.* John P. Galvin, trans.; Philadelphia: Fortress Press.
McNeill, Don, Douglas Morrison, and Henri Nouwen
1983 *Compassion: A Reflection on the Christian Life.* New York: Doubleday.
Mbiti, John
1969 *African Religions and Philosophy.* New York: Frederick A. Praeger.
Miller, John W.
1989 *Biblical Faith and Fathering: Why We Call God "Father."* New York: Paulist Press.
Moltmann, Jürgen
1990 *The Way of Jesus Christ: Christology in Messianic Dimensions.* San Francisco: Harper & Row.
Neufeld, Vernon H.
1963 *The Earliest Christian Confessions.* Grand Rapids, Mich.: Eerdmans.
Newman, Paul W.
1987 *A Spirit Christology: Recovering the Biblical Paradigm of Christian Faith.* Lanham, Md.: University Press of America.

Otto, Rudolph
   1938   *The Kingdom of God and the Son of Man.* London: Lutterworth.
Samuel, Vinay, and Christopher Sugden
   1984   *Sharing Jesus in the Two-Thirds World.* Grand Rapids, Mich.:
          Eerdmans.
Tinsley, E. J.
   ˙ 1960   "The Way of Sonship," *The Imitation of God in Christ.* London: SCM.
Toews, John E.
   1989   *Jesus Christ, the Convener of the Church.* Newton, Kans.: General Con-
          ference Mennonite Church, *et al.*
Tuckett, Christopher, ed.
   1983   *The Messianic Secret.* Philadelphia: Fortress Press.
Trocmé, André
   1973   "Jesus and Jubilee," *Jesus and the Nonviolent Revolution.* Michel Shank
          and Marlin E. Miller, trans.; Scottdale, Pa.: Herald Press.
Van der Goot, Henry
   1984   *Interpreting the Bible in Theology and the Church.* New York: Edward
          Mellen Press.
Visser t'Hooft, Willem Adolph
   1948   *The Kingship of Christ: An Interpretation of Recent European Theology.*
          New York: Harper.
Walls, Andrew
   1985   "Christianity," *A Handbook of Living Religions.* John R. Hinnels, ed.;
          Harmondsworth, Middlesex: Pelican Books.
Yoder, John H.
   1972   *The Politics of Jesus.* Grand Rapids, Mich.: Eerdmans.

CHAPTER 3

The Kingdom of God: Goal of Messianic Mission

John Driver

DURING THE LAST FEW DECADES we have witnessed a growing interest in the biblical image of the kingdom of God.[1] This interest is found among a wide spectrum of Christians. The theme of the 1980 Melbourne Conference on Mission, assembled under the auspices of the World Council of Churches, was "Your Kingdom Come." The Latin American Theological Fraternity, made up of Latin American evangelical scholars, held a consultation in 1972 on the theme of the kingdom of God and its implications for Latin America.

In the wake of Vatican II and Medellin, many Roman Catholics are again being inspired by more biblical images for understanding the nature and mission of the people of God in the world. In this renewal the kingdom of God has become a prime category for reflecting on biblical themes among the Christian base communities in the third world. The reign of God, which fulfills and transcends all human expectations, constitutes a key ingredient in the hope which sustains suffering Christians, particularly in areas of conflict (Catholic Institute for International Relations, 1989:27).[2]

The kingdom-of-God image had become largely inoperative in the church's understanding of its life and mission for several reasons. In traditional Roman Catholicism, the kingdom of God came to be largely identified with the church, robbing it of its capacity to inspire the people of God to a more biblical faithfulness. In the Protestant tradition, a proclivity to bypass the Gospels and to begin with a *solafideistic* reading of Paul tended to result in an individualistic under-standing of salvation and a view of the true church which was largely invisible. In this context the kingdom-of-God image was either ne-glected or largely recast into inwardly spiritual and futuristic terms.

There are a number of reasons for this renewed interest in the kingdom-of-God image in our time. First, in the course of their pasto-ral ministries and theological reflection during the last half of the nine-teenth and the early years of the twentieth centuries in southwestern Germany, Johann Christoph (1805-1880) and Christoph Friedrich (1842-1919) Blumhardt caught a remarkably biblical vision of the kingdom of God. Through his struggle with demon possession in the congregation of which he was pastor, the elder Blumhardt came to un-derstand that because "Jesus is Victor" the kingdom of God has be-come a real possibility for life here and now.

The reality of the kingdom was perceived to be equally relevant in the inner sphere of spiritual warfare and in the concrete socioeco-nomic structures of the day. The insights and convictions which grew out of this overarching concern for the cause of the kingdom were car-ried forward by others, including Eberhard Arnold and the Society of Brothers and the leaders of the Confessing Church in Germany in the early 1930s; they resisted, in the name of the Messiah whom they con-fessed as Lord, the totalitarian and nationalistic claims of the state.

Drawing as they have on this Blumhardtian legacy, Christians have gradually been discerning the demonic dimensions of social structures. Through their experiences during the Second World War, European Christians were able to perceive the essentially demonic na-ture of structures of their social and political life earlier thought to be Christianized. In addition to this, the social and economic analysis of Marxism has undermined even more the fundamentally mistaken view of the sacrosanct nature of Western Christendom and its institu-tions. A more radical reading of the New Testament gospel of the kingdom has provided a framework in which Christians can respond to the challenges of a growing secularism.

Second, due to the extremely difficult social, political, and eco-nomic conditions under which they live, many Christians in the third world are finding the kingdom-of-God motif helpful in understanding God's Word and will for them. Living, as they do, under conditions of political and economic oppression and deprivation, Jesus' proclama-tion of the kingdom—God's new order of justice, peace, and covenant community—has provided for many people a relevant key for under-standing their life and mission as the people of God. It has also furnished them with the hope which sustains them in the midst of persecution. The Book of Revelation, for example, with its powerful portrayal of God's kingdom as his alternative to the kingdoms of this world, provides these brothers and sisters with both encouragement in their pilgrimage and spiritual strength to resist the evil powers.

Third, during recent decades Christians have become increasingly aware of the social dimensions of evil, as well as of the forms which salvation from these evils takes. The highly individualistic ways in which the biblical doctrines of justification and regeneration have been taken for understanding personal salvation have proved to be insufficient, in themselves, for grasping the corporate dimensions of sin and for communicating the social shape of salvation. In this context the kingdom-of-God image provides a more solidly biblical basis for understanding and communicating these realities.

During the final decades of the twentieth century, the question Christians increasingly ask is no longer "Is there life after death?" but "Is there life before death?" In a world plagued by the realities of human misery, oppression, and suffering, Christians are finding in the Bible a message of justice, peace, liberation, and reconciliation.

In the biblical motif of the kingdom of God, we find summed up God's salvific intention for a new humanity within a restored creation characterized by healed relationships with the Creator as well as with fellow humans and the rest of the created order. The biblical view of the kingdom of God responds to the deepest needs of humanity and offers a framework in which to understand more holistically the nature and mission of the messianic community.

The Reign of God in the Old Testament

The kingdom of God is a primary image for understanding the biblical vision of God's salvific activity, first of all in the vocation of Israel and then in the saving mission of his Messiah. While the term *kingdom* is found in all parts of the New Testament, it plays a dominant role in the synoptic Gospels.[3] Although Jesus' messianic mission consisted essentially in "proclaiming the kingdom of God," the precise meaning of the term is nowhere defined in the New Testament. But it is apparent that Jesus' hearers were familiar with the concept. Even though the phrase "kingdom of God" is rare in the Old Testament, the idea of Yahweh's kingship permeated all of life in ancient Israel.

Ancient Israel confessed God's reign over the universe and over the nations, as well as over his own people. God's kingly rule is all encompassing. "The Lord has established his throne in the heavens, and his kingdom rules over all" (Ps. 103:19). God's rule over the nations would manifest itself in both judgment (Amos 1—2) and blessing (Isa. 19:24-25). While the kingdom of God includes his righteous rule over his people, it encompasses all of creation within its scope.

The fact that Yahweh is king over his people Israel is especially prominent throughout the Old Testament. The first specific mention of God's kingship occurs in the context of Israel's exodus experience of salvation. "The Lord . . . has become my salvation. . . . The Lord will reign for ever and ever" (Exod. 15:2, 18). This reality was engraved in the words of the covenant given at Sinai: "You shall be my own possession among all peoples; for all the earth is mine, and you shall be to me a kingdom of priests and a holy nation" (Exod. 19:5-6). There is a close relationship between God's saving activity toward Israel, reflected in the exodus and the covenant, and his rule over all creation.

God's universal kingship is the context of the mission entrusted to God's people. The people of God carry out his salvific mission in a universe in which God is, in reality, King. The mission deals with the question of ultimate loyalties. The evangel calls us to recognize that God alone is King, rather than are the multitude of lesser gods who vie for humanity's loyalties. In this context evangelization consists of the proclamation of the kingdom, as it was incarnated supremely in the Messiah, together with an invitation to enter the kingdom and to participate in its life and mission through radical discipleship.

Human kingship is understood in the Old Testament in the light of God's kingly rule. When Israel demanded a king they were reminded that it was Yahweh who "delivered [them] from the hand of the Egyptians and from the hand of all the kingdoms that were oppressing [them]" (1 Sam. 10:18). God's saving activity was offered as a model for Israel's monarchy. With few exceptions Israel's kings became oppressors rather than saviors. To oppress through the abuse of royal power is to mock the God of Israel.

The exercise of God's kingly rule was not a vague abstraction in ancient Israel. God's kingship does not merely mean a general insistence on moral values as such. God's reign has to do with the concrete forms which life takes among his people. It is in the relationships among God's people that his righteous rule is manifest. The kingdom of God is not abstractly defined in the Old Testament as "wherever God reigns." God's kingdom is manifested in the concrete forms in which social relationships are practiced in response to his intention for his people, in particular, and for all of his creation in general.

Psalms 145 and 146 reflect this view of the kingdom expressed in concrete relationships of covenant righteousness. Here the elements of God's reign include an unflagging covenant faithfulness, bringing justice to the oppressed, providing food for the hungry, setting prisoners free, opening the eyes of the blind, lifting up the bowed, watching over the sojourners, sustaining the widows and orphans. And all of this saving activity is contrasted with the sure ruin which will overtake the wicked. In this text God's rule takes all of these concrete forms (Ps. 146:6-10).

The Old Testament story contains many indications of the concrete social shape God's rule was intended to take among his people. The Decalogue is undoubtedly the most concise and clearest description of God's intention for human relationships under his rule. The preamble makes it clear that life under God's kingship is determined by the very character of God himself who liberated Israel "out of the land of Egypt, out of the house of bondage" (Exod. 20:2; Deut. 5:6).

The Sinaitic covenant consists of grace, law, and promise. It begins with a statement of Yahweh's saving activity on behalf of his people: "I am the Lord your God, who brought you out of the land of Egypt" (Exod. 20:2). This is followed by the Law, Israel's proper response to God's salvific act (20:3ff.) and the promise of reward or the threat of judgment (20:5-7, 12).

The Decalogue, first of all, shows that it is Israel's relationship to a righteous covenant-making God which determines concretely the just practices of the subjects of his divine rule. The covenant has sometimes been called a "kingship covenant." In effect, Yahweh's gracious act of liberation from Egypt was foundational for Israel's existence as a people of Yahweh. The first three words of the Decalogue make it unmistakably clear that Yahweh's exclusive kingship is absolutely foundational for Israel's peoplehood. At Sinai, Yahweh comes to his people, not simply in self-revelation, but as King who rules over them (Lind, 1973:21-24).

The second table of the Decalogue contains specific descriptions of the forms which Israel's response to Yahweh's gracious kingship will take. Covenant law was not a mutually beneficial legal contract but was based exclusively on Yahweh's saving act of grace, liberation from Egypt. The only adequate response to this is obedience. Life under Yahweh's kingship takes the concrete social, economic, and political forms sketched out, in principal, in the Decalogue. Obedience to this law was never intended to be a way to become God's people, but rather, a description of relationships which characterize God's reign.

The sabbatical and jubilee provisions offer another example of the concrete forms which social relationships take under God's rule (Lev. 25; Deut. 15). The land is to be left fallow every seventh year in order to remember that the earth and its resources are the Lord's. And these are given to his people so that all—the poor in particular—may be nourished (Exod. 23:10-11). Indebtedness is to be forgiven periodically because "the Lord's release has been proclaimed" (Deut. 15:2). Indentured slaves among the Israelites are to be released, because God has redeemed Israel from slavery (Deut. 15:12-18). Inheritances lost over the years are to be restored because the earth is the Lord's and everyone in Israel, from the king to the most lowly, was a child and subject of Israel's loving and faithful Lord. Here again the salvific actions of the King are to determine the shape of all relationships, social and spiritual, in the kingdom.

Throughout its history of monarchy, Israel's rulers failed miserably in their understanding of the nature and demands of God's rule. The prophets continually called them to "seek justice, correct oppression; defend the fatherless, plead for the widow" (Isa. 1:17). Contrary to the thinking of many Christians throughout the church's history, the prophets did not perceive of God's rule as a purely spiritual and future reality.

God's kingdom embraced concrete political and social events. This is clear from the biblical descriptions of life under God's rule. It is also clear from the prophetic vision of the future of God's kingdom. They expected God's rule to become universal, including the nations (Mic. 4:1-3). They foresaw a submission to God's rule which would bring about the cessation of warfare as a solution to differences. This would mean the conversion of weapons into instruments for the production of food (4:3). The fear and deprivation, so common under evil rulers, would be superseded under God's righteous rule (4:4).

This kingdom vision shared by the prophets was primarily historical. In all probability they were not thinking of a fulfillment beyond history as we know it. But this does not mean that they envisioned the kingdom coming as a result of mere cause and effect in human history. It would be the result of the sovereign activity of God who had saved his people in the past and whose coming anew was continually awaited. The prophetic vision of God's kingdom of the future is characterized by a radical newness (Isa. 65:17ff.; 66:22). Images drawn from nature, as well as the sphere of social relationships, point to the striking newness of the kingdom envisioned by the prophets (Isa. 11:6-9; 65:17-25). This kingdom which has no end is present in God's just and compassionate ordering of human relationships. God's rule is characterized by the wholeness of life as he has always intended it to be, in marked contrast to the social injustices and the suffering, of which Egypt was a paradigm in Israel's experience.

The great prophets of Israel expected that the messianic age would be characterized by God's sovereignty over his people in a new order of salvation with personal, social, spiritual, and material dimensions. And although the political aspects of this vision of the messianic era easily lent themselves to misunderstandings and were used to nurture the nationalistic spirit of first-century Judaism, the prophetic vision viewed them as ways in which God's reign of peace and righteousness would be extended to the nations.

The prophetic calls to repentance were, in reality, pleas directed to a people whose disobedience was seen as rebellion against the beneficent rule of God over his people. Hope for Israel and Judah lay in their willingness to submit again to God's reign of righteousness and peace. In this context it was expected that with the coming of the Messiah, God's rule would not only be renewed but would be experienced in a way which would surpass all that Israel had known previously. An authentic salvation of covenant love, justice, and peace would become reality because God would dwell in the midst of his people, shepherding them as all good kings should.

God's people returned from Babylonian captivity with high expectations. They understood their return as a new exodus and expected great things from this fresh start. However, their hopes that God's rule would manifest itself in Israel's midst, characterized by covenant justice in internal social relationships and freedom from oppression by national enemies, were not realized. Apocalyptic writers during the period between the two Testaments shared their visions of when and how the kingdom would come. They all but despaired of God acting redemptively within history to restore his righteous rule and concluded that history is dominated by evil. Hope therefore lies only in the future, they said. God would again visit his people to deliver them from evil, but only at the end of history. The earlier prophetic vision of God's rule which held history and eschatology together in a dynamic tension had been all but lost in Judaism.

It was kingdom hope which sustained the pious among Israel in first-century Judaism (cf. Luke 2:25ff.). But it also furnished a point of departure for a wide gamut of movements: the political aspirations of the Sadducees, the revolutionary impatience of the Zealots, and the social withdrawal of the Essenes. This is the broad background against which we must understand the New Testament announcement of the good news of the kingdom of God on the part of John the Baptist, Jesus, and the messianic community in the synoptic Gospels.

Jesus and the Kingdom

Jesus began his messianic mission proclaiming the presence of the kingdom against the backdrop of this wide gamut of prophetic and apocalyptic expectations and the popular tendency to understand God's rule in nationalistic rather than universal dimensions (Mark 1:14). The Jewish people in general expected that the Messiah would establish God's kingdom, vindicating the righteous (the Jewish political and religious establishment) and destroying Israel's enemies.

It soon became clear that Jesus' perception of the kingdom differed from the popular views. He began his ministry making it clear that God's kingdom is for all peoples. In the synagogue in Nazareth Jesus read the prophetic vision of messianic fulfillment from Isaiah 61:1-2a. But he stopped short of the phrase which follows: "and the day of vengeance of our God" (Isa. 61:2b). And instead of announcing divine judgment on Israel's enemies, Jesus went on to recall God's gracious dealings in the past with foreigners including the widow from Sidon and Naaman the Syrian. Jewish opposition was so violent that Jesus seems to have barely escaped with his life. Scholars have suggested that Luke 4:18-30 may well have been intended as a brief preview of Jesus' messianic mission. His announcement of the kingdom of God's new universal community of salvation and his daring willingness to commit himself to its realization did, in fact, eventually lead to his death.

Two more ways in which Jesus' perception of the kingdom differed from popular understandings are reflected in his response to Pilate, "My kingdom is not of this world" (John 18:36, NIV). This text has often been interpreted to mean that the kingdom has nothing to do with social structures. This interpretation is probably more attractive to modern readers than it would have been to Jesus' contemporaries who generally viewed God's rule as a concrete social reality—if not present, then at least future.

First, Jesus' response to Pilate is perceived as a reference to the world to come, in contrast to this world. This view understands the kingdom of God as a reality to be experienced in the distant future, beyond the scope of history. This strongly futuristic view of the kingdom has appealed to many in the church, especially since the fourth century. However, it seems to contradict the plain sense of the words of Jesus recorded by both Matthew and Luke: "But if it is by the Spirit of God that I cast out demons, then the kingdom of God has come upon you" (Matt. 12:28; cf. Luke 11:20). The sense of the verb here leaves no doubt that Jesus viewed the kingdom as a present reality. Thayer has suggested the following translation: "The kingdom of God has come upon you sooner than you expected" (Thayer, 1889:652).

Second, the kingdom is often perceived as an inner, spiritual reality, the right relationship of an individual with God. Jesus' words in Luke 17:21 are interpreted, as indeed some translations have done, "the kingdom of God is within you" (cf. KJV, NIV), as referring primarily to an inner, personal experience. It would seem to be more in line with the intent of Jesus here to interpret Luke's text, "The kingdom of God is among you," or "in your midst" (cf. RSV).

From the context of John 18:36 the meaning of Jesus' words becomes clear. His kingship is not of this world, in that he does not resort to coercive violence, either for self-protection or for the establishment of the kingdom. So God's rule does affect the political, social, and economic decisions of his people who hold values which offer a radical alternative to those of the world, rather than withdrawing into the inner spiritual nature of the person or projecting into a future beyond history. God's rule calls for life in his community as he has always intended it to be.

The collection of Jesus' teachings into the Sermon on the Mount in Matthew's Gospel would seem to show that the early community understood Jesus' proclamation of the kingdom in the light of the Sinaitic Covenant: Yahweh's act of liberation and the Decalogue which ordered social relationships under his sovereign reign. In Matthew's Gospel, the description of Jesus' salvific ministry and the giving of the Sermon on the Mount offer a remarkable parallel to the Sinai experience. In effect, life under God's kingship takes the concrete social, economic, and political forms sketched out in the Sermon on the Mount. Jesus did not abolish the covenant righteousness reflected in the Decalogue and the sabbatical provisions which characterize Yahweh's kingship. Rather, he radicalized it, discerning its deepest meaning by going to its very root in God's intention (Matt. 5:21, 27, 31, 33, 38, 43).

In Jesus' parables of the kingdom we catch a glimpse of his understanding of the reign of God. Here the so-called parables of growth (Dodd, 1961:140-56) are especially helpful: the sower, the seed growing secretly, the tares, the mustard seed, the leaven, the dragnet. The parables of the mustard seed and the leaven show "that out of the most insignificant beginnings, invisible to human eye, God creates his mighty kingdom, which embraces all the peoples of the world" (Jeremias, 1963:149). With the coming of the Messiah, God's hour has already begun. And in this beginning, the full fruition of God's kingdom is already implicit (Jeremias, 1963:153).

The focus of the parables is not so much on growth, as such, nor on its gradual evolution, nor on human efforts to speed its consummation, but on the movement of God's salvific kingdom purpose toward its consummation. Meanwhile, the meaning of the kingdom is visible only to the eyes of faith. Its dynamic and its values remain a mystery to those who have not caught the messianic vision of reality and entered the kingdom. The kingdom perspective reflected in these parables undermines the optimistic strategies and the grandiose visions which have been a characteristic part of the church's Constantinian heritage.

The kingdom does not come as a calculated result of human activity. The parables point to a consummation which defies human efforts to predict or to precipitate its appearing. Parables such as the thief in the night, the waiting servants, and the ten maidens urge a stance of active waiting and discerning vigilance. In a world characterized by conflict with anti-kingdom forces, the citizens of the kingdom are called to vigilance and preparedness. The consummation of the kingdom calls, not so much for active militancy in the hope of bringing the kingdom as it does for steadfast resistance against the powers of anti-kingdom. In kingdom conflict this is the most powerful witness which Jesus' followers can give (Rev. 12:10-11; 13:10).

According to the New Testament, the power of the new order is already operative in Jesus. Everything he said and did was related to the coming of God's kingdom. Jesus' exorcisms are prime examples of the way the rule of God is being inaugurated. In his messianic mission Jesus has assailed and overcome the evil one (Luke 11:21-22). The imagery of Jesus' struggle against the tempter and the wild beasts in the wilderness furnishes us with a vision of the "second Adam" who begins to reverse the effects of the disobedience of the first Adam. In effect, the mission of Jesus has been to reverse the consequences of evil in the world: disease; demon possession; the hostility of nature; social, religious, and ethnic rivalries; hunger; economic exploitation; empty religiosity; alienation; and death. The conflict which characterized Jesus' ministry was, in reality, the struggle of the new order to displace the era of sin and death. Therefore, all who trust in wealth, power, and prestige for security react violently because the values of the new order threaten their false sources of security.

Wherever the kingdom of God is dynamically present the values and structures of the present age will be radically reversed (Luke 1:51-53). Therefore, Jesus' followers rejoice at the signs of Satan's fall. Wherever the values and structures of evil are being effectively challenged and are being radically turned around, there we see a sign of the dynamic presence of God's kingdom.

It has sometimes been said that while Jesus came proclaiming the kingdom of God, the mission of the early church was to preach Christ. At best this is a dangerous half-truth. To preach Christ certainly does not mean to be silent about the kingdom which Jesus proclaimed at the cost of his very life. The prominent place which the kingdom occupied in the life and preaching of Jesus was continued in the mission of the twelve (Luke 9:2) as well as in the wider group of Jesus' followers (Luke 10:9-11). The early story of the messianic community recorded in Acts opens and closes on this note (Acts 1:3; 28:23, 31). And even though the term occurs only eight times in Acts, it appears that Luke saw the proclamation of the kingdom of God as the core of the early church's message.

The relative infrequency of references to the kingdom of God in Pauline writings is sometimes noted as well. Although we search in vain for a clear reason for the relative scarcity of the term (fourteen times), several observations may be pertinent.

Paul may have simply taken Jesus' teaching about the kingdom of God for granted. It seems perfectly natural for him to center his message to the Jewish leaders of the community in Rome in the kingdom of God which Jesus had announced. We may be sure that the gospel which Paul shared in Rome was the gospel of the kingdom and not "another gospel."

Paul mentions the kingdom of God in Romans 14:17 in the context of a discussion about problems arising out of Jewish ritualistic practices in the Christian community. Based on the life and teachings of Jesus (Matt. 5—6), Paul was convinced that the coming of the kingdom of God had cancelled out an earlier era concerned about the details of ritual purity. First Corinthians 15:24-28 mentions the kingdom in the context of Jesus' resurrection victory over the powers of the present evil age which is passing away. The allusion here is to Psalm 110 in which the enthronement of the Messiah marks the defeat of God's enemies, the last of which is death.

Furthermore, it appears that Paul used other images to refer to exactly the same reality expressed by the term *kingdom*. These include

Paul's teaching about the first and second Adam, the two ages, the redemption of creation (Rom. 8:18ff.), the victory of Christ over the powers (Rom. 8:38ff.; Col. 2:15), and the life of the new community (Gal. 3:28; Eph. 2:13-18; Col. 3:10-11). All of these are logical extensions of what we learn elsewhere about the kingdom of God. It would appear that Paul's understanding of the meaning of Jesus Christ can be best grasped against the backdrop of the kingdom of God. After all, as an orthodox Jew, Paul could not possibly have accepted the fact that Jesus was the Messiah without recognizing that the kingdom had, in fact, come with him (Kirk, 1983: esp. 55-57).

Kingdom, Church, and Mission

The section which follows summarizes the concept of the kingdom of God found in the New Testament and notes the principal implications of this image for the church's self-understanding and mission.[4]

Political Kingdom and the Kingdom of God

The contrast between the Gospels' understanding of the kingdom of God and the vision which characterized popular Jewish expectations is remarkable. The Gospel accounts of the temptations essentially recount Jesus' response to popular nationalistic messianic expectations. The disciples' request for primary consideration in the kingdom (Matt. 20:21) and their question about the restoration of the kingdom to Israel (Acts 1:6) show that even they shared the popular nationalistic expectations right up to Pentecost. It was well nigh impossible for Jews to conceive of the restoration of Israel under God's righteous rule apart from a restoration of political power and economic well being. This was the context in which the eschatological coming of the nations to worship Israel's God was expected. According to this vision, they would first be subjected by the Zealots' warrior Messiah. But Jesus did not offer this kind of national salvation.

In contrast to this vision, the suffering servant of the prophetic vision of Isaiah became the messianic model. Jesus saw himself as a servant who comes in weakness and humility. The majority within Judaism, and their religious leaders in particular, found Jesus' messianic claims so sharply divergent from all that they had hoped for that they dismissed his view of the kingdom of God as incredible. The kingdom, as Jesus presented it, was a mystery to the masses and religious leaders alike. On the other hand, people from the most unlikely sectors of Jewish society thronged to Jesus. Judaism's outcasts—the tax collectors and the prostitutes, the poor and disinherited, Galileans and Samaritans, the humble and the "little ones"—crowded to enter into the kingdom which was rejected by their leaders (Matt. 21:31).

God's rule of righteousness was so mysteriously different it was rejected out-of-hand by Israel's authorities. Of course, the kingdom which Jesus inaugurated was so radically different it was also soon discarded by major sectors of the Christian church. The concept of the kingdom was redefined to make it compatible with the interests of the powerful and the prosperous. This was done by practically identifying the kingdom with the church, or by conceiving of the kingdom as almost entirely future. The kingdom of God was thus stripped of its power, and its message was no longer good news.

In the biblical vision, the kingdom of God presupposes a people of God. The kingdom community is God's restored people who live under his salvific rule. God's character and will determine both the identity and the mission of his people.

The meaning of this radically upside-down kingdom (Kraybill, 1978) can be perceived only through the eyes of faith. It is a matter of "hear[ing] the word and understand[ing] it," i.e., grasping it in obedient faith (Matt. 13:23). Of course, the possibility of perceiving the secrets of the kingdom of God is in itself a gift of God's grace (13:10-12). Even so, the disciples had to be told repeatedly what the kingdom was about. The nature of the kingdom is such that its story must continually be retold in the community of faith lest it become deformed or be forgotten. To those who respond to the invitation to life under the righteous rule of God he grants the gifts of obedient faith and hope. Although clarity and credibility in its communication surely enhance the church's witness to the kingdom, there are no sure strategies to insure its growth. The kingdom comes as a gift of God and is received in childlike faith and obedience (Mark 10:15). The unbounded joy of one who stumbles onto a hidden treasure and then gives up everything so that it can be his or hers is certainly one of the best pictures of the way in which the kingdom comes (Matt. 13:44).

The Kingdom of God: The Presence of the Future

In the mission of Jesus, the future has been brought into our midst. This does not mean that the future has already been realized in the coming of the Messiah and thereby has been bereft of its significance. The ministry of Jesus is only the beginning of the end. All that he did points to the consummation of all things which he will usher in at his parousia. This messianic presence of the future fills the church with hope and determines the mission of the messianic community.

The eschatological character of the kingdom determines the way the church will carry out the mission with which it has been charged. Jesus, in his incarnation, has furnished the authoritative signs whereby the essential character of God's reign can be recognized and distinguished from all other kingdoms. In his parousia Jesus will bring to consummation God's glorious reign in all of its fullness. Faithfulness in mission depends on the church's aligning itself with God's eternal salvific purposes. Sensitivity to this pull of the future will protect the church from a distracting concentration on lesser goals, such as pragmatic concerns for the best missionary strategies, activism in behalf of good causes, other matters which are not of ultimate significance, and even its own growth in terms of numbers and apparent influence.

When mission is held in eschatological perspective, the church will find resources of power which will ultimately carry it to triumph over the powers of death which characterize the kingdoms of this world. When this vision of the kingdom coming in fullness and power is lost, mission becomes characterized by confusion, false activism, and goals which are decidedly secondary when they are evaluated by kingdom criteria.

The Kingdom of God: Already, But Not Yet

The preaching and teaching and kingdom activity of Jesus do not only point to the rule of God which will become effective sometime in the future. In a real way God's rule began to be realized in the ministry of Jesus: "But if it is by the Spirit of God that I cast out demons, then the kingdom of God has come upon you" (Matt. 12:28; cf. Luke 11:20; 17:21).[5]

The kingdom of God is not a strictly future reality, nor is it primarily an inner reality limited to the hearts of individuals. Jesus' intention was that the rule of God be fully established, that it come visibly into appearance. This tangibility of God's rule requires a restored people who experience the salvific rule of God, who reflect its character, and who show forth God's intention for all humanity.

The New Testament call to repentance is an invitation to be freed from the dominion of Satan to enjoy life in the kingdom of God. Experiences of forgiveness, of healing, and of liberation from all sorts of bondage are evidence of the fact that God's rule is already operative in the world.

To say that the kingdom of God is eschatological is to understand that the earthly ministry of Jesus already marked the beginning of the end. The Sermon on the Mount is not merely a utopian program for the future. It describes realistically the community of those among whom the righteous and peaceful kingdom of God is present. Rather than simply looking forward to the time when God's reign of peace will be fully established, kingdom people are already beating "their swords into plowshares, and their spears into pruning hooks" (Isa. 2:4) and are already living together in "justice and with righteousness" (9:7). Life in the community of the Messiah already offers a foretaste of the fulfillment to come.

While the rule of God has already been inaugurated by Jesus, it still awaits fulfillment. All of Jesus' kingdom activity on earth and all that he commissioned his disciples to continue to carry out points forward to the consummation of the kingdom. The full meaning of the parables of the kingdom cannot be understood apart from the parousia and the fulfillment of God's kingdom purpose. The presence of the future fills God's people with authentic hope and keeps the church's sense of identity and mission clear.

The inability of the church to live faithfully with the tension between the "already" and the "not yet" of the kingdom of God in its life and mission has been the source of much of its confusion and indirection. Whenever the church had concentrated unilaterally on the "already" aspect of the rule of God, it has tended to lose its power and sense of direction. It has historically identified the church with the kingdom. When this happens, the church itself becomes the center of its own concern and activity. The attitude of the church becomes marked with triumphalism, and the church sees itself as an agent of the kingdom and the dispenser of salvation rather than a sign of the kingdom and a witness to God's amazing grace.

On the other hand, a one-sided concentration on the "not yet" aspect of the kingdom exercises an equally pernicious influence on the church. In its "other worldliness," the church is tempted to flee from the real world—which is the object of God's love—into an unreal and spiritualized sphere. Instead of offering a message of hope for the present, the church tends to limit its offer of hope to the future.[6] To relegate the pertinence of Jesus' kingdom teachings and activity to the future is to offer a partial gospel for the present. Some have conceived of the Sermon on the Mount as primarily intended for the future. But this is to deprive the church of kingdom blessedness here and now. Others who view God's rule of righteousness as fundamentally future have assumed a largely defeatist attitude toward sin.[7] The alternative need not be a stance of legalistic perfectionism. A full-orbed vision of the kingdom offers abundant resources to sustain God's people who submit willingly to his righteous rule here and now, in view of the glorious future which has been promised.

The consummation of the kingdom is still to come. This is the context in which the church carries forward its commission as witnesses to the kingdom which has been initiated in Jesus and which will be consummated on his return. The interim between the incarnation and the parousia is characterized by conflict between the two kingdoms, the kingdom of Satan and the kingdom of God. The kingdom message of the church includes witness to its historic coming in Jesus, its authentication in the life of the messianic community, and the continuing promise of the future which God will usher in.

The Primacy of the Kingdom

In our attempt to understand the identity and mission of the church we must begin where the New Testament begins—with the kingdom. The primacy of the kingdom of God is stated quite explicitly: "Seek first his kingdom and his righteousness" (Matt. 6:33). In other parts of the New Testament, the priority of the kingdom is implied. Jesus begins his messianic mission in the synoptic Gospels with his proclamation of the kingdom. The confession that Jesus is Lord (also "King of Israel" in John 1:49) presupposes the priority of the kingdom.[8] The focus of the New Testament is primarily on the kingdom and secondarily on the church.

The kingdom is God's righteous rule in human history to which people are invited to respond in loyal commitment. God reigns in a radically new order. Those who responded to Jesus' call were incorporated into a messianic community, a new people of God, the church. Therefore, the church may be understood as the people of the kingdom. The kingdom and the church are closely related; however, they are not identical. The church preaches and teaches the gospel of the kingdom. It continues Jesus' kingdom activity. It exercises kingdom authority (Matt. 16:18). It must maintain its integrity as a community which lives under God's righteous rule. The church occupies a central place in God's intention for the advancement of his kingdom: "that through the church the manifold wisdom of God might now be made known to the principalities and powers in the heavenly places" (Eph. 3:10). But in the perspective of the New Testament, the kingdom remains primary. The church is the community of the kingdom.

The authority of the church is ultimately the authority of the kingdom. Jesus entrusted to his disciples the amazing authority which he himself exercised in God's kingdom. But this authority is by no means to be exercised in arbitrary ways. The church is to proceed in exactly the same way as Jesus did in its use of the keys of the kingdom. The authority which the church exercises is not its own. It is kingdom authority. And to this authority the church itself is submitted.

Therefore, the church must never forget its servant role. It is at the service of the King and of his righteous reign. To commit oneself to the kingdom of God will ordinarily involve participation in the community of the King. However, participation in the church is never an absolute guarantee that people are living under the rule of God. Kingdom criteria, of which Jesus was the prime expression, must always be primary.

The Kingdom of God and the Kingdom of Satan

The biblical context of God's rule of righteousness and peace is one of conflict. Jesus had to struggle with temptations to be a different kind of Messiah, to participate in a different kind of kingdom (Matt. 4:1-11). Jesus' kingdom activity was characterized largely by conflict with the demonic powers which caused so much human pain and suffering, as well as with the personalized power of evil in Judaism's religious leadership.

The mission of the messianic community was likewise characterized by conflict. The mission of the twelve involved being sent out "as sheep in the midst of wolves" (Matt. 10:16) and was characterized by confrontation, conflict, and persecution (10:16-39). The mission of the seventy was also interpreted in terms of conflict. "The seventy returned with joy, saying, 'Lord, even the demons are subject to us in your name!' And he said to them, 'I saw Satan fall like lightning from heaven. Behold I have given you authority . . . over all the power of the enemy' " (Luke 10:17-19). The plot of the parable of the wheat and the tares is characterized by conflict: "[the] enemy came and sowed weeds . . . and the enemy who sowed them is the devil" (Matt. 13:25, 39).

According to the biblical vision there are two kingdoms, the kingdom of God and the kingdom of Satan. These two kingdoms are engaged in mortal combat. This warfare leaves its mark on the entire New Testament. To participate in the kingdom of God is to engage in the war of the Lamb. In this conflict citizens of the kingdom of God will suffer in the same way that Jesus suffered at the hand of the antikingdom and can expect persecution. The weapons of this warfare are the same as those employed by Jesus. This calls for the "endurance and faith of the saints" (Rev. 13:10).

The context of mission, therefore, is this cosmic warfare between the kingdom of God and the kingdom of this world. Jesus Christ is already replacing Satan's rule with his own. This struggle is being carried out in the arena of human history. To preach the gospel of the kingdom is to be engaged in battle with the kingdom of this world. The triumph of God's kingdom is assured to those who see reality through eyes of faith. However, this does not make the conflict any less real. The conditions of our warfare call for unfailing loyalty, clarity of vision, depth of commitment, and willingness to suffer persecution.

Jesus warned his followers that "no one can serve two masters" (Matt. 6:24). Jesus calls people to renounce their allegiance to the "prince of this world" and to submit to the rule of God. Just as in the case of the Messiah himself, faithfulness in the witness of the church will take the form of a cross. The warfare section of Jesus' missionary discourse in Matthew 10 concludes with the promise that "he who loses his life for my sake will find it" (10:39b).[9] According to the New Testament, there is no other path to faithfulness in mission. In the New Testament, as well as in the subsequent history of the church, suffering and growth have gone hand in hand.

God's Kingdom and God's Mission

Just as Jesus in his person as well as by his preaching, teaching, and activity communicated the good news of the establishment of God's reign, he also commissioned the messianic community to continue the same kind of witness. This means that the church must understand its role in instrumental terms rather than in managerial and imperial images, as has often been the case. The church does not build the kingdom. According to the New Testament use of the image, God is the builder and the church is the building. The church is not the agent or representative of the kingdom. According to the pertinent New Testament images, the church is servant and messenger of the King.

The church's witness does not build or establish the kingdom. God alone can do this. As firstfruits of the kingdom, the messianic community can joyfully testify to God's rule of salvation. Its message is good news because it is effectively salvific. By its recital of God's saving deeds in history and its picture of the future in which God's kingdom will be fulfilled, the church communicates forcefully the essential character of God's reign in the present. In its kingdom activity the church offers a credible demonstration of the reality of God's kingdom.

Rather than simply reporting kingdom truths and kingdom

events objectively, as a news reporter would do, the church shares a story and a hope in which it is a participant. The church concretely continues Jesus' messianic mission. In the process the church is caught in the same kind of struggle Jesus experienced. It is tempted to take the same messianic shortcuts which lead to false kingdoms. Likewise, only in its obedience unto death will the church prove, just as Jesus did, to be fully faithful in its witness. This kind of witness and solidarity with the kingdom are gifts of the Spirit of God.

Spirit, Kingdom, and Church

According to the prophetic vision, the messianic restoration of Israel would take the shape of a "new covenant," with God's law written upon new hearts of flesh and a new Spirit enabling his people to walk in his statutes (Jer. 31:31-33; Ezek. 36:26-27; 37:24).

Pentecost is essential to a biblical understanding of kingdom, church, and mission. Pentecost is often interpreted in a largely individualistic way, in terms of personal holiness and charismatic experience. And these personal aspects of Pentecost are certainly not to be disparaged. However, it is noteworthy that Acts sets Pentecost in a kingdom context. And it is in this context that the church and its missionary role are best understood.

Jesus "presented himself alive after his passion . . . appearing to them during forty days, and speaking of the kingdom of God. And . . . he charged them not to depart from Jerusalem, but to wait for the promise of the Father . . . 'you shall be baptized with the Holy Spirit' " (Acts 1:3-5). Then in response to the disciples' question about the restoration of the kingdom to Israel, Jesus replied, "You shall receive power when the Holy Spirit has come upon you; and you shall be my witnesses in Jerusalem and in all Judea and Samaria and to the end of the earth" (1:8). The words "the Holy Spirit will come upon you" were addressed to Mary when Jesus was given a physical body (Luke 1:35). Here they are addressed to the disciples, who, in the power of the Spirit, have been created into a new body—the church. At the heart of the Pentecost experience is the creation of a new body—the body of Christ, the community of the kingdom (Lederach, 1980:34).

The response to kingdom expectation is the creation of a community commissioned with the task of witnessing in the power of the Spirit to the kingdom and to its Lord, King Jesus. Peter's Pentecostal call to repentance is a call to abandon the kingdom of Satan and to enter the kingdom of God. To be saved from "this crooked generation" (Acts 2:40) was to become incorporated into a new people who live under the rule of God. "The kingdom is where the presence and the power of the Holy Spirit are manifested in the midst of a new people" (Lederach, 1980:36).

The Pentecostal era of the Spirit is characterized in Acts as the age of mission, the church's witness to the kingdom. The relevance of Pentecost can best be appreciated as a corporate event, and mission can be best understood as the church's witness to the kingdom and to its King. This vision, of course, has far-reaching implications for the church's understanding of its identity and mission. Rather than separating the kingdom and the church, as dispensationalism has done, the identity of the church must be defined by its relation to the kingdom. And rather than separating church and mission, as Constantinian Protestantism had done, the role of the church is defined as mission, full-orbed witness to God's kingdom, in the power of his Spirit.

The Gospel of the Kingdom

The gospel which the church shares is the gospel of the kingdom. This was the message which the early church communicated to Jews (Luke 10:9), to Samaritans (Acts 8:12), and to everyone (Acts 28:31). The church does not preach itself, no matter how attractive its life may be or how appealing its program is. As we noted earlier, it has sometimes been alleged that Jesus proclaimed the kingdom, but the church's task is to preach Christ as the early church did. It is supposed that there is a substantial difference between the two messages. At best this is a dangerous half-truth which has sometimes permitted the church to cheapen its offer of salvation.

The Christ of the church's preaching has often become the Christ of the Apostles' Creed: conceived by the Holy Spirit, born of the Virgin Mary, suffered under Pontius Pilate, crucified, dead, buried, descended into Hades, risen from the dead, ascended into heaven, sitting at God's right hand, and coming judge. The overriding concern in the proclamation of this Christ is orthodox theology rather than discipleship in Jesus' kingdom activity and participation in kingdom mission.

Again, the Christ of the church's preaching has sometimes been the spiritualized and unreal Christ of the mystics. And here the overriding concern has been the cultivation of individual religious experience and personal piety of a mystical nature.

Still again, the church has preached a Christ who was essentially the good Master of Galilee. And here the center of attention has been the formation of good people of solid character who fit well into the social and religious structures of Western Christendom.

None of these visions does justice to the Messiah of the New Testament. All of these approaches bypass the specific preaching and teaching and kingdom activity of Jesus described in the New Testament. All are in reality deformations of the gospel of the kingdom preached by Jesus and the early church. All proclaim a Christ who has been co-opted and placed at the service of the church.

To preach Christ is to proclaim the kingdom in which Christ is Lord. Within the context of this kingdom the church confesses that Jesus Christ is Lord. The New Testament gospel is not the church's gospel. It is the gospel of the kingdom. Therefore, to evangelize is much more than to promote the interests of the church, i.e., church extension, no matter how worthy this goal may be. The gospel of the kingdom is the good news of God's reign of righteousness, peace, and salvation. The New Testament refers indiscriminately to the gospel as the gospel of the kingdom (Matt. 4:23; 24:14; et al.), a gospel of salvation (Eph. 1:13; Rom. 1:16), a gospel of peace (Acts 10:36; Rom. 10:15; Eph. 6:15), a gospel of grace (Acts 20:24), and by implication, a gospel of righteousness (Matt. 6:33; Rom. 14:17). To be aware that the gospel which the church shares is the gospel of the kingdom is to recognize that the concern of the church in mission is as broad and as deep as God's concern for humanity.

> The gospel is not to be treated lightly. It is not the possession of the church. The church itself was created by the gospel and can remain true to its calling only by sharing the gospel of the kingdom with others, for the King's message is for all people. The church experiences its most vital solidarity with the King when carrying out the King's wishes (Shenk, 1979:25).

The gospel of the kingdom is best proclaimed by the church when, in the power of the Spirit of the King, it preaches, teaches, and dedicates itself to authentic kingdom activity in the confident hope that God's universal salvific reign of righteousness and peace will be manifest within the church itself, among all humankind, and over all of creation. This is the context of the church's fervent prayer, "Thy kingdom come, Thy will be done, On earth as it is in heaven" (Matt. 6:10).

Notes

1. The biblical term, *kingdom of God,* is liable to be misunderstood due to the secular meaning of the term *kingdom.* A kingdom refers, first, to a government or country

headed by a king and, second, to a realm or domain; it is understood primarily in a concrete spatial sense. In its biblical usage, however, the term carries a dynamic concept. It does not refer to a place but to God's reign, to his kingly activity, to his rule, to his order. Hans Küng defines the kingdom of God simply as "God's cause" in the world (1976:215). In the course of the church's history, the concept of the kingdom of God has suffered a number of serious deformations (see Arias, 1980:37-53). Here it must suffice to note that kingdom is fundamentally a political term and implies a wide range of social relationships. Kingdom of God refers to a social order, God's new order. In the course of this chapter, we shall refer to the kingdom of God using a variety of terms which point to the essentially dynamic sense in which the New Testament perceives the reality of God's kingdom.

Taking his cue from Targum Isaiah, where kingdom means the saving revelation of God himself, Bruce Chilton (1984:126) has suggested that the kingdom of God is, in effect, "God come in strength." Rather than seeing the kingdom of God simply as an apocalyptic regime, or as a political movement, or as a program for social improvement, we perceive in his reign "God revealed in consummating strength" (Chilton 1984:126).

In Sinai we witness the coming of Yahweh to rule over his people. In Jesus' proclamation of the kingdom of God, we perceive the saving activity of God present in the person and word/deeds of Messiah (Luke 11:20; cf. Matt. 12:28). The essential element in the messianic proclamation of the evangel is "your God reigns" (Isa. 52:7).

2. An example of this increased interest in the kingdom of God is seen in "A Response to Lausanne: Theological Implications of Radical Discipleship," a document drawn up by an ad hoc group made up largely of third-world, Australian, and young evangelical participants. This four-page statement (1975) contains ten references to the "kingdom of God." In contrast, "The Lausanne Covenant," the ten-page official statement of the 1974 Lausanne Congress, contains only four references.

3. The approximate number of occurrences of *basilea* (kingdom) in the New Testament is as follows: Matthew, 51; Mark, 16; Luke, 41; John, 5; Acts, 8; Pauline Epistles, 14; Hebrews and Catholic Epistles, 4; Revelation, 4. Biblical references used in this chapter are from the Revised Standard Version unless noted otherwise.

4. In this section I am indebted to Wilbert R. Shenk (1979:21-26).

5. The primary sense of the Greek verb *phthano* is to "come before, to precede" (Bauer 1979:856). Thayer suggests the following translation of Matthew 12:28 and Luke 11:20: "The kingdom of God has come upon you sooner than you expected" (Thayer, 1889:652).

6. Dispensationalism, a theology which has been quite popular among evangelicals, emphasizes the importance of the kingdom. But its understanding of the kingdom is almost totally futuristic. From the standpoint of the history of Christian doctrine, dispensationalism is a recent development. J. N. Darby and others popularized the view about 150 years ago. The kingdom is viewed as altogether future, and the church is conceived of as a parenthesis between the dispensation of law and the coming kingdom.

7. Traditional Lutheranism and much of mainstream Protestantism have historically fallen in this category. Luther's one-sided emphasis on salvation by faith alone and his understanding of the Christian as *simul justus et peccator* have contributed to this attitude.

8. Other royal messianic titles applied to Jesus include "Son of David," "Son of man," "Son of God" (see Lederach, 1980:26-28).

9. These words must have impressed Jesus' followers. They are repeated six times in the Gospels (Matt. 10:39; 16:25; Mark 8:35; Luke 9:24; 17:33; John 12:25).

References Cited

Arias, Mortimer
    1980   *Venga tu reino.* Mexico: Casa Unida de Publicaciones.

Bauer, Walter
   1979   *A Greek-English Lexicon of the New Testament and Other Early Christian Literature.* William F. Arndt and F. Wilbur Gingrich, trans. and adapt.; Chicago: University of Chicago Press.

Catholic Institute for International Relations
   1989   *The Road to Damascus: Kairos and Conversion.* London: Catholic Institute for International Relations.

Chilton, Bruce
   1984   *The Kingdom of God in the Teachings of Jesus.* Philadelphia: Fortress Press.

Dodd, C. H.
   1961   *The Parables of the Kingdom.* New York: Scribner.

Jeremias, Joachim
   1963   *The Parables of Jesus.* S. H. Hooke, trans.; New York: Scribner.

Kirk, Andrew
   1983   *The Good News of the Kingdom Coming: The Marriage of Evangelism and Social Responsibility.* Downers Grove, Ill.: InterVarsity Press.

Kraybill, Donald B.
   1978   *The Upside-Down Kingdom.* Scottdale, Pa.: Herald Press.

Küng, Hans
   1976   *On Being a Christian.* Edward Quinn, trans.; Garden City, N.Y.: Doubleday.

Lausanne Committee for World Evangelization
   1974   "The Lausanne Covenant," official statement of the Lausanne Congress.

Lederach, Paul M.
   1980   *A Third Way: Conversations about Anabaptist/Mennonite Faith.* Scottdale, Pa.: Herald Press.

Lind, Millard
   1973   *Biblical Foundations for Christian Worship.* Scottdale, Pa.: Herald Press.

"A Response to Lausanne"
   1975   "Theological Implications of Radical Discipleship," a response to "The Lausanne Covenant" from the International Congress on World Evangelization, 1974, printed in *Mission Trends No. 2: Evangelization.* Gerald H. Anderson and Thomas A. Stransky, eds.; Grand Rapids, Mich.: Eerdmans.

Shenk, Wilbert R.
   1979   "Church Growth and God's Kingdom," *Mission Focus* 7:2 (June).

Thayer, Joseph Henry
   1889   *A Greek-English Lexicon of the New Testament.* New York: American Book Company.

CHAPTER 4

Holy Spirit: Source of Messianic Mission

Roelf S. Kuitse

THE HOLY SPIRIT has not been at the center of theological reflection in Western Christianity. Otto Dilschneider, a German theologian, speaks about "eine akute Geistvergessenheit" (1979:332-35), an acute amnesia with regard to the Holy Spirit, in Western theology. John Taylor writes, "We had . . . relegated the Holy Spirit to the merest edges of . . . theology (1973:5).

For a long time most attention has been focused on Christology. Theological issues have been christological issues. This Christocentric focus has not left much room for the work of God as Creator and for the work of the Holy Spirit. Pentecost is overshadowed by Christmas, Good Friday, and Easter. Cross and resurrection seem to be the last decisive and saving acts in God's encounter with the world.

In the Roman Catholic Church, the Spirit was subordinated to the church, the continuation of the incarnation. The Spirit became the possession of the church, working in and through the ruling, teaching, and sacrificing ministry of the hierarchy. The Spirit became, as has been said, institutionalized.[1]

Churches of the Reformation put emphasis on the Spirit as an instrumental entity which opens the human heart for the proclaimed Word and in this way applies the salvation received in Christ to the individual. Word and Spirit, the preached Word and the Spirit, were closely connected. Out of fear for an individualization and subjectivation of the work of the Spirit, the Spirit was later closely linked to the written Word, especially in Calvinistic circles. A shift from the spoken Word to the written Word took place, a development which has its parallel from prophets to scribes in the Old Testament. Divine inspiration became verbal inerrancy. Instead of the holy, infallible institution, the church, came the holy, inerrant book, the Bible.

Among certain groups of the so-called Radical Reformation the Spirit was seen at work primarily in the heart of the believer. There was supposed to be a direct inner relation of the soul with God via the Holy Spirit. In this way the Spirit was detached from the Word, the present from the past. This led to aberrations such as the story of Münster. James Dunn is convinced that this story was the reason why in Western Christianity the Spirit was neglected: "The Spirit . . . did not return to prominence largely owing to Protestant suspicion and hatred of the Anabaptists" (Dunn, 1970:225).

Not much attention was paid, either in Roman Catholic or in Protestant circles, to the relation of Spirit and mission. The divine Spirit was not primarily seen as a missionary Spirit.

Rediscovery of the Holy Spirit

It seems that in our days a new chapter is being written in the history of human reflection on the work of God in the world. In movements inside and outside the church, new attention is given to the work of the Holy Spirit. There are different signs of this rediscovery of the Holy Spirit.

The birth and development of the Pentecostal movement since the beginning of this century should be mentioned as a first sign. This movement has led to a remarkable growth of Pentecostal churches. It has also had an impact on Roman Catholic as well as Protestant churches in and through the charismatic movement. The Pentecostal movement is an expression of a strong desire for a direct experience of the divine reality and presence. There is also a deep longing for an inspiring community. In the Pentecostal movement we can discern a reaction against an objectivization of the gospel in institutes and doctrines, a reaction also against an overemphasis on the transcendence of God.

A third aspect of the Pentecostal movement is mission as work of the Spirit. The percentage of mission workers from Pentecostal background has increased considerably during the last decades. According to David Barrett (1988:119-30) Pentecostal and charismatic movements cover 20 percent of World Christianity (320 million members).

The greatest number of people related to Pentecostal churches can be found in the so-called two-thirds world, especially in Latin America and Africa. Writing about the movement in Latin America, David Martin (1990) expresses his view that Pentecostalism, a North American "periphery religion," may one day become the core culture in Latin America, just as nonconformists, once a periphery religion in Britain, supplied the core culture of North America. In Africa it is in the African independent churches where the Spirit plays a significant role. Andrew Walls once characterized these churches as the "Anabaptists of Africa" (Walls, 1979:48-53).

Will the so-called Third Church (Bühlmann, 1976) become the church of the Holy Spirit? Is the Third Church in Africa, Asia, and Latin America the place where a theology of the Holy Spirit will be developed? The First Church (Eastern Orthodoxy) is many times characterized as the Church of the Resurrection, the Church of Easter, with a *theologia triumphans*. And the Second Church, in the West, has been characterized as the church where the cross, a *theologia crucis*, has played a dominant role. Especially Hollenweger (1975) has called our attention to the importance of the Holy Spirit in oral cultures where the Christian faith is not expressed in concepts and doctrines but in hymns and stories circling around the experiences of divine presence in human life.

John H. Yoder (1967) has pointed to a parallel between early Anabaptists and the rise of Pentecostalism in our century.

> The Pentecostal movement is in our century the closest parallel to what Anabaptism was in the sixteenth: expanding so vigorously that it bursts the bonds of its own thinking about church order, living from the multiple gifts of the Spirit in the total church while holding leaders in great respect, unembarrassed by the language of the layman and the aesthetic tastes of the poor, mobile, zealously single-minded (Yoder, 1967:78; cf. 1979:41-48).

Eastern Orthodoxy puts a heavy emphasis on the resurrection of Christ, on Easter. Yet, one of the theologians of this church (Bulgakow, in Heiler, 1971:119) speaks about Eastern Orthodoxy as a religion of the Holy Spirit. The encounter with Eastern Orthodox spirituality can be seen as a second sign of a new attention given to the Holy Spirit. In Eastern Orthodoxy a total subordination of the Spirit to Christ, a pneumatological subordination, is rejected. Stress is put on the independent work of the Spirit in the cosmos as well as in history. That makes it easier for Eastern Orthodoxy than for many Protestants to see the divine Spirit at work in other non-Christian, religious communities. Bulgakow points to the fact that Eastern Orthodox Christians in their spiritual life call upon the Spirit as much as they call upon Christ.

The Spirit is also closely related to the worship of the Orthodox church. Prayer and intercession play a significant role in the worshiping community. Urged by the Spirit, the church does what the world does not yet do: praise and glorify God. This emphasis on intercession for the world and worship on behalf of the world leads to a concept of mission which is different from the Western, activistic concept. Growing contacts with Eastern Orthodox churches and continuing discussion about the *filioque*[2] issue have contributed to a renewed attention in Western Christianity to the work of the Holy Spirit.

A third example of a renewed attention for the work of the Spirit is feminist theology. In feminist theology we see an attempt to overcome a one-sided, male way of speaking about the divine reality. The Holy Spirit is seen as a female manifestation of God, stressing closeness, presence, warmth, consolation, and love (Van de Beek, 1987:174-78). A Roman Catholic theologian wrote a pneumatology with the title *The Divine Mother* (Gelpi, 1984).[3] This way of speaking about God as immanent is put over against a male way of speaking about God as transcendent and distant in concepts and doctrines.

The rediscovery of the Spirit in the life and work of the church has also had an impact on other aspects of theology. In one of his last writings, Karl Barth (quoted in Dilschneider, 1979:333) writes about his dream in regard to the future of theology. This dream is a theology of the Holy Spirit, a pneumatological rewriting of theology. Some theologians, Roman Catholic (Mühlen, 1967) as well as Protestant (Berkhof, 1988),[4] have already made a beginning with this rewriting. It seems that the period of neglect of the Holy Spirit in theological reflection has ended. Has this development also had an impact on missiology?

The Holy Spirit and Missiology

There has been much discussion about where in theological reflection mission belongs. Should it be part of Christology, ecclesiology, or eschatology? More and more in our day mission is related to pneumatology. This is a result of the rediscovery of the Holy Spirit in church and theology. This pneumatological perspective on mission also does justice to the other three aspects: the Spirit is the Spirit of Christ (Rom. 8:9), the Spirit creates the church (2 Cor. 13:13), and the Spirit gathers the first fruits of the harvest (Rom. 8:23).

Developments in mission have also contributed to a stronger emphasis on the Holy Spirit. Here the name of Roland Allen (1868-1947) should be mentioned. Allen was a witness of the repercussions of the Boxer Rebellion in China at the end of the nineteenth century. What happened to many churches after missionaries had to leave was an eye-opener to Allen. Many churches collapsed after missionaries left. These churches had been too dependent on the presence and work of missionaries. These negative developments brought Allen back to the Bible, especially to the writings of Luke and Paul. He was impressed by the important role played by the Holy Spirit in Luke's writings, especially in the book of Acts. In these writings mission is seen, according to Allen, as work of the Spirit. The Spirit of God is a missionary Spirit, crossing boundaries to bring people in relation to Christ.

What this rediscovery of the missionary Spirit of God means for the way and goal of mission has been described by Allen in different books (1949, 1962). Not much attention was given to these books right after they were published; Allen's thoughts and ideas were seen as idealistic and unrealistic. That changed after the Communist revolution in China brought mission into a new crisis. Since then more attention has been given to the work of Allen and to his emphasis on the essential role of the Holy Spirit in the mission of the church.

The encounter with independent churches on different continents and their ways of doing theology has also contributed to a new way of looking at the missionary enterprise. Theologies developed in other contexts pay more attention to the Holy Spirit than do theologies developed in Western contexts.

Missiologists such as Boer (1961), Newbigin (1958, 1978), Taylor (1973), and others have, in their own independent ways, contributed to a renewed way of thinking about mission from a pneumatological perspective. Also in regard to missiology it is not possible anymore to speak about a neglect of the Holy Spirit or, to say it in German, "eine akute Geistvergessenheit" (Dilschneider, 1979:332-35). The renewed emphasis on the Holy Spirit has contributed to a more balanced view of mission as the work of the triune God.

Fire and Wind

The Bible speaks in different ways about the divine Spirit. In the languages of the Bible, Hebrew and Greek, spirit is the same as breath, wind, air. *Ruach* in Hebrew is feminine, and *pneuma* in Greek is neuter.

Without air, without breathing, life is not possible. Air is around us: air is in us. Yet air or breath is not something that we can catch, keep, or possess. The same is true in regard to the breath of God, the Spirit. Without the breath of God, without the Spirit of God, life is not possible and renewal of life cannot happen: yet the Spirit of God cannot be kept or caught in our thoughts and words, concepts and definitions. The Spirit of God is not at the disposal of human beings and cannot be manipulated.

The Spirit is the wind of God. "The wind blows where it chooses, . . . you do not know where it comes from or where it goes" (John, 3:8).[5] We learn to know the wind through what it brings about, through its effects. The wind is invisible and elusive; the effects of the wind are visible and discernible. The same is true in regard to the divine Spirit, the wind of God. The effects of the work of God's Spirit can be discerned in lives of people, individually and as community. In the book of Acts one important effect of God's wind, God's Spirit, is emphasized: mission. Luke 24:49 uses the word *power*: "power from on high," which changes disciples into apostles. In the Gospel of John, life is seen as the result of the working of the Spirit: "energy for life" (Stendahl, 1990), new life of divine quality. Paul mentions several fruits of the Spirit, two of which are freedom and love (Gal. 5:13-25).

Fire is an image used to describe the work of the Spirit. The Spirit of God is like a fire, warming and purifying. Purification and judgment belong to the working of the Spirit in human lives. In the story told in Acts 2 about the Spirit descending on the disciples, the coming of the Spirit is accompanied by "a sound like the rush of a violent wind, and . . . divided tongues, as of fire" (Acts 2:2-3; cf. Matt. 3:11).

Jesus is described in the synoptic Gospels as the *pneumatophorus*, the one who is endowed with the Spirit. Jesus is the Christ, the Anointed one, anointed with the Holy Spirit. In Matthew and Luke, his birth is related to the Holy Spirit. In Matthew, Mark, and Luke, we read about the Spirit descending on Jesus "like a dove" (Matt. 3:16) at the time of his baptism. The dove is the symbol of peace, of hope for new life. As in the primal flood, the catastrophe is not final; the destructive forces don't have the final word (Gen. 8:6-12). After Jesus' baptism there is the temptation in the desert, the place of demonic powers, the reverse image of paradise (Matt. 4:1-11). In Christ "the reversal of the expulsion from paradise is in the making" (Stendahl, 1990:25). In this reversal healing and exorcism play an important role. They are signs of the kingdom of God, signs of the working of the Holy Spirit (Matt. 12:28). The Spirit of God is stronger than the power of evil. In Hebrews (9:14) and Romans (1:3-4) the sacrifice and the resurrection of Jesus are related to the Spirit.

Jews held the view that the Spirit had been withdrawn from Israel after the last prophet had spoken. The hope was alive that the Spirit would return again, descending on the one who would inaugurate a new era (Isa. 11:1-2; 42:1; 61:1-2). According to Luke 4:18-19, this hope has found fulfillment in Christ: "The Spirit of the Lord is upon me, because he has anointed me to bring good news to the poor. He has sent me to proclaim release to the captives and recovery of sight to the blind, to let the oppressed go free, to proclaim the year of the Lord's favor" (cf. Matt. 12:18).

The New Testament not only speaks about Jesus as endowed with the Spirit, but also about Jesus as the one who gives the Spirit, who endows others with the Spirit. This view of the Anointed One becoming the Anointing One is not part of Jewish expectations. It is a new aspect.

The Last Days

Christ inaugurated a new era. The Anointed One becomes the Anointing One. The risen Lord bestows the Spirit on his disciples to prepare and equip them for their work as apostles among the nations. The apostles are called to be witnesses among the nations, telling the story of God's work in Christ and inviting people to turn around and participate in the new way of living revealed in Christ.[6]

The last days have arrived in the coming of Christ and in the descending of the Holy Spirit. The last days are the days of the Spirit, mission, and church. These three cannot be separated; they belong together. According to the writings of Luke, mission has priority in the order of the works of the Spirit.

Why did the kingdom of God not manifest itself in full glory during Jesus' life? Why did history continue after Christ? What is the meaning of the interim period between the coming of Christ and the return of Christ, between incarnation and parousia? What is the meaning of "the last days" between the first revelation of the reign of God in Christ and the final revelation of God's reign at the end of time?

The life, work, death, and resurrection of Christ are *euaggelion*, good news. They disclose the way God rules, the way God deals with the world in compassionate love. The life of Christ, culminating in cross and resurrection, shows how far God in loving concern for the world goes to overcome human alienation, to bring human beings back to communion with God and with each other.

The good news is embodied in one person, living at a certain time and in a certain place. The good news about God's loving concern for the world is good news for all people at all times and places. Therefore the good news has to reach to others and be told to others living in other times and places. It is the Spirit who, via mission, brings the good news embodied in the one to the many. It is the Spirit who, via mission, crosses boundaries of time and place to let people in other nations and cultures share in the good news. The Spirit keeps the memory of Christ and the dream of God's reign, revealed in Christ, alive at different times and at different places in the world.

In "the last days," the Spirit focuses the attention of a small group of disciples of Jesus on the ends of the earth. A broadening of horizon takes place. From the kingdom restored to Israel (Acts 1:6), the attention is shifted to "the ends of the earth" (1:8). The interim period between incarnation and parousia is the time when people are invited to move in the direction of the kingdom of God, to move toward God in reconciliation and toward each other in a new community which speaks a new language, the key words of which are derived from the story of Jesus. The last days are the days of the Spirit and therefore the days of mission and church.

Luke especially emphasizes this. In the last chapter of his gospel, he describes the disappointment and despair, the confusion and doubt, of Jesus' disciples because of what happened to their Master. These disciples are not depicted as heroes of faith, but as weak, vulnerable persons who fail to act in the right way at decisive moments. They are an image of the church! And yet Jesus joins with these disciples who fail time and again. They are called to be his witnesses among the nations. They are called to be his representatives in the world. This emphasis on the weakness and vulnerability of the disciples makes it impossible to regard mission merely as a human enterprise. More is needed than human initiatives, planning, and programs. After having been called to be Christ's witnesses, the first thing the disciples had to do was to wait for the coming of the Spirit, the power from on high (Luke 24:49). Mission starts with waiting. The emphasis is on the weakness and vulnerability of the disciples, and the emphasis on waiting leaves no room for human triumphalism. There is only room for grateful surprise that the Spirit of God is not ashamed to use weak, failing human instruments—the surprise of grace!

The mandate and promise of Christ mentioned in Luke 24 are repeated in the first chapters of Acts. The Spirit does not direct people's attention to another world, away from this world where Christ was crucified: "Why do you stand looking up toward heaven?" (Acts 1:11). The Spirit induces disciples to look at this world in a new way, in the light of the resurrection and the kingdom of God.

The fulfillment of Christ's promise is described in Acts 2, where we read how disciples are anointed with the divine Spirit. Wind, fire, and speaking in other languages are the visible signs of the descending of the Spirit at Pentecost.

Pentecost was originally a harvest festival, the festival of weeks (Exod. 23:16; 34:22), the festival of the firstfruits. The coming of the Holy Spirit is the beginning of the harvest, the gathering of the new humanity.

Later Pentecost became a festival in memory of the receiving of the Law at Mount Sinai at the day of assembly (Deut. 4:10; 9:10; 10:4). According to a Jewish tradition based on Exodus 20:18, God's voice was heard on the day of assembly at the ends of the earth (Weinfeld, 1978:7-19). The new Pentecost also has universal meaning. The good news of God's saving acts is heard in different languages. The one story reaches people of different cultures, in different languages. The Spirit crosses boundaries. The gospel is translatable.

Another link to the Old Testament is made when Acts 2 is read in the light of the story in Genesis 11 which tells how descendants of Noah tried to stay together and make a name for themselves by building a city with a tower reaching into the heavens. The result of this human initiative is division and confusion. In Acts 2 we read about the countermove of the divine Spirit overcoming division and confusion by creating a new community.

The Spirit is linked to the Word. Through the Word the Spirit touches and renews human lives. Luke does not write much about the work of the Spirit as a private, individual religious experience. The emphasis is on witness as work of the Spirit. Before witness is possible there has to be a personal encounter with the Spirit. Without the Spirit, without the Spirit opening heart and mind, it is impossible to confess that the suffering servant is Lord, that the crucified one is the victorious one, that God's love and not evil has the final word in human history. The emphasis in Luke, however, is not on personal, religious experiences, on conversion stories. The emphasis is on the call to witness, to convey the message of Christ to others. Acts records different speeches or addresses given by apostles to Jews and to Gentiles. All these addresses are missionary addresses except one, the farewell address of Paul to the Ephesian elders (Acts 20:17-36).

A word several times connected to witness, to the proclamation of the Word, is *boldness* (Greek: *parresia*, Acts 4:13, 29, 31; 9:27; 14:3; 18:26; 19:8; 28:31). It is especially used where the apostles face a more-or-less hostile audience. Members of the Sanhedrin are amazed by the way Paul and John speak: "When they saw the boldness of Peter and John and realized that they were uneducated and ordinary men, they were amazed" (4:13). The secret of this boldness is not education or knowledge. The secret of the boldness is the Holy Spirit (4:8; Luke 12:11-12).

The Spirit brings people together in a new community, the church. However, Spirit and church are not identical. Many times the Spirit is far ahead of the church. The Spirit continues to challenge the church to be what the church, according to God's intention, should be. The church in Jerusalem was reluctant to cross boundaries, to move on the way to "Judea and Samaria, and to the ends of the earth" (Acts 1:8). The persecution of believers in Jerusalem is used by the Spirit to bring the word of life to Samaria (8:4-8) and Antioch (11:19-25). Philip was led by the Spirit to the eunuch from Ethiopia (8:29). The Spirit set Paul and Barnabas apart for the work among Gentiles (13:2). Where the Spirit works, things start moving; there is surprise and the unexpected happens. The Spirit leads to new initiatives, new beginnings; human planning and programs are thwarted. Paul had to change his plans; the Spirit led him to Europe (16:6-11).

The Spirit struggles with human misconceptions. One of these misconceptions is related to the tendency to absolutize one's own response to the gospel and to impose that response on others. The Spirit respects the freedom of people to respond in their own way to the gospel. The story of Peter and Cornelius is not only a story of the turning around of Cornelius; it is also the story of Peter's conversion as the result of the working of God's Spirit. The Spirit broadened Peter's horizon and corrected his exclusive way of thinking, his absolutizing of his own response to the gospel. Again, the Spirit surprises the church; the Spirit is ahead of the church. The importance of the lesson learned by Peter is stressed by the attention given to this story in Acts 10:1—11:18. The struggle between Paul and members of the church in Jerusalem about law and grace, about circumcision and the validity of Mosaic Law for Gentile Christians, is another example of the struggle of the Spirit and exclusive modes of thought. The solution of this crisis is seen as work of the Spirit: "It has seemed good to the Holy Spirit and to us" (15:28).

Martin Kähler (1971:112-15) has pointed to the difference between propaganda and mission and has warned that mission should not degenerate into propaganda. Propaganda, according to Kähler, is making carbon copies of ourselves, trying to mold other people after our way of thinking and behaving. In propaganda something else, belonging to our context, is always added or linked to the gospel: the gospel and our culture (Christendom), the gospel and a particular confession, the gospel and a certain lifestyle. The Spirit, as the source of mission, does not work that way. The Spirit does not impose things on people; the Spirit creates the freedom to respond to the gospel in one's own way, from within one's own cultural context.

Roland Allen, in his "boundless confidence in the power of the Holy Spirit" (Boer, 1961:211), points in a similar direction. Paul transfers responsibility for newly established churches to the members of these churches as soon as possible. He does not make these churches dependent on the persons who were instrumental in creating the new communities. Where people come to faith, the Holy Spirit is at work, and this divine Spirit will guide the new believers in their individual and community life. This spiritual independence should not be curtailed by the spiritual dominance of those who brought the good news. Paul's missionary methods, according to Allen (1949), were totally different from missionary methods of modern missions.

Acts emphasizes three points concerning witness. First is the person of Jesus Christ, especially his suffering, death, and resurrection. Neither doctrines nor laws are the content of the Spirit-guided proclamation; but a person, Jesus Christ, is. The Spirit, via the Word, points to Christ: "He proclaimed . . . the good news about Jesus" (Acts 8:35; cf. 5:42; 28:31).

The second point emphasized is what God has given to humankind, to Jews and Gentiles, in and through Jesus, what Jesus' coming and life mean for people living in this world. Different words are used to disclose the meaning of Jesus' life and ministry. A few of these words describing God's gifts in Christ are forgiveness, eternal life, grace, reconciliation, peace, salvation. Forgiveness of sins and the Holy Spirit get special attention in Acts (9:17-18; 22:16). Life in Christ is not dominated anymore by the past and the sins of the past; life in Christ is life open to the future, life in the power of the Spirit. In the first sermon after Pentecost, in Peter's sermon, these two gifts—forgiveness and the Spirit—are mentioned (2:38).

The third aspect of Spirit-guided proclamation is the invitation to make a decision for the God who in Christ has made a decision for humanity. A human decision for God means "repentance toward God and faith toward our Lord Jesus" (20:21), and, as a sign of the new life and the incorporation into a new community, baptism (2:37-41).

These three essential parts of the witness, as described in Acts, are clearly expressed in Peter's sermon after Pentecost. In Peter's sermon the Word is added to the Spirit, the Word explains the event of the descending of the Spirit. For Peter, Pentecost is the fulfillment of the prophecy of Joel about the pouring out of the Spirit of God, in the last days, upon all flesh. The close connection between Spirit and witness is stressed by Peter in the addition made to the text of Joel; the words "and they shall prophesy" are added to the text (Acts 2:18).

The Church

The Spirit of God is a missionary Spirit. The Spirit-guided witness, the proclamation of the gospel, leads to the establishing of communities of believers. One of the fruits of the work of the Spirit is the creation of a new community, a new way of relating to each other. This new community is the church. There is one body and one Spirit (Eph. 4:4). Second Corinthians 13:13 speaks about the communion or fellowship of the Holy Spirit. These words can be interpreted in two ways: the community created by the Holy Spirit or the community of people participating in the Holy Spirit. Something from on high, the Holy Spirit—not ties of blood or nationality, ideology, or economic interests—links people together in this community. That makes the church a community which cannot be identified with any other community.

Sociological categories cannot adequately describe the character of this community. That is one of the reasons why the New Testament uses so many different images for the church. The mystery of the church is beyond definition. Images such as body of Christ and fellowship in the Spirit are used to point to the mystery of the church. In his well-known book, *Images of the Church in the New Testament*, Paul Minear (1960) deals with 96 different images used in the New Testament to describe the church.

One does not belong to this new community by birth, but by rebirth, birth from above (John 3:3), birth of water and the Spirit (3:5). It is a community, which, like Tertullian said, does not grow from "the loins of people," but by "the waters of baptism." It is a community of people who, guided by the Spirit, respond positively to the grace of God disclosed in Christ and who in gratitude for this grace decide to walk in the way of Jesus as obedient disciples of Jesus.

The church is not the end station of God's way with the world. The final goal is the glorious manifestation of the reign of God, the coming of the kingdom of God. Two things should be said about the church: the church is both result of the missionary work of the Spirit and instrument of the missionary work of the Spirit; the church is both sign of the kingdom of God and instrument of the kingdom of God. Both fruit and instrument, being and acting, belong together. The one should not be separated from the other. Only by emphasizing both aspects can we avoid the Scylla and Charybdis of quietism and passivity on the one side and activism and aggressiveness on the other.

The church as body of Christ keeps the memory of Christ alive in the world by being gathered around Word and sign (baptism, communion) which point to Christ. The church as royal priesthood (1 Pet. 2:9) does on behalf of the world what the world does not yet do: praise and glorify God. The church as priesthood for the world is the place where in intercessory prayer the needs of the world are brought before God. The church as new humanity (Eph. 2:15) is the place in the world where the wall separating nations is broken down and the nucleus of a new humanity is manifested. The being of the church in worship and fellowship is a witness, a sign of the kingdom, an expression of the work and the impact of the Spirit.

In the Johannine writings, special attention is given to the missionary presence of the church in the world. The unity of the church (John 17:20-23) and the love of the members toward each other (1 John 2:7-17) are a witness to a divided world. The members of the church have received the anointing of the Holy Spirit. All sisters and brothers in the church share in the same way in the Holy Spirit (1 John 2:26-28). They don't need anybody to rule or teach them; they are ruled and taught by the Holy Spirit. This community in the Holy Spirit, this community of loving mutual care, confronts the world with another way of being or living together, with another pattern of life. The difference between church and world is stressed in the Johannine writings. The word *boldness* (Greek: *parresia*) is not used here, as in Acts, for the way the apostles proclaim the gospel in a hostile world, but for the way believers can approach God in prayer (1 John 5:14).

Acts of the Apostles also points to the missionary dimension of the presence of the church in the world. Mission is not merely activities, not only going, but also being. The primary witness is the new reality of people brought together in a new community by the Spirit. This new way of being cannot remain unnoticed: "Having the goodwill of all the people . . . day by day the Lord added to their number" (Acts 2:47). Adolf von Harnack (1915) stated that the growth of the church in the first centuries was caused mainly by the attraction of the new way of being, the new way of presence of the followers of Christ in the world.

The epistle to the Ephesians calls attention to another aspect of this missionary dimension of the church's presence in the world. In the new humanity (Eph. 2:15) those who were far off and those who were near are brought together in one body by one Spirit (2:17; 4:3-6). The head of the body is Christ. Christ is also called the head over all things (1:20-23). The church as body of Christ is the fullness of him who fills all in all.

Here is an indication of a special relation of church and world. The church is the fullness (Greek: *pleroma*), the domain of the risen Lord, the domain of him who fills all in all, the domain of him who is the head of the world. The church is the place in the world where Christ as Lord is known, acknowledged, and confessed. The church is the place in the world where the rule of Christ, which sometime will comprise the whole world, begins. What will become visible at the end of time in the kingdom of God is now already discernible in the church, where Christ is confessed to be Lord and where people accept each other as sisters and brothers in Christ. In the church freedom is celebrated; it is the freedom attained by Christ, the Lord, in his unmasking of the powers of sin and death.

The emphasis on the church as part of the message, this emphasis on the missionary being or presence of the church in the world, has been neglected by some modern ecclesiologies which tend to reduce the church to its functions, to what has to be done and accomplished in the world. All the emphasis is put on "acting"; "being" tends to be neglected. However, the church is more than its functions.

> The basic reality is the creation of a new being through the presence of the Holy Spirit. This new being is the common life (*koinonia*) in the Church. It is out of this new creation that both service and evangelism spring, and from it they receive their value. . . . And even the most impressive preaching is sterile if it does not spring from and lead back into that new reality. This new reality—namely the active presence of the Holy Spirit among men—is the primary witness, anterior to all specific acts whether of service or preaching. These different acts have their relation to one another not in any logical scheme, but in the fact that they spring out of the one new reality (Newbigin, 1958: 20).

It is difficult to give equal attention to both being and acting, to the church as fruit of the Spirit and to the church as instrument of the Spirit. There is always the danger of overemphasizing the one or the other. If being is overemphasized, there is the danger of identification of church and kingdom of God. If acting is overemphasized, the impression is created that the coming of the kingdom of God is dependent on human activities. If being is overemphasized, the church tends to be seen as the end of God's ways with the world. If acting is overemphasized, there tends to be the danger of neglecting essential elements in the life of the church, such as worship, intercession, and the celebration of freedom received in and through Christ, the Lord.

How being and acting are interrelated, how witness and service spring out of the new Spirit-created reality in Christ, can be seen if we look at the church as a community of faith, love, and hope. Faith, love, and hope are fruits of the Spirit. The Spirit relates a person to God's story with the world, a story which culminates in the Christ event (faith). The Spirit relates people of different backgrounds to each other (love). The Spirit opens human hearts and minds for the future, for the coming of the kingdom of God (hope). Past, present, future, faith, love, and hope are linked by the Spirit. This linking becomes clear and visible in the celebration of the Lord's Supper.

Faith ties people to Christ. It is the choice and willingness to accept Christ as Lord and to base one's life on Christ's teachings and directions as expressed in the Sermon on the Mount. Faith is the positive, Spirit-guided response to the story of Christ. The outward sign of this choice for Christ, the way of Christ and the community or body of Christ, is baptism. Baptism signifies dying with Christ, cutting of ties with the powers of sin, and being raised with Christ in newness of life, a life guided by the Spirit and shared with others in the fellowship of believers. Being leads to acting; being in Christ leads to witness, to attempts to relate others to the story of Christ. In the Bible, faith and silence do not go together.

Love is the new reality to which faith leads. The encounter with Christ in faith is an encounter with God's compassionate love embodied in the life of one person. This unconditional and unrestricted love guides the believer in his or her relations to fellow human beings and to God's created order. This love is not and cannot be confined to the inner circle of the Christian community. Such a love would not reflect God's love for the world. Here again being leads to acting; being the object of divine love leads to acting in love toward others. Mission is sharing faith with others; mission is acting in love toward the neighbor who is in need of help and support.

The new reality in love to which faith leads has to struggle with the old reality, the reality of sin, in human lives and in the structures of this world. In this struggle with the flesh, the church is not left without help and hope. The helper is the Holy Spirit, who creates hope in human hearts. The Spirit is called the firstfruits (Greek: *aparche*, Rom. 8:23) of the harvest, the pledge or first installment of what is to come (Greek: *arrabon*, 2 Cor. 1:22; Eph. 1:14). This hope is not wishful thinking or dreaming. It is the inner conviction, based on the resurrection of Christ and the descending of the Spirit, that God will have the final word in human history. What started in Christ will find its fulfillment in the expected kingdom of God, where God is all in all (1 Cor. 15:28) and where "steadfast love and faithfulness will meet; righteousness and peace will kiss each other" (Ps. 85:10). In the struggles and defeats of the day, the Spirit keeps hope alive.

This hope is not dreaming away from the world. Hope, as fruit of the Spirit, determines the ethos, the way of acting in the world. Expecting the full disclosure of God's reign, expecting the kingdom of love, peace, and justice, means working in this world for reconciliation, peace, and justice. The prayer for the coming of God's kingdom, in the Lord's Prayer, is followed by the prayer for God's will being done on earth. Being in Christ is living in hope, giving account of the hope in us (1 Pet. 3:15), keeping the future open for humanity. Being and acting go hand in hand.

The church as a community of worship, fellowship, freedom, faith, love, and hope lives in tension with the world. The church as a community gathered by the Spirit and as fruit and instrument of the Spirit must continuously struggle with the flesh, with the powers that alienate people from God and from each other. This tension can be broken and has many times been broken in the course of history in two ways. The church can separate itself from the world, withdraw from the world as much as possible. If that happens an essential element of the gospel is lost: Christ, in whom God's love for the world was embodied, was crucified for the world, for the healing of the world. The church can also uncritically identify itself with the world, become a mirror of the world. If that happens, again an essential element of the gospel is lost: Christ, in whom God's love for the world was embodied, was crucified by the world. The cross symbolizes the tension in the life of the church, gathered by the Spirit, in relation to the world.

The Spirit is not a captive of the church. The Spirit cannot be manipulated. Rather, the Spirit of God is free and sovereign. That leads to the question whether the Spirit works in the world, whether there are marks of the work of the Spirit in the world.

The World

So far our main attention has been paid to the Spirit in relation to Christ and to the community gathered around Christ, the church, in its mission to the world, a mission of being and acting. The main focus has been on the New Testament, on "the last days" inaugurated by Christ and the descending of the Spirit.

We can also read about the Spirit in the Old Testament. The Old Testament speaks about the Spirit in the different contexts (Vriezen, 1964:7-40) of the story of Israel, in relation to the future (Joel 2:28-32; Isa. 11:1-2; 42:1; 61:1-2), and in relation to the created order and to human culture.

Especially in the Psalms and in Job, the breath of God, the Spirit of God, is described as a creative force at work in the world (Pss. 33:6; 104:29-30; Job 26:12-13; 34:14-15). Without the Spirit, without the breath of God, life is not possible. Not only human life (Gen. 2:7), but also the life of other creatures (Ps. 104) is dependent on the breath or Spirit of God. Moltmann (1985:12) describes the world, the created order, as God's "house" where human beings live together with other creatures. The care for this house is the special responsibility of human beings, created in the image and likeness of God. The mission of the church is to call attention to God's work, God's acts in the history of Israel and in the story of Jesus, but also to God's work, the work of God's Spirit in the created order. To care for and to protect God's creation, God's house, is a special responsibility of the fellowship of believers, especially in our days of violent abuse and destruction of God's gifts in the world around us.

The New Testament does not give much attention to the natural, created order related to the breath or Spirit of God. When the New Testament speaks about creation it is always in direct relation to the new creation in Christ (Col. 1:15-20). In Romans 8, Paul writes about life in the Spirit over against life according to the flesh. In the context of this chapter, he writes about the decay and disorder caused by life according to the flesh, a decay and disorder in which the creation shares (Rom. 8:18-25). Paul points to the close relation between creation and those "who have the first fruits of the Spirit" (8:23): there is in both the groaning and longing for "the revealing of the children of God" (8:19).

In the Old Testament, the Spirit is not only brought in in connection with the natural or created order; the Spirit is also linked to human creativity, to human culture. The divine Spirit gives "ability, intelligence, and knowledge in every kind of craft, to devise artistic designs" (Exod. 31:3; cf. 35:31). In Job it is said that "the breath [Spirit] of the Almighty . . . makes for understanding" (Job 32:8). Ruling and administering justice are also seen as a gift of the Spirit (Num. 11:17, 25). Human wisdom, result of an attentive and understanding attitude in life, is a gift of God. Many examples of this human wisdom can be found in the Old Testament: in the wisdom literature, in parables, in the Joseph story.

Neither the Old Testament nor the New Testament gives a closed, systematic theory about the Spirit of God and the work of the Spirit in the world. The Spirit, God in action, is seen at work in the story of Israel (judges, kings, prophets). The Spirit is expected to be given to the Messiah (see Isaiah), and the Spirit is expected to descend on all flesh (see Joel). But the Spirit, the breath of God, is also discerned in what Israel shares with others, the created order and the ability to gain understanding and knowledge, to be culturally active and creative. "Beauty and forgiveness are cousins in the family of the Holy Spirit" (Stendahl, 1990:21).

For mission the cultural issue is important. Human beings are cultural beings. Cultures are products of human creatures endowed by the Spirit with the ability to be creative. Cultures are also creations of human beings, alienated from God. Each culture is therefore a mixture of positive and negative elements. No culture can be identified with the divine message, the divine Word. No culture should be made absolute. The divine message, the divine Word, cannot reach people without making use of cultural elements as instruments. There is no culture which cannot be used by the Spirit as an instrument to bring people in contact with the divine revelation in Christ, with the Word of God that has become flesh. The Spirit judges and uses human culture: the Spirit can change and transform culture.

The Spirit of God works in the church, yet cannot be identified with the church. The Spirit of God is also at work outside the church. Wherever and whenever persons transcend their self-absorption—in working for peace and justice, for reconciliation and healing—and wherever and whenever people are fighting against dehumanizing forces in the world and for human dignity, there and then we can see marks of the work of the Spirit and we can discern the breath of God. The criterion for the discernment of the Holy Spirit at work in the world is the Word of God, as it has become visible in the life and work of Christ (Luke 4:18-19). Word and Spirit do not contradict each other. Several times in history the church has refrained from acting, speaking, or helping where it should have acted, spoken, or helped in the name of Christ. Others did or said what the church should have done or said. At times resistance and protests against evil structures which caused suffering to many have come from movements outside the church, whereas the church accepted and used the Bible to justify these structures. In these movements the Spirit was at work.

In discussions about religious pluralism, that is, the relation of the gospel and world religions, the question in regard to the presence of the Spirit is important. There is a movement away from a theology of rejection or confrontation in respect to other religious traditions. Attempts are being made to develop a theology which takes seriously the sovereignty of the Spirit of God, at work in the world in ways that surpass human understanding. Max Warren (1971:16ff.) called for a "theology of attention," a theology which gives attention to the ways in which God is present and works among adherents of other world religions. Mission is not only speaking and acting; mission is also waiting and listening, giving attention to the signs of God's presence in the worldwide family of human beings created in the image and likeness of God.

Listening and speaking, attention and witness, humility and boldness are essential features of the missionary calling. Without listening, attention, and humility, mission easily becomes an expression of religious arrogance and pride. Without speaking, witness, and boldness, religious relativism becomes the dominant pattern in the encounter of religions. Without listening, attention, and humility, the neighbor of another religious tradition is not taken seriously. Without speaking, witness, and boldness, the revelation of God in Christ is not taken seriously. David Bosch summarizes the tension in this way:

> We do not have all the answers and [we] are prepared to live within the framework of penultimate knowledge, but we regard our involvement in dialogue and mission as an adventure, [we] are prepared to take risks, and are anticipating surprises as the Spirit guides us into fuller understanding. This is not opting for agnosticism, but for humility. It is, however, a bold humility—or a humble boldness. We know only in part, but we do know. And we believe that the faith we profess is both true and just, and should be proclaimed. We do this, however, not as judges or lawyers, but as witnesses; not as soldiers, but as envoys of peace; not as high-pressure salespersons, but as ambassadors of the Servant Lord (Bosch, 1991:489).

Grieving the Holy Spirit

The Holy Spirit is not the captive of the church. The Holy Spirit cannot be identified with the church. The church sometimes moves in directions which are contrary to the way of God's Spirit. The church, in its being and acting, is sometimes far away from what it, according to divine intention, should be. Theologians are sometimes accused of speaking or writing about the church as if they deal with a Platonic idea, far away from the earthly reality, far above the vicissitudes of history. The New Testament is very honest in the way the church is described. The church is not idealized. The dark spots are not covered; what is wrong is not concealed. There is an awareness that the saints have feet of clay, that the treasure of the gospel is kept in earthen vessels.

Yet this does not mean that the discrepancy between divine intention and human reality is accepted as something which cannot be changed. The epistle to the Ephesians speaks about "grieve[ing] the Holy Spirit of God" (4:30), and 1 Thessalonians 5:19 speaks about "quench[ing] the Spirit." God is not an unmoved onlooker at what people do to each other, to the world, and to the body of Christ. The Spirit of God can be grieved; the Spirit of God can be hurt. That's the reason why things that are contrary to the work of the Spirit in the life of the church should not be taken for granted, but should cause disquiet and disturb the members of the body of Christ.

There are many lamentations about the church and about mission: disunity and competition, dogmatism and ritualism, moral pride and self-righteousness, accommodation to the world, the irrelevance of preaching. Lamentations and criticism can also grieve the Spirit, when only negative categories are used to describe the church and its mission, when only dark colors are used to paint a picture of the church. When that is done the commitment of many to the cause of Christ is overlooked, and the faithfulness of many whose names are not known to a wide circle of people is neglected. There is unfaithfulness, but there is also faithfulness; there is self-righteousness, but there is also deep awareness of the necessity of God's grace; there is bickering about trivial things, but there is also ultimate concern for and devotion to God's work in this world.

Not to see or not to be disturbed about the dark colors in the picture of the church leads to a contentment which grieves the Spirit, because then God's intention for the church is forgotten. To see and to give attention only to the dark colors in the picture of the church also grieves the Spirit, because the transforming work of the Spirit in the lives of many people, known and unknown, is overlooked.

Modern mission, as it started at the end of the eighteenth and beginning of the nineteenth centuries, has to face much criticism in our day. It is sometimes described as religious or ecclesiastical imperialism, as a servant of the colonial powers, as an expression of religious pride, arrogance, and intolerance. It cannot and should not be denied that the modern missionary enterprise has had its negative features: there has been a lack of critical distance in respect to colonial powers, there are examples of efforts to build ecclesiastical kingdoms, there have been and are cases of arrogance and intolerance.

That is, however, not the whole picture. The modern missionary movement was an expression of renewal in the church, caused by the Holy Spirit. The movement toward the world, in witness and service, was a movement in which many persons, touched by the Spirit, participated. This Spirit-endowed movement has had an impact on the lives of numerous people on different continents and has made the church a worldwide community. Not to recognize and acknowledge this is not taking into account the work of the Spirit and grieves the Spirit.

At the heart of the new life in Christ is prayer, prayer for the coming of God's kingdom, for the manifestation of God's reign, and that God's will be done on earth. The one is not possible without the other. Two other foci of the prayer of the community of believers are asking for forgiveness and asking for the renewing power of the Spirit. Again, the one is not without the other. Prayer for forgiveness leads to prayer for renewal, for the renewing power of the divine Spirit. As long as the church exists, in "the last days" between incarnation and parousia, this prayer with two foci—forgiveness and renewal—will be necessary. The prayer for forgiveness is an expression of the awareness that the kingdom of God does not come as a result of human endeavor. The prayer for the renewing power of the divine Spirit expresses that, in spite of human failure and weakness, the Spirit of God is not ashamed to use human beings as instruments to move history in the direction of the kingdom of God.

On the church's way to the kingdom, the prayer for forgiveness and for renewal by the Spirit will always accompany a living church. Where guilt is explained away and where brokenness is trivialized, where guilt and brokenness are not in sincerity confessed before God, there urgent longing vanishes for the purifying and renewing power of the Spirit of God, which continues to call the church to become, in Christ, salt of the earth and light of the world (Matt. 5:13-16).

Notes

1. Documents of the Second Vatican Council, like *Lumen Gentium,* put less emphasis on the "institutionalization" of the Spirit. In 1990, however, Pope John Paul II characterized the criticism of the hierarchical structure of the church by some theologians as "grieving the Holy Spirit."

2. The *filioque clause* (the Holy Spirit proceeding from the Father *and the Son* [filioque]) was added to the Nicene-Constantinopole Creed in the Western church. This addition to the creed was rejected by the church in the East.

3. Zinzendorf also spoke about the Holy Spirit as Mother.

4. In the second edition of Berkhof's book, Uwe Gerber has written an epilogue on developments in the reflection on the Holy Spirit in recent decades.

5. Bible quotations in this chapter are taken from the New Revised Standard Version.

6. Eduard Schweizer has written several essays and a book about the Holy Spirit in the New Testament (1963; 1968:389-455; 1978).

References Cited

Allen, Roland
    1949   *The Spontaneous Expansion of the Church and the Causes Which Hinder It.* (2nd ed.), New York: World Dominion Press.
    1962   *Missionary Methods: St. Paul's or Ours?* Grand Rapids, Mich.: Eerdmans. (First published 1912.)

Barrett, David B.
    1988   "The Twentieth-Century Pentecostal/Charismatic Renewal in the Holy Spirit, with Its Goal of World Evangelization," *International Bulletin of Missionary Research* XII:3.

Berkhof, Hendrikus
    1988   *Theologie des Heiligen Geistes.* (2nd ed.), Neukirchen: Neukirchener Verlag.

Boer, Harry R.
    1961   *Pentecost and Missions.* Grand Rapids, Mich.: Eerdmans.

Bosch, David
    1991   *Transforming Mission: Paradigm Shifts in Theology of Mission.* Maryknoll, N.Y.: Orbis Books.

Bühlmann, Walbert
    1976   *The Coming of the Third Church: An Analysis of the Present and Future of the Church.* Maryknoll, N.Y.: Orbis Books.

Dilschneider, Otto A.
    1979   *Der Geist fuhrt in die Wahrheit.* (Evangelische Kommentare) Stuttgart: Kreuz Verlag.

Dunn, James D. G.
    1970   *Baptism in the Holy Spirit: a Re-examination of the New Testament Teaching on the Gift of the Spirit in Relation to Pentecostalism Today.* London: SCM Press.

Gelpi, Donald L.
    1984   *The Divine Mother: A Trinitarian Theology of the Holy Spirit.* Lanham, Md.: University Press of America.

Heiler, Friedrich
1971   *Die Ostkirchen*. Munchen: Kaiser Verlag.

Hollenweger, Walter J.
1975   *Glaube, Geist und Geister*. Frankfurt am Main: Verlag Otto Lembeck.

Kähler, Martin
1971   *Schriften zur Christologie und Mission*. Munchen: Kaiser Verlag.

Martin, David
1990   *Tongues of Fire: The Explosion of Pentecostalism in Latin America*. Oxford: Basil Blackwell.

Minear, Paul S.
1960   *Images of the Church in the New Testament*. Philadelphia: Westminster Press.

Moltmann, Jürgen
1985   *Gott in der Schopfung*. Munchen: Kaiser Verlag.

Mühlen, Herbert
1967   *Der Heilige Geist als Person*. Münster: Aschendorf.

Newbigin, Lesslie
1958   *One Body, One Gospel, One World: The Christian Mission Today*. New York: International Missionary Council.
1978   *The Open Secret: Sketches for a Missionary Theology*. Grand Rapids, Mich.: Eerdmans.

Schweizer, Eduard
1963   "Gegenwart des Geistes und eschatologische Hoffnung bei Zarathustra, spätjudischen Gruppen, Gnostikern und den Zeugen des Neuen Testaments," *Neotestamentica: Deutsche und Englische Aufsätze 1951-1963: German and English Essays 1951-1963*. Zürich: Zwingli Verlag.
1968   *Theological Dictionary of the New Testament*, vol. VI, s.v. "pneuma." Gerhard Friedrich, ed., Geoffrey W. Bromiley, trans. and ed.; Grand Rapids, Mich.: Eerdmans.
1978   *Heiliger Geist*. Stuttgart: Kreuz Verlag.

Stendahl, Krister
1990   *Energy for Life: Reflections on the Theme "Come, Holy Spirit—Renew the Whole Creation."* Geneva: WCC Publications.

Taylor, John V.
1973   *The Go-Between God: The Holy Spirit and the Christian Mission*. Philadelphia: Fortress Press.

Tengstrom and Fabry
       Theologisches Worterbuch zum Alten Testament, vol. VII, s.v. "ruach." Stuttgart: Verlag W. Kohlhammer.

Van de Beek, A.
1987   *De adem van God*. Nijkerk: Callenbach.

Von Harnack, Adolf
1915   *Die Mission und Ausbeitung des Christentums in den ersten drei Jahrhunderten*. Leipzig: J. C. B. Mohr.

Vriezen, Theodorus C.
1964 "De Heilige Geest in het Oude Testament," *De Spiritu Sancto*. Utrecht: Kemink.

Walls, Andrew
1979 "The Anabaptists of Africa? The Challenge of the African Independent Churches," *Occasional Bulletin of Missionary Research* III:2.

Warren, Max A. C.
1971 *Face to Face: Essays on Inter-faith Dialogue*. London: S.C.M. Press.

Weinfeld, Moshe
1978 *Pentecost as Festival of the Giving of the Law*, No. 8. Jerusalem: Immanuel.

Yoder, John H.
1967 "Marginalia," *Concern: A Pamphlet Series for Questions of Christian Renewal*, No. 15. Scottdale, Pa.
1979 "The Enthusiasts and the Reformation," *Concilium: Conflicts about the Holy Spirit*. Hans Küng, ed.

CHAPTER 5

The Church as Messianic Society: Creation and Instrument of Transfigured Mission

Larry Miller

CHRISTIANS seldom doubt that the church is both created by and is an instrument of Christ's mission in the world. Yet just as rarely, perhaps, do we agree on which churches actually measure up to divine expectations for the life and work of the church. After all, as any critical look at church history or contemporary ecclesiastical life shows, every church is the product and vehicle of some cause or kingdom.

But which ones indeed are the creation and instrument of Messiah's mission to establish God's new order of righteousness, justice, and peace? What type of church results from and extends the mission of the martyred Messiah who reigns as Lord? The reading of the New Testament reported here suggests that transfigured mission produces and continues through those churches which take the form of micro-societies present in and daily interacting with the existing sociopolitical order.

Messianic Movement

For the past fifteen years at least, historians have borrowed tools from the sociologist and the anthropologist to construct their analyses and descriptions of earliest Christianity. This work has produced a relatively broad consensus, held across confessional lines, that primitive Christianity was a millenarian or messianic movement.[1]

Definitions and descriptions of millenarianism vary. The word is generally used to designate phenomena which arise in situations of sociopolitical crisis and are shaped by hope for radical change in the established order which issues sooner or later in the transformation of all things. This change "is to be brought about by the creation of a new man and a new social order together with the creation of new assumptions, attitudes, and the renewal of all other aspects of [human] social life" (Tidball, 1983:28). Millenarian movements—whether originally political, social, or religious—are so numerous and significant in world history that one anthropologist calls them a distinguishing characteristic of humanity. "The pain of the millennium belongs only to man. It is why he is man, when the time comes, he has to make a new man" (Burridge, 1969:3).[2]

Messianism, in the words of French sociologist Henri Desroche, is "a plan for a Kingdom, conceived in the lands of Exile" (Desroche, 1979:112). In less biblical language, messianism is millenarianism which affirms that the agent of radical change is a person who maintains a privileged relationship with God. In the midst of oppression or domination, a messiah appears as God's instrument to announce or establish divine rule which encompasses and renews all dimensions of human existence. Those who follow the messiah break more or less clearly with the established order to form more or less formally messianic groups which are thought to prefigure in some sense and announce the coming kingdom.

Sociopolitical Situation[3]

Anthropological and sociological descriptions of messianic movements in general provide a window on the particular messianic movement of interest here, the one tracing its origins to Jesus the Galilean. In a situation of protracted foreign domination, the Jewish community at the turn of the millennium manifested an increasingly insistent hope for the restoration of God's direct rule through messianic liberation. It was, in New Testament perspective at least, the "fullness of time."[4]

Foreign domination. Successive periods of domination by foreign powers shaped the life of the first-century Judaism into which Jesus of Nazareth was born. Following the Babylonian exile, Persia, Greece, and Rome had all imposed their authority on the Jews.

Rome, of course, was the dominant factor on any map of power in the first century. When brought under Roman rule, Palestine experienced politically what it had been subjected to economically and culturally at least a century earlier. The Hellenistic kingdoms of Alexander's successors had brought systematic economic exploitation and cultural imperialism. Rome perpetuated and extended that situation as it reimposed foreign rule following the Hasmonaean dynasty.

Roman political domination began with violent conquest and continued through a long period of destructive power struggles. In the initial and later conflicts, the Romans treated inhabitants of Jewish Palestine harshly. Jews expelled from the Greek cities along the coast, in the Decapolis, or in Galilee lost their trade and property when they were forced to settle in already overpopulated Judea. Oppressive client kings were followed by direct Roman rule through provincial governors; Jews had not experienced anything of the sort since the initial Babylonian and Persian conquests. Official Roman policy, of course, was to maintain Jewish autonomy in religious matters. But there was no longer complete freedom to practice Jewish law which encompassed all of life. At the same time, successive attempts to reorganize the country led to a lower standard of economic life, even impoverishment, particularly for the socially disadvantaged.

The situation appears to have been particularly difficult under Herod and his successors. After subduing Jewish resisters with the help of Roman troops, Herod maintained tight control over the people by means of foreign mercenaries, strategically placed fortresses, and a secret service. He eliminated members of the old Sadducean aristocracy and fostered a new, more loyal elite. Unitary governance–simultaneously sociopolitical and religious—was broken apart when Herod separated the high priesthood from temporal rule and brought into it non-Zadokite families loyal to himself. He put an end to effective participation by the Jewish people in the political processes, thus reducing the Pharisees, for example, to a loose association of religious brotherhoods. And to pay for the many building projects reportedly motivated largely by his passion for Hellenistic civilization, Herod imposed a heavy tax burden. The common people suffered most.

Although the majority of the Jewish population continued to cooperate with the established authorities, whether grudgingly or willingly, more and more came to resent the domination of the Romans and their collaborators. At Herod's death resentment turned to active resistance. About the time Jesus was born a few kilometers down the road, Roman military interventions ended in Jerusalem with the crucifixion of two thousand Jewish prisoners (4 B.C.E.), adding to the legacy of resentment and resistance passed on to Herod's successors. The insensitivity of Roman governors like Pontius Pilate exacerbated the problem during the next five or six decades. Rebellions flared up several times and were repressed. In Palestine, one Zealot-like raid came out of the desert and apparently nearly captured Jerusalem; it was masterminded by "the Egyptian" who was still a concern to the authorities at the time of Paul's arrest (Acts 21:38). Another exploded into a war of liberation (66 C.E.), led to the destruction of the temple, and was finally crushed with difficulty by the Romans at Masada.

During this period, Jews of the Diaspora experienced local but severe conflicts. In Alexandria in the year 38, the Roman prefect ignored a series of mob attacks on the Jewish population. Appeals to the Roman emperor brought eventual relief but no permanent solution. The beginning of the second century would see Jewish revolts against Roman rule in Egypt, North Africa, on Cyprus, and in parts of Mesopotamia. "Roman armies put down these revolts so ruthlessly that in portions of North Africa and Egypt the Jewish communities simply ceased to exist" (Meeks, 1986:68).

In short and in the words of sociologist Desroche (1979), the sociopolitical situation of first-century Judaism—both in Palestine and the Diaspora—was one of "Exile." It was also the context for conception of "a plan for a Kingdom" (Desroche, 1979:112).

Messianic hope. Situations of oppression can lead to despair or serve as a crucible out of which come hope and action. There is little or no evidence for lively messianic hope during the period of Persian and Hellenistic domination. But expectations of an anointed royal figure began to revive during the Hasmonaean period of independence and expansion (142-63 B.C.E.). The early Roman period and the return of foreign domination saw further resurgence of hope for the reestablishment of theocracy on earth as in heaven. And, as has already been implied, discontent with Herod seems to have focused longing for a king who would renew all things, both religious and sociopolitical.

> Living under an oppressive and illegitimate king installed by an alien power, the people were ready for an "anointed" charismatic leader from among the peasantry, like David of old. . . . As soon as Herod died, the pent-up frustrations of the people burst forth precisely in the form of messianic movements (Horsley and Hanson, 1985:109).

Stereotypical descriptions of early first-century Jewish response to foreign domination seldom focus on these popular messianic movements. They center rather on the main Jewish parties formed by the intellectual or literate elite—Sadducees, Pharisees, Essenes—and one later group of more popular origin, the Zealots. In this typology, Sadducees represent the religiously conservative, aristocratic establishment favoring prudent collaboration with the Romans as a means to national survival or reform. Pharisees appear as pious people promoting religious purity within society as the path to national renewal. Essenes, at least in their Qumranian form, symbolize passive withdrawal from society in anticipation of Yahweh's holy war of national redemption. And the Zealots are presented as those who take up arms to drive out the oppressors in national revolution. Recently, some specialists have begun to pay more attention to the wider variety of popular socioreligious movements which may provide the most fruitful points of comparison for a description of Jesus' own response to foreign domination.

Indeed, there were a number of messianic movements in first-century Palestine composed mainly of peasants. Charismatic leaders—usually men of humble origin—appeared on the scene to announce liberation from foreign domination and return to God's direct rule encompassing all dimensions of human existence. Several of these messiahs generated popular support and were acclaimed "king" by their followers (Horsley and Hanson, 1985:ch. 3). Others were designated "prophet" by the groups that gathered around them (Horsley and Hanson, 1985:ch. 4).

These differences of language point to divergent perspectives on how the vision advocated by a messianic king or prophet should be carried out. Indeed, like any messianic movements, first-century ones in Palestine had to respond more or less self-consciously to the fundamental questions of mission, of project implementation: how will the kingdom come on earth as in heaven (Desroche, 1979:92-97)? Will it come from "above" in revolutionary manner thanks primarily to divine deliverance or from "below" through effective human action? Will the kingdom come already in the present, or is it reserved primarily for the future? Will it come through takeover and transformation of the existing macrosociety or through the creation of a messianic microsociety where members live transformed lives already and which can therefore function as an instrument of the kingdom in relation to the established order? And does the coming of the kingdom require use of violence or recourse to nonviolence?

Answers to each of these questions varied from group to group. "Kingly" messianic movements, for example, usually attempted to impose their project by armed rebellion, while the "prophetic" type generally promised miraculous divine intervention instead. What all of them seem to have held in common was an intense desire for the kingdom to come now.

The "fullness of time." The New Testament calls this period of crushing foreign domination and surging messianic hope the "fullness of time." There was an urgency about finding life-giving solutions to death-producing sociopolitical problems. Why would God choose this risky time and place to intervene directly and personally—in an unprecedented way, according to all Christian confessions of faith—in human affairs? Why would Yahweh choose once again, as he usually had from the beginning of the story told in the Old Testament, to work through those in sociopolitical exile or oppression? If God's mission is to transform the nations on the basis of conventional power, these choices are senseless. Was there after all a design behind them? Is there something normative about this strategy for the setting and nature of all Christian mission?[5] In any case, this was the situation into which Messiah was sent to accomplish the *missio Dei*.

Messiah's Response

Like the action of other first-century messiahs, Jesus' intervention can be understood as a response to conditions of oppression and hope for change. Indeed, in sociopolitical perspective at least, every move he made had explicit or implicit sociopolitical implications. Appearing on a Palestinian scene determined by foreign domination and competing parties or movements, Messiah proclaimed the restoration of God's direct, holistic rule: "The time has arrived; the kingdom of God is upon you. Repent, and believe the gospel" (Mark 1:15).[6] His own mission, he claimed, was to "announce good news to the poor, to proclaim release for prisoners and recovery of sight for the blind; to let the broken victims go free, to proclaim the year of the Lord's favour" (Luke 4:18). Briefly, his too was a plan for a Kingdom.

Since other chapters of this book describe Jesus' responses to the fundamental questions of project implementation, we will not do so in depth here. We suggest only that his message and action reveal more confidence in Yahweh's intervention than dependence on human activity. They manifest the conviction that God's revolution—the transformation of all things—is already underway but not yet complete; Messiah's ministry itself is held to be in some sense the real "presence of the future" (Driver, 1993a:9). While he may initially have considered attempting to transform the established Jewish macrosociety from within, the creation of a distinctive microsociety seems finally to have been Jesus' instrument for proposing the kingdom project to the existing order. In any case, he rejected violence as a tool to implement or even protect the project.

While not unique in every respect, Jesus' message of "good news to the poor" (Luke 4:18) and his choices in respect to implementation of the vision gave his action a particular identity. They distanced him not only from the more elitist Sadducees, Pharisees, and Essenes in specific ways but also from those popular messiahs of the kingly variety who opted for armed rebellion, Indeed, according to Gerd Thiessen, this characteristic differentiates the Jesus movement from all other similar movements of the time, including messianic movements of the prophetic type.

> The Jesus movement differed most clearly from all comparable radical theocratic movements by virtue of its ethos. Resistance fighters and Essenes demanded hatred of foreigners. This aggressive feature was lacking in the Jesus movement. Whereas other prophetic movements went back to the exodus as a model of liberation from foreign rule, Jesus connected his vision of the future with the sphere of Judaism: the temple building would be the type of what was to come" (Thiessen, 1978:64).

Everything about the movement, continues Thiessen, "points to a readiness for reconciliation which transcends frontiers and culminates in the requirement to love one's enemy (Matt. 5:43ff.). The Jesus movement was the peace party among renewal movements within Judaism" (Thiessen, 1978:64).

Messianic Groups[7]

Jesus' shalom action provoked contrasting reactions, both opposition and support. What attracts our interest here is the observation that those who accepted his leadership not only joined the movement but also entered more or less formally constituted groups composed of others committed to follow the Messiah. In other words, while Jesus reportedly was tempted to implement his vision through takeover and transformation of the established order, he chose instead as his mission strategy the creation of a new community composed of people already living transformed lives.

From the very beginning, the nature of these groups varied considerably. While the original group of most intimate disciples was itinerant, most others—apparently composed of sympathizers in given localities—were less mobile. They multiplied relatively rapidly, spilled over the boundaries of Palestine, and spread across much of the Roman Empire by the turn of the century. Most importantly for us, however, is the fact that whatever their form or location, these groups were directly or indirectly created by the Messiah, and the task of continuing his mission fell to them. But how, more precisely, did these groups—both creation and instruments of Messianic mission—look and act?

Microsociety

If we are to believe the New Testament documents, the first Christians were not simply human individuals interacting with superhuman powers. When reading the New Testament text in socioreligious and sociopolitical context, messianic groups look as much like small societies as other first-century religious communities.

Like any society, messianic groups were concerned not only with religion but with all of life. They were totalistic in a way no pagan cultic association was. Their goals, having to do with "salvation" in a comprehensive sense, were less segmented. Almost any reading of Scripture shows them to be people with a common social life shaped by common convictions, values, and models. A closer look at the foundational Christian documents suggests that their life together included potentially every category of human relations: peoplehood, friendship, family, politics, economy, education, piety, ritual, festival, and all the rest.

Yet, unlike many societies, messianic groups were microsocieties. The word *micro* points not only to the size of these groups but also to the fact that they established boundaries between themselves and the dominant macrosocieties—whether Jewish, Greek, or Roman—in relation to which they lived daily. Viewed sociologically, messianic groups constituted—more or less consciously, explicitly, comprehensively, and radically—an alternative to the established socioreligious order. In New Testament perspective, it was the only viable alternative in a broken and dying world.

Alternative society. Each layer of the normative tradition bears some trace of the conviction that messianic groups were called to provide in some sense and to some degree an alternative to established society; *alternative* peoplehood, *alternative* friendship, *alternative* family, *alternative* politics, *alternative* economy, *alternative* education, *alternative*

piety, *alternative* ritual, *alternative* festivals. Messiah's followers were to
live life in another manner than it was normally lived in macrosociety.

The most concisely formulated vision of this different approach
to life, of course, is the Sermon on the Mount. "You have heard that
our forefathers were told. . . . But what I tell you is this . . . ," Messiah
repeatedly said (Matt. 5:21-48). Does established society tell you not
to commit murder? I tell you not even to nurse anger against your
brother. Does society tell you not to commit adultery? I tell you not
even to look at a woman lustfully. Does society tell you not to break
your oath? I tell you not even to swear at all; plain "yes" or "no" is all
you need to say. Does society tell you to love your neighbor? I tell you
to love also your enemy. Does society use charity and piety as means
to social recognition? I tell you to do good, to pray, and to fast secretly;
God who sees what is done in secret will reward you appropriately.
Does society encourage you to accumulate possessions or wealth? I
tell you not to do so; seek God's justice and you will receive what you
need (cf. Matt. 5—7).

Such was the vision of Messiah. But what shape did the vision actually take when implemented in messianic microsocieties during the
years following Jesus' sermon? Time and space limitations preclude a
fully adequate response to the question here. A glance at three of the
more basic categories—peoplehood, politics, piety—of social existence as lived in these groups may provide some hints.

1. Alternative peoplehood. "Once you were not a people at all;
but now you are God's people," Peter wrote to messianic groups in
Anatolia sometime during the middle third of the first century (1 Pet.
2:10). Pagans, too, soon came to view Christians as somehow forming
another people, neither pagan nor Jewish. A "third race" was their expression for the Christian movement which brought together typical
people in atypical ways.

The "otherness" of messianic peoplehood was not only religious
or ethnic. People previously separated by social or economic boundaries united in messianic groups. Luke's description of the microsociety in Jerusalem (Acts 1—6) suggests that city folk with some financial resources soon joined the core group of rural, relatively poor
Galileans. Hellenists—Greek-speaking Jews of the Diaspora—converted and entered the first messianic community; culturally, they
were probably a far cry from the simple Galileans and looked down
upon by many Jews. This sort of heterogeneity continued to distinguish the messianic movement as it spread across the Roman Empire.

Christian groups were more inclusive in terms of social stratification and other socioeconomic categories than were the pagan cultic associations or other groups in which people shared a common daily life.

At the same time, few if any members of messianic groups came from the dominant layer of the established order. The early converts in Palestine did not represent established Judaism. Not a single high priest, for example, is mentioned as a convert. Paul is the only Pharisee known to have embraced the faith. In Greek and Roman cultural settings, the extreme top of the social scale seems absent in the messianic groups. Apparently, there were no landed aristocrats, no senators, no knights, no decurions (the highest local authorities). The messianic groups gathered most of their adherents from among the socially disinherited of the empire: slaves, freedmen, freeborn Roman citizens of low rank, non-Romans. If one can hazard a hypothesis based on scanty evidence, even the wealthier members of the groups exhibited some signs of social deprivation; they had high income but low social prestige.

The relative socioeconomic heterogeneity of messianic microsociety coupled with the lack of socially prominent members apparently did not impede solidarity within the group. Quite the contrary. The establishment of alternative structures of solidarity strikes the observer of Roman history as another distinguishing characteristic of messianic peoplehood.

> One rarely finds in the history of the ancient world such an explicit need to mobilise . . . so fully a feeling of solidarity between members of a threatened community. One finds even more rarely in ancient literature . . . the permanent fear that participants will not consecrate themselves totally to such a demanding enterprise (Brown, 1985:243).

This "feeling of solidarity" manifested itself in concrete ways. Community gatherings and agape meals are one example. "For many members, especially those of the humbler social strata, the Christian assemblies and meals provided a more than adequate substitute for benefits, both physical and social, than they might otherwise have obtained from membership" in other groups or from the municipal festivals (Meeks, 1983:104). The "feeling of solidarity" issued also in the "language of belonging" spoken within messianic groups. "Especially striking is the language that speaks of the members of the Pauline groups as if they were a family. They are the children of God and also of the apostle. They are brothers and sisters; they refer to one another as 'beloved' " (:86).

Messianic solidarity was not limited to the local microsociety. The essential and distinguishing mark of messianic peoplehood was its linking of the local messianic group to the universal messianic movement. The "intimate, close-knit life of the local groups was seen to be simultaneously part of a much larger, indeed ultimately worldwide, movement or entity" (:73). This vision of international interdependence became real in many small and practical ways: exchanging letters on issues of faith and life vital to the survival and mission of messianic groups, hospitality offered to Christian travelers, visiting believers imprisoned for their faith or practice far from home, sharing of decision making and resources as possible translocally. Indeed, one might say that in New Testament perspective, messianic peoplehood was always both local and international; otherwise it was not messianic. Before long this vision resulted in a situation where the Roman state was no longer the only empire-wide entity; there was also the church universal.

2. Alternative politics. The development of a people—particularly a heterogeneous people interdependent worldwide—presupposes the existence not only of structures of solidarity but also of structures of governance. Sooner or later every group explicitly or implicitly mandates authorities, defining for them legitimate roles and power.

A study of structures of governance in the macrosocieties where first-century Christians lived suggests the existence of several kinds of authority at the disposal of recognized leaders. In both the public and private spheres of life in Greek and Roman societies, at least two fundamental authority roles recur: authority to direct members of a group by proposing or imposing norms for acceptable action and authority to judge or sanction the action of group members in light of established norms. Commonly, one person or one group of interrelated people assumed both authority roles. In the private domain, for example, the male head of an extended household not only could tell his wife, children, and slaves what to do; he could also judge and punish or reward them for their subsequent conduct. In the public sphere, the emperor could not only command all of his subjects in all areas of life if he so chose; he could also exercise directly or indirectly all judicial authority over them.

. The attribution of authority roles included definition of legitimate power. In other words, when society attributed authority to individuals, it also explicitly or implicitly authorized them to use one or several types of power to accomplish their mission. Power could be coercive in nature, whether physically or psychologically so. Or it could be noncoercive. Generally, authorities in established macrosocieties of the first-century Mediterranean world were free within broad limits to use coercion if they judged it necessary in the exercise of their role. In the private domain, for example, the lord of the household could so dominate his subjects through social, economic, and religious pressure that they had little choice but to obey or perish. Recourse to physical coercion was acceptable in varying degrees; generally more in relation to a slave and less with a wife. In the public sphere, the emperor not only possessed the legal right of life and death over all of his subjects; his direct or indirect control of police and army meant he could enforce by coercion his decisions to permit life or destroy it.

Early in the history of his movement, according to the Gospels, Jesus appealed for and provided in his messianic community an alternative to the model of governance found in macrosocieties. "You know," he said to the first messianic group,

> those who are regarded as rulers of the [nations] lord it over them, and their high officials exercise authority over them. Not so with you. Instead, whoever wants to become great among you must be your servant, and whoever wants to be first must be slave of all. For even the Son of Man did not come to be served, but to serve, and to give his life as a ransom for many (Mark 10:42-45, NIV).

Was the appeal to governing by service and self-sacrifice heard by Messiah's followers? Was his example followed in messianic communities? A lack of hard data makes response difficult. What can be said with certainty is that the New Testament documents reflect an understanding of legitimate authority and power for leaders of messianic groups which differs from normative governance patterns in the established macrosocieties of the first century.

Early Christian writings indicate the existence of authorities who guide or direct local messianic communities. As in established society, there are people who make recommendations or issue commands, articulate shared values or norms, and help manage conflict. The earliest Christian document refers to people filling this function as "those who are working so hard among you, and are your leaders and counsellors in the Lord's fellowship" (1 Thess. 5:12). In other texts, a variety of names are used to designate the same or a similar role: shepherd, bishop, president, elder. Some of these leaders exercise their mandate across the entire messianic movement or at least translocally. Peter is an example of this when he writes to messianic groups in the

Anatolian provinces not only as apostle but also as fellow-elder (1 Pet. 5:1), offering direction to communities experiencing harassment at the hand of pagan neighbors disturbed by messianic nonconformism.

Were these same authorities—those who guide and direct messianic communities—or others authorized to sanction group members by punishing them for deviant conduct or convictions? Apparently not. This governance role seems generally to have remained with the group as a whole rather than delegated to any one individual or subgroup. While every member was supposed to go and show the sinful member his fault so that he may be saved, the decision to discipline unrepentant deviants seems to have belonged to the community itself (see Matt. 18:15-17; 1 Cor. 5:1-13).

In any case, use of coercive power—whether physical or psychological—was proscribed in messianic groups. The only legitimate power at the disposal of leaders was the power which comes from the suffering, serving, exemplary leadership modeled by the Messiah. Peter—reflecting, incarnating, and noncoercively shaping the emerging normative tradition—summarizes it this way for the leaders of the Anatolian groups:

> I appeal to the elders of your community, as a fellow-elder and a witness of Christ's sufferings, and as one who has shared in the glory to be revealed: look after the flock of God whose shepherds you are; do it, not under compulsion, but willingly, as God would have it; not for gain but out of sheer devotion; not lording it over your charges, but setting an example to the flock. So when the chief shepherd appears, you will receive glory, a crown that never fades (1 Pet. 5:1-4).

3. Alternative piety. In the world in which Christianity emerged, one of the terms most frequently used to designate religious attitude and practice was piety. Ancient piety—whether public or private—expressed itself concretely in numerous ways: shrines, temples, cult statues, public festivals, pilgrimages, reading sacred writings. But sacrifice and prayer were its most characteristic forms. Just as specified victims were offered on the altar at the Jewish Temple in Jerusalem, so Greeks and Romans made sacrifices on the altars in front of temples of their gods. Just as set prayers were recited at regular times in the Jewish community, so official prayers were written down and repeated without variation in the pagan world. Romans were particularly careful in making sure that gods understood their petitions; they thought that "if one syllable or one ritual gesture was performed incorrectly, the prayer might well be invalid" (Stambaugh and Balch, 1986:129).

Why did proper piety matter so much in the first century? Was it because people felt they lived in a life-threatening universe where daily protection and provision for family or nation came from above? In that context, religion was not an autonomous dimension of life; it belonged to the deep structure of state and society. Indeed, as John Scheid writes near the end of a sociohistorical analysis of religion in the Roman world, "piety was the foundation of the imperial regime" (Scheid, 1985:124). Dominant Judaism for much of the first century was similar: sacrifice, prayer, and correct interpretation of the Torah grounded the *de facto* rule of the priestly aristocracy and its Roman overlord. If piety was the foundation of the established social order, to challenge or reject established religion was to undermine—consciously or unconsciously, explicitly or implicitly—the existing sociopolitical order which seemed to make life possible.

Were Messiah's people pious people? Were messianic groups religious groups? A first-century observer might not have thought so. "Not only did the first-century Christians lack shrines, temples, cult statues, and sacrifice; they staged no public festivals, dances, musical performances, pilgrimages, and as far as we know they set up no inscriptions" (Meeks, 1983:140). Of course, they did pray. Yet even their prayers, addressed exclusively to the messianic "Father in heaven" while rejecting the gods or "idols" upon whom pagan neighbors counted for protection and provision, sometimes departed from recognizable norms. Prayers in the free, charismatic order of worship of some messianic groups, for example, could be said either "rationally" or "by tongue" (1 Cor. 14:13-15). The contrast between inspired improvisation and Roman repetition would probably have been evident to anyone watching. And other early Christian practices such as coming together regularly in citywide "assemblies" [*ekklesiai*] for singing, speaking, teaching, ethical decision making, and eating, which a late twentieth-century social scientist can label religious ritual (cf. Meeks, 1983:ch. 5), may not have looked very religious to first-century Jews and pagans.

In some eyes at least, Messiah's followers may have looked more like subversive atheists than cooperative pietists. With their rejection of established piety and proposal of an alternative, messianic groups implicitly rejected the foundations on which state and society rested. Is it surprising that their movement soon faced opposition and, in some cases, repression?

Voluntary society. As alternative society, messianic groups were not "natural" society. Unlike the host macrosocieties within which they lived, people entered microsociety neither by birth nor geography. Opposition from outsiders potentially constituted a further obstacle to the recruitment of new adherents. So the Christian communities had to deal with the question of membership. Should entrance and participation in messianic society be imposed in some way on people? Or should the conversion and resocialization implied by life in alternative society happen voluntarily? Several "kingly" messiahs active in the first-century Palestinian resistance movement appear to have chosen this option in their own relation to macrosociety; they violently rejected the established Judeo-Roman system and sought to impose God's direct rule on people (Thiessen, 1978:61). By contrast, messianic microsociety was voluntary society.

Messianic groups were voluntary society at least two ways. First and most obviously, entrance into these groups presupposed a voluntary decision to join, since membership was not imposed on people by natural or social ties. Baptism—spoken of as "dying and rising with Christ" in some biblical texts—gave visible expression to that decision; it marked both a break with the dominant order and integration into microsociety. Second and perhaps more importantly, life in messianic groups was based on voluntary decision making by the group itself rather than on imposed obedience to some external authority (Gager, 1975:33). Messianic groups reserved for themselves the right to grant, refuse, and withdraw membership. They defined their own objectives and the means to achieve them. They themselves determined what it meant to believe in and to follow the Messiah, what was true and what was false, what was right and what was wrong. None of these decisions were supposed to be left to outside authorities, powers, or cultures. The Lord's Supper, with its appeal to remember the lordship of the Messiah and to "discern the body" before eating (see 1 Cor. 11:23-32), manifested and helped to maintain this kind of "free church."

Later, dominant Christianity abandoned life as voluntary society and as free church. From the fourth century at least, methods based on coercion—"flattery and battery," in the words of one eminent historian (MacMullen, 1984:19)[8]—were widely used in winning and subduing adherents to Christianity. Messianic microsociety was replaced by Christendom macrosociety—inclusive society "established through the forced conversion of entire groups of peoples and held intact through the coercive powers of state and church controlling the whole of life" (Shenk, 1993a:4). As a result the church was filled by "partial converts," people who "made such adaptations as were really necessary and kept what they could" (MacMullen, 1984:116-17). In other words, the demise of voluntary society meant the (temporary) end of alternative society. Had Christians been in but not of the world (John 17)? Now many were in but not of the church. This deformation of messianic society spelled also the death of messianic mission, at least for several centuries. After all, as Jesus had once said, "If the salt loses its saltiness, how can it be made salty again? It is no longer good for anything, except to be thrown out and trampled by men" (Matt. 5:13, NIV).

Microsociety in Macrosociety
Although messianic groups manifested the characteristics of voluntary alternative society, their members did not systematically withdraw from social structures and relationships within the host macrosocieties. This refusal to live quietly on the margins of the existing order obliged the first Christians to deal with the fundamental problems of living in but not of the world.

Missionary society. Messianic microsociety soon had to face the question of its relation to a dominant society which did not accept *en masse* the messianic message. Hypothetically at least, a voluntary alternative society in this kind of situation can choose to withdraw systematically from the established order or to make war—revolutionary or liberationist war—against it. Messianic groups chose instead to relate to the dominant society primarily through missionary witness, an alternative to both withdrawal and war.

Despite uncertainties about many aspects of emerging Christianity, the sources are unanimous in reporting an enthusiastic dedication to missionary witness as the basic characteristic of the relation to macrosociety. Early on there may have been discussion about the focus of the mission. Should the focus be on rural areas like Galilee where the movement started or on the urban centers of the empire? Should it be directed exclusively to Jews or inclusively to "all nations?" But there seems to have been little doubt that messianic groups should neither systemically withdraw from dominant society nor crusade against it. The mandate was to witness peaceably from within the structures of macrosociety to the Messiah who had himself lived and died within the established order before being raised by God to lordship over it.

True, there seems to have been no organized missionary program. To a significant degree, the messianic movement spread unprogrammatically through the natural mobility of its members and their daily interaction with unbelievers. For example, when Christian artisans or tradespeople moved to a city where there was no messianic group, they might start meetings in their homes and draw in neighbors or friends. According to one historian, in any case, there is no evidence "of a mission directed by church leaders . . . we cannot name a single active Christian missionary between St. Paul and the age of Constantine" (Lane Fox, 1986:282). From the time of Jesus onward, of course, evangelistic preachers and prophets wandered purposefully about, sometimes starting new messianic groups. But whatever their origin, it was the messianic groups themselves which seem to have been the fundamental instruments of mission. Stated more precisely, "early Christianity achieved its chief [mission] goals by means of its total corporate life" (Hinson, 1981:2).

How were messianic groups missionary? Fundamentally, they were so by living as alternative societies in the midst of a dominant society in crisis. Little by little the *Pax Romana* ceased to make sense to many people. What was visible to all by the third century had begun much earlier. The "imperial coinage was being debased, order was breaking down, and society was becoming increasingly hierarchical, as the urban rich were being economically and legally distanced from the rest of society. Hopelessness was widespread, and the gods seemed powerless to address the crisis" (Kreider, 1990:35). In this setting, as has already been suggested, messianic groups offered alternative ways of living and believing. Transformed peoplehood, transformed politics, transformed piety, and all the other dimensions of transformed lives, were the basis of messianic mission.

But living alternatively within the boundaries of voluntary micro-society was not the entire picture. In the hot, dry, crowded cities of the eastern Mediterranean, people lived in close quarters—whether they wanted to or not—both outdoors in public places and in private houses or apartments. In this situation, it was "simply not possible or necessary to conceal one's prayers or worship from everyone's eyes" (Lane Fox 1986:316). Whether possible or not, members of messianic groups did not seem to want to operate inconspicuously on the margins of the established order. Refusing to withdraw voluntarily from the households and workplaces which constituted fundamental social structures in Mediterranean society, they interacted continuously with neighbors or associates and witnessed naturally to them. In a word, Christians were present in the ordinary, everyday settings of life "where their character and common life were evident to people who knew them, and on other grounds, trusted them" (Kreider, 1990:34).

If their presence was missionary, so also was their talk. While intermingling with family and neighbors—Jew and pagan, in public and private, at work and leisure—members of messianic groups talked about their faith and life. They talked about the one God, denouncing all others as impotent idols. They talked about God's Messiah who had already come, accepted crucifixion in order to reconcile enemies "in one body through the cross" (Eph. 2:16, NRSV), been raised to life at God's right hand, and who would soon return victoriously to judge the world.

In the meantime, the early Christians asserted, Messiah's Spirit is present, saving individual believers from the hopelessness of their old life and giving them the experience of new life in a worldwide family of local groups prefiguring the coming kingdom. Messiah's advocates talked "about lifestyle—they claimed, a critic complained, that 'they alone . . . know the right way to live.' Where their neighbors were facing crises, they offered their congregations' resources of prayer and power over illness and demonic forces" (Kreider, 1991:6). The Messianic message apparently exercised a powerful attraction on outsiders and held the enthusiasm of converts in spite of hostility, rejection, and persecution (Stambaugh and Balch, 1986:56).

Pacifist society. From the very beginning of the messianic movement, reaction to it was mixed. While transfigured mission attracted growing numbers of people, it offended others. From the vantage point of the general populace across most of the Roman Empire, messianic missionaries who promoted life in alternative society must have seemed like deviants, both religiously and socially. If Christians had systematically withdrawn from social interaction to live on the margins of macrosociety, there may have been little problem. But they chose instead to engage in missionary witness to those around them. That amounted to active propagation from within the existing order of an alternative to it. Not surprisingly, this action provoked the hostility of those who had something at stake in the way things were.

While violent repression of the messianic movement was sporadic and local until the middle of the third century, the threat of it remained relatively constant from the days of Jesus the Messiah onward. Occasionally the danger to members of messianic groups came from established authorities taking judicial or police action against them. More often, however, the menace took the form of social pressure—suspicion, verbal abuse, discrimination—which could lead to physical violence against Christians.

How should members of messianic groups respond to the attempted repression of their movement and mission? The first letter of Peter is the earliest Christian writing to focus on that question. How should the followers of the Messiah living in Anatolia in the second half of the first century respond to the unjust repression which their alternative and missionary lifestyle had provoked? Suffering and blessing the adversary like the Messiah himself did, responds Peter, is the Christian calling:

> . . . when you have behaved well and endured suffering for it, that is a sign of grace in the sight of God. It is your vocation because Christ himself suffered on your behalf, and left you an example in order that you should follow in his steps. . . . Do not repay wrong with wrong, or abuse with abuse; on the contrary, respond with blessing. . . . Dear friends, do not be taken aback by the fiery ordeal which has come to test you, as though it were something extraordinary. On the contrary, in so far as it gives you a share in Christ's sufferings, you should rejoice; and then when his glory is revealed, your joy will be unbounded (1 Pet. 2:20-21; 3:9; 4:12-13).

Peter's perspective was typical of messianic teaching. There is today a broad consensus among historians that primitive Christianity taught and practiced pacifism. The messianic movement was the peace party across the Roman Empire just as it had been in Palestine during Messiah's lifetime. Not only were messianic groups voluntary, rejecting coercion as a means to win members and transform macrosociety. They also chose to resist by suffering instead of violent self-defense when facing repression of their alternative and missionary society.

For some members of messianic groups during the first centuries, the decision to suffer "as Messiah suffered" led to forced labor, prison, even martyrdom. "Many Christians were condemned to the mines or marble quarries. Many more were imprisoned, and Roman imprisonment was particularly brutal. Prisoners were often kept in underground cells without light or sanitation; they were frequently chained to the wall or to the floor" (Walsh, 1986:237). For some, prison was a stop on the path to martyrdom. The most common method of execution seems to have been beheading, not lions in the Roman Colosseum as later martyr mythology might suggest. But whatever "the manner of death, those Christians who were executed seem to have gone willingly to meet their Lord" (:238) in the spirit of Peter's exhortation.

In early Christian perspective, this kind of pacifism was messianic witness. For it was precisely by remaining faithful to the Messiah in innocent suffering or death that many seem to have believed, that Christians received the most "unique opportunity to reveal openly where the logic of God was leading them. Martyrdom, therefore, was the most perfect form of witness which Christians were called to give in the world—witness to the death and resurrection of Christ" (Minnerath, 1973:311). From this point of view, the pain and the blood of those who responded to violence with "blessing," beginning with the martyred Messiah himself, were indeed the seed of the church.

From the First Century to the Twenty-First: Messianic Churches in Messianic Mission

What sort of churches were the creation and instrument of Messiah's mission to establish God's new order of righteousness, justice, and peace? A sociologically informed reading of the New Testament suggests that it was churches which took the form of a messianic movement clustered in interdependent messianic groups whose members were present in and continually interacting with the established societies of the day.

It is not unreasonable to believe that mission done today in Messiah's way still leads to the creation of churches of the same type. As long as mission has something to do with the renewal of all things, the churches it produces will resemble little societies whose life together potentially addresses all areas of human existence in this world—and some pertaining to the next. As long as mission has to do with an introduction to a new way of life destined to replace all other ways of life, the churches it spawns will be alternative societies, incarnating a system of values in tension with established systems. As long as mission rejects seduction and coercion in favor of free response to God's grace, the churches it creates will be composed of voluntarily converted participants. As long as this kind of mission calls converts to witness in the world rather than to withdraw from it or make war on it, new churches themselves will be missionary—in lifestyle, in action, and in word. And as long as mission calls believers to follow the path of the suffering Messiah, mission churches will respond peacefully to repression, preferring martyrdom to violence.

Is it unreasonable to believe that only churches with this particular identity—alternative, voluntary, missionary, pacifist microsocieties—can be instruments of Messiah's transfigured mission? After all, only churches whose goals have something to do with salvation in a comprehensive sense, who embrace not only religion but all of life, stand in the tradition of the Messiah. Only churches which are alternative societies, transformed in relation to existing society because they are already conformed to Messiah's vision of the future, can demonstrate the nature of life in the coming kingdom. Churches which reproduce life as lived in the present order reveal only what the world is already like, not "what the world could be like if it, too, repented and submitted to God's will" (Shenk, 1991:106). And, as church history seems to suggest, only churches which are voluntary societies have some chance of living as alternate societies. Compelled membership and participation filled the churches of Christendom century after century with people who continued to live as much as possible in conformity "to the pattern of this present world" (Rom. 12:1).

Of course, even churches which live as voluntary, alternative, microsocieties cannot communicate Messiah's gospel of peace if they withdraw from society or make war on it. If Messiah is the message and model of mission, the only choice—even in the face of repression—is nonviolent witness in society. The only choice is, as Peter might have put it, to "always be ready . . . to justify the hope which is in you" but to do so with "courtesy and respect" (1 Pet. 3:15).

Notes

1. See, for example, Gager (1975), Horsley and Hanson (1985), Meeks (1983), Rowland (1985), Thiessen (1978). Derek Tidball agrees that earliest Christianity was a millenarian movement in many respects but adds that this point of view "does not exhaust the whole picture" (Tidball, 1983:40).

2. Kenelm Burridge (1969:3) contends that "millenary activities predicate a new culture or social order coming into being. . . . Certainly it is more scientific to regard these activities as new cultures-in-the-making, or as attempts to make a new kind of society or moral community than as oddities, diseases in the body social, or troublesome nuisances to efficient administration—though of course they may be all of these as well" (also quoted by Gager, 1975:1).

3. This summary is based primarily on books by John G. Gager (1975), Helmut Koester (1982), Wayne Meeks (1986), Christopher Rowland (1985), and John E. Stambaugh and David L. Balch (1986).

4. The idea here, if not the exact words, are found in Mark 1:15, for example. Scripture references in this chapter are taken from the Revised English Bible (1989) unless noted otherwise.

5. For an implicit affirmative response, see comments on "subversive evangelism" in the chapter by John Driver, "Messianic Evangelization" (Driver, 1993b).

6. On the biblical understanding of the kingdom of God, see Driver (1993a).

7. Fundamental terms or categories in the following descriptions of messianic groups are inspired by and adapted from writings of Henri Desroche and Jean Séguy, key figures in the Groupe de Sociologie des Religions, Centre national de la recherche scientifique, Paris. See Desroche (1979; 1968:56-74). See also Séguy's perspectives (1971; 1980; 1984).

8. For a synopsis and analysis of MacMullen, see Alan Kreider (1990).

References Cited

Brown, Peter
    1985   "Antiquite tardive," *Histoire de la vie privee, v. 1, De l'Empire a l'an mil.* Paul Veyne, ed.; Paris: Seuil.

Burridge, Kenelm
    1969   *New Heaven, New Earth: A Study of Millenarian Activities.* New York: Schocken Books.

Desroche, Henri
    1968   *Sociologies religieuses.* Paris: Presses Universitaires de France.
    1979   *The Sociology of Hope.* Carol Martin-Sperry, trans.; Boston: Routledge & Kegan Paul.

Driver, John
    1993a "Kingdom of God: Goal of Messianic Mission," *The Transfiguration of Mission.* Wilbert R. Shenk, ed.
    1993b "Messianic Evangelization," *The Transfiguration of Mission.* Wilbert R. Shenk, ed.

Gager, John G.
    1975   *Kingdom and Community: The Social World of Early Christianity.* Englewood Cliffs, N.J.: Prentice-Hall.

Hinson, E. Glenn
    1981   *The Evangelization of the Roman Empire: Identity and Adaptability.* Macon, Ga.: Mercer University Press.

Horsley, Richard A., and John S. Hanson
    1985   *Bandits, Prophets, and Messiahs: Popular Movements at the Time of Jesus.* Minneapolis: Winston Press.

Koester, Helmut
    1982   *History, Culture, and Religion of the Hellenistic Age.* Philadelphia: Fortress Press.

Kreider, Alan
    1990   "The Growth of the Early Church: Reflections on Recent Literature," *Mission Focus* 18:3 (September).
    1991   "Neither Induced Nor Compelled: Christian Mission in an Exhilarating Period," unpublished.

Lane Fox, Robin
    1986   *Pagans and Christians.* London: Penguin Books.

MacMullen, Ramsey
    1984   *Christianizing the Roman Empire (AD 100-400).* New Haven, Conn.: Yale University Press.

Meeks, Wayne A.
    1983   *The First Urban Christians: The Social World of the Apostle Paul.* New Haven, Conn.: Yale University Press.
    1986   *The Moral World of the First Christians.* Philadelphia: Westminster Press.

Minnerath, R.
   1973   *Les Chretiens et le monde (Ier et IIe Siecles)*. Paris: J. Gabalda.
Rowland, Christopher
   1985   *Christian Origins: From Messianic Movement to Christian Religion*. Minneapolis: Augsburg.
Scheid, John
   1985   *Religion et piete a Rome*. Paris: La Decouverte.
Séguy, Jean
   1971   "Une Sociologie des societes imaginees: monachisme et utopie," *Annales, E.S.C.* (March-April).
   1980   "La socialisation utopique aux valeurs," *Archives de Sciences Sociales des Religions* 50:1 (July-September).
   1984   "Pour une sociologie de l'ordre religieux," *Archives de Sciences Sociales des Religions* 57:1 (January-March).
Shenk, Wilbert R.
   1991   "Missionary Encounter with Culture," *International Bulletin of Missionary Research* 15:3 (July).
   1993   "Introduction," *The Transfiguration of Mission*. Wilbert R. Shenk, ed.
Stambaugh, John E., and David L. Balch
   1986   *The New Testament in Its Social Environment*. Philadelphia: Westminster Press.
Thiessen, Gerd
   1978   *Sociology of Early Palestinian Christianity*. Philadelphia: Fortress Press.
Tidball, Derek
   1983   *An Introduction to the Sociology of the New Testament*. Exeter: The Paternoster Press.
Walsh, Michael
   1986   *The Triumph of the Meek: Why Early Christianity Succeeded*. San Francisco: Harper & Row.

CHAPTER 6

Messianic Mission and the World

Wilbert R. Shenk

MESSIANIC MISSION IS INEXTRICABLY LINKED to the world.[1] God the Creator instituted the *missio Dei* because the creation was alienated from its Creator. The God of Creation is also the God of redemption. God sent Messiah into the world for one compelling reason. God's love is world-embracing. Jesus the Messiah was mandated to liberate and redeem the world from the power of sin and death, reconciling it to God (Isa. 49:8-13; 61:1ff.; Matt. 4:23; Luke 4:18-19; 19:10; John 10:10b; 2 Cor. 5:20). This is to be accomplished by establishing God's order where there has been fundamental disorder.[2] As noted in chapter 3, God's kingdom alone represents this new possibility. This is the "good news."

Messianic mission thus is kingdom-driven toward the consummation of God's purpose for the world in the parousia. The world is the scene of messianic mission but the goal of mission transcends the world. The mission must always be held within this eschatological framework.[3]

Messiah's advent in the world met a mixed reception. The Gospel of John describes this event in sharp contrasts. This Word of God was the light and yet the people closest to the Word could not see. Even the people who knew Jesus the Messiah most intimately did not recognize him for who he was. "But to all who received him, who believed in his name, he gave power to become children of God" (John

1:12).[4] These latter experienced a fundamental and decisive change of relationship with God and world.

Similarly, Simeon's song refers to the role of Messiah as that of "a sign that is spoken against" (Luke 2:34b) in order that the truth of the human situation will be disclosed and brought to judgment. Without judgment there can be no new beginning, for judgment starts with *krisis* or clarification as the first step toward the new.[5]

The relationship between Messiah and the world is marked by a tension of cosmic proportions. The mission of Jesus led to his death by crucifixion at the hands of those who bitterly opposed his liberating and redemptive ministry. And the course of messianic mission down through history has always included long passages of persecution and martyrdom. Indeed, it has been estimated there have been more martyrs for the faith in the twentieth century than in all previous centuries.[6] Martyrdom remains the ultimate mark of faithful missionary witness. Jesus anticipated such opposition and tried to prepare his disciples for it, since their discipleship was to be exercised "in the world" even though they "were not of the world" (John 17; 20:19-22).

This meant that the messianic community was called to give its unequivocal allegiance to Messiah rather than to any earthly power. Every other authority was made relative to the authority of Jesus. The earliest confession of faith was: "Jesus Christ/Messiah is Lord." This was in direct response to the challenge of emperor worship the first Christians faced at the hands of the Roman authorities. Throughout history wherever the church has rendered unswerving allegiance to Jesus there has been strong—and frequently violent—reaction by contending authorities and competing lords. This tension is thus an authentic stamp of messianic mission. It represents a prolongation of the struggle between Jesus Messiah and the religious and political authorities in the days of his earthly ministry.

The Context for Messianic Mission

Several terms are used interchangeably in discussing the relationship between God and world. These terms are rich in meaning and defy easy definition. For the purposes of this chapter three terms are of special importance: culture, world, and worldview.

Culture
Culture consists of the learned patterns of behavior which enable an individual to participate in a society acceptably. A culture is a system

of folkways, values, and preferences which a people hold in common and by which they live. It is this elaborate body of shared experience and conventions that one generation seeks to pass on to succeeding generations and which makes one group of people distinct from all others.[7]

It is necessary to distinguish between cultures in terms of the rich diversity that marks the human species. Each one follows its own historical trajectory and is marked by a whole range of features that set it apart from all other cultures. Of course, humankind is characterized by nonnegotiable universals which establish an essential unity that transcends acquired cultural differences. One can speak of the fundamental unity of humankind in terms of shared biological, psychological, sociocultural, and spiritual features.[8] Every human being has at least some sense of personal conscience. The dread of death is universal. In common with all animals, human beings struggle to live and to avoid danger, pain, and death. All people seek to answer the question of the meaning of life. There is universal appreciation of beauty expressed through a variety of art forms. But all of these universals are mediated through the particularities of cultures. These cultural differences have continually exerted enormous influence in human existence and have often contributed to conflict between peoples.

The study of culture is of unquestioned importance to the conduct of mission especially where we are concerned with cross-cultural communication of the gospel. By definition, a cross-cultural missionary is a cultural outsider who typically never completely overcomes the telltale signs of foreignness—speaking the language of the host culture with an accent, not being fully familiar with the idioms and nuances of a culture that are characteristic of one who is "native born," perhaps having a different pigmentation. Indeed, that can have a positive value the missionary should use to advantage. But "foreignness" may remain only on the level of the exotic or even become a barrier to relationship if the outsider fails to learn the language of a people or is insensitive to cultural values and customs. To gain rapport a missionary must respect and appreciate a people and their culture. The incarnation established the standard for all missionary adaptation and identification with a people in their culture.

Culture is essential to human existence as a life-support system. The human being begins life as a complex, vulnerable, and highly dependent organism that cannot survive without much care from immediate family and society. In this sense it is not possible to describe a person apart from culture. The human being is always "in culture."

Every culture is a comprehensive system for organizing and sustaining human life as a society throughout the entire life cycle from birth to death. The Bible affirms that God has provided for human well-being by the ordering of life through social and political institutions which give society structure.

Human beings are endowed with expressive gifts and create cultures of endless variety. A culture never remains static: it is constantly changing in response to the challenge of external circumstances and internal impulses. Culture is an important means of expressing human autonomy from the Creator and may become an act of rebellion (Gen. 11:1-9). The Bible does not evade this tension between culture as an expression of human striving toward God and of culture as an expression of human rejection of God. This paradoxical relationship pervades the whole of human experience.

Significantly, the Bible does not discuss culture as such.[9] A theology of culture can only be inferred and extrapolated from Scripture. Certain religiocultural practices are treated. The people of God were given a comprehensive ritual law by which they were to live and worship. When Paul discusses the question of "food offered to idols" (1 Cor. 8), he is trying to mediate between Jewish ritual law and Gentile religiocultural sensitivities. But the Bible does not designate a particular culture as a "holy" culture. Indeed, this was the great missionary issue that tested the mettle of the new church to the limit. Paul brought to the council in Jerusalem the matter of whether Gentile converts to the messianic movement had to become cultural Jews before they were fully "messianic." The council reached a momentous decision: each people in their culture may enjoy God's benediction by bringing their lives under the rule of God without repudiating their culture as such (Acts 15).

World

The term "world" is widely used in the Bible in at least five distinct senses. First, it is used to refer to the **physical universe** described in the creation accounts in Genesis 1—2. Certain Psalms exult in the goodness and wonder of God's creation of the physical world (Pss. 8:2-3; 104:1-23; 148). Acts 17:24 speaks of God and the universe: "The God who made the world and everything in it, being Lord of heaven and earth," a phrase echoing the Old Testament.

The Bible speaks of the **human inhabitants of the earth** as the world. Psalm 9:8 says God "judges the world with righteousness" (cf. Pss. 96:13; 98:9). In Isaiah 13:11 God promises to "punish the world for its evil, and the wicked for their iniquity." In explaining how it came about that Jesus was born in Bethlehem, Luke reports "a decree went out from Caesar Augustus that all the world should be enrolled. . . . And all went to be enrolled, each to his own city" (Luke 2:1-3). Accordingly, Joseph and Mary went to their ancestral city.

In a third sense, world refers to the **scene of human activity**. The world is the theater of human actions—for good and for ill: "For godly grief produces a repentance that leads to salvation and brings no regret, but worldly grief produces death" (2 Cor. 7:10). Jesus warned the disciples, "For what will it profit a man, if he gains the whole world and forfeits his life?" (Matt. 16:26).

In the fourth place, world signifies the **forces arrayed against God and God's purposes**. This usage encompasses fallen and unrepentant peoples as well as spiritual forces (Eph. 3:10). Hebrews 11:38 speaks of the martyrs "of whom the world was not worthy." The epistle of James refers to "religion that is pure and undefiled" as requiring the keeping of "oneself unstained from the world" (James 1:27). Second Peter 1:4 warns of "the corruption that is in the world." Paul draws a sharp contrast between the world and the things of God (1 Cor. 2:7-8, 12; 3:19; Gal. 6:14). Paul attributes the condition of the world to the fact of sin (Rom. 1:18-32; 5:12-14; 1 Cor. 15:21-22). The Johannine writings are even more emphatic in warning against the evil powers at work in the world (1 John 5:19; John 8:23; 12:25; 13:1; 18:36; and numerous other passages). First John 2:15-17 exhorts the community of faith not to love "the world or the things in the world." Accordingly, the disciples must expect to be hated because their Master was hated by the world (John 7:7; 17:14).

Theologically, this would seem to be rooted in human rebellion against God's purpose. A key word in the New Testament is *kosmos*, meaning "order" or "arrangement." This represents the *kosmos* God established for the universe. Human reaction to God's *kosmos* is not so much *chaos* as it is *anti-kosmos*. The structures and institutions of society serve to hold in check this rebellious bent. Occasionally, human society plunges into chaos, a situation so terrifying that a people will accept as leader an Adolf Hitler or Mao Tse-tung precisely because they promise to restore order. It is in this area—*anti-kosmos* and *chaos*—that the "principalities and powers" operate.[10]

Finally, the world is the **object of Messiah's mission**. The world that hates God is the world God has loved to the extent of giving "his only Son, that whoever believes in him should not perish but have eternal life" (John 3:16). Messiah is acclaimed "Savior of the world"

(John 4:42; 1 John 4:14; cf. John 12:47). Paul summarizes the work of the Messiah, saying: "God was in Christ, reconciling the world to himself" (2 Cor. 5:19). When the world is redeemed it will be restored to its rightful relationship to God (Rev. 11:15; 21:1).

We conclude this section with several summary observations. First, for the purposes of this chapter, we will focus on the fourth of the five definitions noted above: **the world signifies the forces arrayed against God and God's purposes**. This is the realm which does not acknowledge God's authority for it is under the sway of Satan and the powers acting in rebellion against God and the Messiah.

In the second place, the Bible pictures the relationship between the kingdom of God and the kingdom of this world as one of continuous conflict which will only be resolved at the parousia when the Messiah of God completes the redemption of the world.

Third, the mission of the Messiah is to enter the vortex of this conflict between the two kingdoms. Messiah, in turn, calls the disciple community to be full participants in that mission task. Messiah's mission becomes the mission of the messianic community.

The fourth observation is that in the Bible the operative term is "world" rather than "culture." Because we frequently use "culture" in the sense in which the Bible refers to "world," and vice versa, it is important that we clarify definitions in light of biblical usage.[11]

Worldview

We have already noted the main features of culture. It is a complex system consisting of patterns of behavior controlled by values and preferences. Culture is essential to human welfare and survival. The older generation invests substantial amounts of time and resources in attempting to prepare the new generation for life by passing on this cultural deposit. Tied up in culture are identity, personal and group well-being, and destiny.

It is instructive to visualize a culture as consisting of several layers.[12] At the heart of culture is its worldview. A second layer is comprised of the values and controls which regulate human relationships. The outer layer is made up of a series of institutions which furnish the framework for human activity—family, economy, laws, policies, education.

These layers are interconnected. The second layer directly reflects the core, that is, the worldview; the third layer represents a working out in social institutions of the values of the second. But the worldview is being modified over time by changes in the experiences

CULTURE

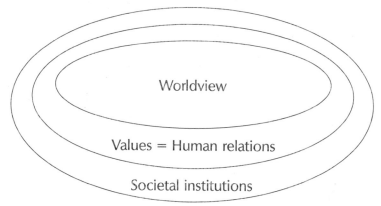

of the members of a cultural group. For example, all cultures have felt the impact of the forces of modernity, and the process of modernization has affected all three levels of cultures, not least worldview.

No one can say exactly when or how a particular worldview emerged. It is the result of the interaction of a group of people with a particular space/time environment and trying to make sense of life in its totality. Of special concern are the suprahuman—such as the forces of nature—and supranatural powers which are perceived to exert decisive influence over human existence. A worldview furnishes a conceptual map of reality and guidelines for human response within such a "world."

Charles Kraft suggests that a worldview performs five functions. First, it **explains** matters of ultimate concern to members of a culture: What is the universe and the place of human beings in it? What makes things happen for good and for ill? What is the meaning of human existence? Who controls the universe?

The second function of a worldview is that of setting a standard by which members of a culture **evaluate** life and the important questions that are raised by human experience. Sanctions may be imposed against certain views while others are approved. In a culture based on communist ideology, free enterprise is disallowed as a part of the very worldview. Conversely, in a society based on free enterprise central planning and control are rejected by the worldview.

Third, a worldview offers **psychological reinforcement** for the members of a culture. This is particularly important at times of crisis and transition when personal anxiety rises. A society may provide ritualized ways of dealing with these experiences—birth, death, marriage, rites of passage, natural catastrophe—so that the individual is helped to cope.

Fourth, a worldview helps to **integrate** perceptions of reality. Members of a group inevitably encounter a range of experiences which raise questions about life. A worldview provides the framework within which these questions can be answered and the whole of the individual's experience (re)integrated.

Finally, because a culture does not remain static but evolves over time, a worldview helps a culture's members **adapt** to fundamental change by coming to terms with contradictions and conflicts that threaten disintegration unless resolved. The various "fundamentalisms" that have arisen in the twentieth century are essentially reactions on the part of various groups to the threat posed to particular worldviews by massive conceptual and structural changes as a result of modernity. In this case, the usual response is to resolve the contradiction by redefining the nature of the new phenomenon to conform to the traditional worldview. In other instances, inner coherence is re-established by adjusting the worldview so as to be congruent with the external environment as it is perceived.

The worldview of a culture is the "command center" out of which emanates cultural impulses. A worldview shapes and animates the way a particular culture views the world. Yet a worldview always remains a fallible and one-sided view of the world. A worldview reflects the limitations of all human constructs. It cannot deliver itself of human bigotry, bias, and partiality for it is the product of historical and human processes.

This is the point at which the biblical notion of "world" and what we commonly call "culture" meet and merge. When Paul made his twofold appeal to the Christians at Rome to "present" themselves wholly to God while refusing to "be conformed to this world" (Rom. 12:1-2), he clearly called for a basic reorientation—a re-centering—of this "command center." This was to be accomplished through a transformation of their minds, that is, their worldview. In other words, conversion must begin at this fundamental level if the thorough renovation Paul envisages is to be actualized. The messianic community was being called to understand that God has a radically different view of the world and this was the view that was to be normative in the life and witness of this community even though it would not always understand perfectly what "the will of God" was for them and the world.

"In But Not of the World": The Essential Tension

On any reading of the Bible it becomes evident that a pronounced tension is present. Indeed, we must insist that this tension is essential to biblical faith and its mission in the world. It is a tension that emerges right at the beginning and is dissolved only in the Apocalypse at the end. For our purposes we will highlight some of the important features of this unfolding drama.

Old Testament

The human predicament. The primal paradigm against which the biblical account is rendered is set forth in Genesis 3:1-7. The *dramatis personae* consists of four characters—Satan, the human couple, and God. The plot is permanently set. Satan proffers a proposition the human couple find irresistable—to become godlike by asserting their independence of God's providence. At the instigation of the tempter, the human couple rejected God's will in favor of following their own.

Scene after scene, the Bible unfolds the implications of human attempts to become godlike, attempts that end either pitifully or tragically (Gen. 4:1-16; 6:5—8:22; 11:1-9). The great irony which the Bible reveals is that human beings are least godlike when they most vehemently assert their independence of God by rejecting an accountable relationship to God. By contrast, God models true interdependence. God, who is totally independent of creation, including humankind, in *agape* chooses to be in relationship with humankind, demonstrated most fully and concretely in Jesus the Messiah. The human rejection of God ends in the embrace of and deepening dependence on other powers. These powers, which we will investigate later in this chapter, are in rebellion against God; they are powers which cannot give life or liberate from creaturely limits.

The Old Testament assumes the fundamental problem to be this conflict between God's will and human willfulness. Human beings are powerless to save themselves. The temptation to become godlike is in fact an attempt to save self independently of God. The paradox is that salvation becomes possible only when humans admit their creatureliness and turn to the Creator/Redeemer God who alone can restore the dignity for which they were destined as sons and daughters of God.

Covenant and election. In view of the human predicament, God takes a series of initiatives. In the Old Testament the most significant step is the calling out of Abraham to be a means of blessing (Gen. 12:1-3) to the peoples of the world. Abraham is called into covenant relationship with God. Covenant indicates the privilege of responsibility both to God and to the peoples. It is not a covenant based on self-interest or self-aggrandizement.

The covenant people have a special vocation to the world. Their calling is to be a holy people: "the mark of holiness is the highest expression of the covenant relationship between a holy God and his people" (Williams, 1984:515).[13] To be holy is to be set apart from the ordinary. The covenant bound the Abrahamic people to God. The human quest for godlikeness, which consistently ends in futility, is now transmuted. God takes the initiative and binds this people in covenant to God. Holiness involves becoming godly precisely by rejecting the world's way of rebellion against God and entering into covenant relationship.

God's strategy for redeeming the world is *pars pro toto*, the one for the many, reaching the peoples through God's own people. The responsibility of Israel to the nations comes to greatest clarity in Isaiah where Israel's role is pictured through various messianic images: "ensign to the peoples . . . for the nations" (Isa. 11:10, 12); "a covenant to the people, a light to the nations" (Isa. 42:6; cf. 49:6; 51:4; 61:3); "oaks of righteousness" (Isa. 61:3); "The holy people, The redeemed of the Lord . . . Sought out" (Isa. 62:12). In other words, the people of God were to display before the peoples of the world the fruit of the way of life based on God's righteousness. As other peoples saw this new possibility incarnated in the world, they would be attracted to covenant relationship too.

Covenant compromised. In spite of such a grand calling, the people of the covenant repeatedly failed to honor their special relationship and role. They compromised their calling. The meaning of the covenant was distorted by attempts to reinterpret the means of blessing as being chosen because of special favor. The Old Testament gives a full account of this desultory history, the clash between God's will and human willfulness.

The story reaches a decisive point when the people of Israel demand a king. This is the scene. The elders of Israel approached the aged Samuel with a demand. Samuel had appointed his two sons to assist him in governing Israel, but they proved corrupt. The elders, therefore, insisted that Samuel institute kingship. Samuel argued strenuously against this step on both theological and political grounds (1 Sam. 8; cf. Deut. 17:14-20). Theologically, this step would shift Israel's primary loyalty from Yahweh to the king. Politically, this form of kingship would subject the people to all manner of oppression and exploitation, against which they would have no recourse.

But the elders were determined. Nothing Samuel said changed their viewpoint. They insisted: "No! but we will have a king over us, that we also may be like all the nations, and that our king may govern us and go out before us and fight our battles" (1 Sam. 8:19b-20). The history of that kingship—the outcome of becoming "like all the nations" and adopting the way of the world—is recorded in 1 and 2 Kings.

Prophetic critique. The prophetic writings of the Old Testament provide an extended critique of Israel's bent toward covenant breaking manifested through the worship of idols, moral compromise, and unfaithfulness to their vocation as the people of God. Israel comes under judgment for living like the other peoples rather than as people of the covenant with God as leader. The prophets repeatedly issue the call to "repent!" and return to Yahweh as true leader. Failure to heed this call, the prophets warned, would result in perpetual bondage and death. Only *metanoia*, turning to God, would bring redemption from their present bondage.

These prophetic interventions were not limited, however, to concern for Israel's salvation. The prophets tried to recall the people of Israel to their covenant relationship with a view to their again becoming a blessing to the nations. With privilege went responsibility. Blessing was the result of faithfulness to the covenant. Thus, the key to a restored Israel was covenant renewal: "be holy for I am holy" (Lev. 11:44; cf. 19:2; 20:7).

An important theme in the prophets' preaching was the coming of Messiah. The people were encouraged to look for Messiah who would transform their present predicament into a new age of justice/righteousness characterized by *shalom* and put their enemies to flight. It is important to bear in mind that the people perceived the enemy as being external, more precisely the neighboring nations. The prophets uniformly emphasized the enemy within—the peoples' hardheartedness toward God and weaker members of society, the widow, orphan, and alien. The prophetic prescription was the transformed heart, an inward conversion, for that alone could produce the fruits of social righteousness consistent with the original covenant (Mic. 6:8; cf. Amos 5:21-24; Jer. 31:8, 12-13, 17, 31-34).

New Testament
Messiah's coming. If anything, the New Testament heightens the tension between human willfulness—or the world—and God's will. The

Messiah, Jesus, is interpreted as the one who embodies God's new order fully. This order presents a stark contrast to the order of this
world, thus underscoring the tension.

In Matthew's account of the inauguration of Jesus' ministry, Jesus
is confronted by the possibility of resolving this tension through compromise, that is, by submitting himself to the authority of Satan (Matt.
4:1-11). This Jesus resolutely resisted. Immediately following this
temptation experience, Matthew reports, "Jesus began to preach, saying, 'Repent, for the kingdom of heaven is at hand' " (Matt. 4:17; cf.
Mark 1:15). Jesus' response gives us the clue as to how this tension
will be worked out within the New Testament. God's concession to Israel, allowing them to have a king, is now abrogated.

John's witness. The Johannine writings highlight this tension.
The Gospel of John opens with an assertion of God's claim on the
world by creation (John 1:1-3) but recognizes at the same time that
this claim is contested (1:10ff.). God enters the world, becoming incarnate in the human situation, identifying fully with the human predicament. The pivotal statement in John's Gospel comes in 3:16 where
God makes an unconditional commitment to the salvation of the
world in the sending of the Son as God's Messiah.

It is significant that the Gospel of John's version of the great commission makes a point of saying that the relationship of the disciples to
the world is the same as that of Jesus himself—linking his own martyrdom with the commission to the disciples to go into the world (John
20:20ff.). The Johannine epistles continue to address this God/world
tension in the context of faithful discipleship with the appeal: "Do not
love the world or the things in the world. If any one loves the world,
love for the Father is not in him" (1 John 2:15). The Revelation of John
is a sustained dramatic depiction of this struggle by the forces of evil
against God. The struggle is resolved only when the Lamb triumphs
and delivers a transformed world into the hands of God.

Apostles' witness. The Acts account of the first days of the messianic community is replete with this tension. The early witness is
made against a backdrop of continual opposition, often leading to confrontation, frequently ending in punishment and sometimes death.
The fundamental position of the apostles is staked out early. Following the arrest of the apostles in Jerusalem and their arraignment before the religious court, the high priest sought to silence them. The
apostolic response: "We must obey God rather than men" (Acts
5:29b). They went on to describe Jesus the Messiah as the "Leader and
Savior" of Israel. For the apostles there could be no retreat from this

position. The outcome of history hinged on the lordship of Jesus Messiah.

This brief survey of the tension between God and world in the New Testament has highlighted the fact that the coming of Jesus Messiah into the world intensified the God/world conflict as he challenged the coalition of religious and political leaders for their false piety and unjust administration.

In contrast to this kind of religion, Jesus calls for a discipleship based on holy living, thus renewing the Old Testament emphasis on being a holy people.

The Opposition Forces

In his exhaustive study of the language of power in the New Testament, Walter Wink remarks how pervasive the concern with power is and how surprising it is that this fact has been largely overlooked in preaching and teaching.[14] "On every page of the New Testament one finds the terminology of power" (Wink, 1978:99). In that respect the Scriptures reflect reality. Life cannot be lived and the world cannot operate apart from power exercised in all sorts of ways. Maintenance of *kosmos* itself is dependent on the exercise of power. Human society depends on a vast system of institutions, positions, authorities, and procedures by which to legitimate and regulate the use of power. In every realm it is only by the exercise of some form of power that change is effected.

The Scriptures offer no apology for this preoccupation with power. Paul made the remarkable declaration that he was "not ashamed of the gospel: it is the power of God for salvation" (Rom. 1:16). The implication is that there are other powers at work that will lead to the opposite of salvation. Therefore, the apostle is an unhesitating apologist for the gospel. Indeed, we can say that central to messianic mission is the question of the power of God engaging other powers. An important part of the apostolate for Paul was that of bringing the powers of the cosmos under the reign of Messiah.

The Powers

Old Testament background. It is of more than casual interest that the first two commands of the Decalogue define the relationship of Yahweh to the "gods" or powers and forbid any form of idolatry (Exod. 20:3-4). This is the essence of biblical faith. The struggle in the Old Testament is cast in terms of God's summons to the people of Israel to break with the prevailing pattern of the worship of the many gods of their neighbors, tied as they were to specific cultures, fertility rites, and the conquest of their military rivals. Evil is not clearly personified. Satan—which means "obstruct, oppose"—seldom mentioned, is not a demonic figure (see Caird, 1956: chap. 2; Gaster, 1962:224-28). In the Old Testament "satan" is used of obstructing someone's path (Num. 22:22, 32), opposing war (1 Sam. 29:4), prosecutor (Ps. 109:6), and adversary (Job 16:9).

New Testament shift. The New Testament presents some important contrasts with the Old. At the center stands the figure of the Messiah, and there is a sharply defined opposition (Matt. 4:1-11). The leader of the opposition is Satan who is also referred to by other terms such as the devil and obstructor. Satan is also referred to as the tempter (Matt. 4:3; 1 Thess. 3:5), the accuser (Rev. 12:10), enemy (Matt. 13:39; Luke 10:19), adversary (1 Pet. 5:8), prince of demons (Matt. 9:34; 12:24; Mark 3:22; Luke 11:15), ruler of this world (John 12:31; 16:11), prince of the power of the air (Eph. 2:2), Beliar = Belial (2 Cor. 6:15), Beelzebul (Matt. 10:25; 12:27; cf. Mark 3:22; Luke 11:15, 18-19). As God's opponent, Satan also has a "throne," but it is not located in a realm above or a place below. Rather it is in the institutions of society (Rev. 2:12-13).

The New Testament depicts Satan as a personality interacting with humans and responsible for inspiring evil actions. Satan is the implacable opponent of God and God's people. However, Satan is not alone but rather stands at the head of a contingent of powers.

The Powers Defined

A classic text which speaks of the identity and role of Jesus Christ/Messiah is Colossians 1:16-20, which includes these key phrases: "for in him all things were created, in heaven and on earth, visible and invisible, whether thrones or dominions or principalities or authorities—all things were created through him and for him. . . . For in him all the fulness of God was pleased to dwell, and through him to reconcile to himself all things, whether on earth or in heaven, making peace by the blood of his cross."

Included in this text is a comprehensive statement of the powers. First, we observe that they are heavenly and earthly, divine and human, spiritual and political, invisible and structural. Second, there are good powers and evil. Third, all powers, regardless of status, are God-created for the divine purpose and owe their existence to God's sufferance. Fourth, because some of these powers are in rebellion against

God and the purpose for which they were created, the great work of the Messiah is to effect a cosmic reconciliation, "making peace by the blood of his cross" (v. 20).

Many scholarly studies of the powers have focused on the Pauline writings because of the way Paul recognized these realities. It will be useful to note the way Jesus referred to the powers, as compared to that of Paul, and then consider summary definitions by biblical scholars.

Jesus and the powers. In the ministry of Jesus, the clash between Jesus and the powers is most intense in relation to the religious leaders and the state.[15] Jesus' sharpest exchanges took place with the religious establishment. His teaching so threatened their *authority* that they began early to plot his assassination (Mark 3:6). It was the Roman government that acted in collusion with the religious leaders and arranged the crucifixion of Jesus. Jesus encountered other powers as well. He cast out demons as a demonstration of the power of the kingdom of God over evil, he healed, he challenged the reigning worldview that kept people enslaved. Finally, he engaged and triumphed over death, the "last enemy" (1 Cor. 15:26).

Paul and the powers. The Pauline phrase "principalities and powers" captures in the popular mind Paul's thought about the powers—these are sinister forces bent on subverting and destroying the work of God in the world. Paul himself felt that Satan was frustrating his mission (1 Thess. 2:18; 2 Cor. 12:7). And Paul believed elemental spirits held the world in bondage (Gal. 4:3; Col. 2:8, 20). The god of this age blinds the minds of those who do not believe so they will not receive the gospel (2 Cor. 4:4).

Only by the work of Jesus the Messiah were the Ephesians brought to life after having been in captivity to "the prince of the power of the air, the spirit that is now at work in the sons of disobedience" (Eph. 2:2). Paul lived in the hope of that final triumph when every kind of authority is submitted to Jesus Christ (1 Cor. 15:24). But, as noted above, based on Colossians 1:16-20, Paul also knew these powers were created by and for God's Messiah, that "every tongue [should] confess that Jesus Christ is Lord" (Phil. 2:11a). God had a purpose for all the powers, even those that have become erstwhile rebels.

Summary definitions. In *Christ and the Powers*, Hendrikus Berkhof (1977) does not offer a comprehensive definition but keeps adding further dimensions as he moves along. After surveying the key Pauline texts, Berkhof sums up his findings: "Paul observes that life is ruled by a series of Powers. He speaks of time (present and future), of space (depth and height), of life and death, of politics and philosophy, of public opinion and Jewish law, of pious tradition and the fateful course of the stars" (1977:22). Berkhof sees the powers as falling into four categories: nature, state, mammon, and demons. In Jesus Christ these powers have been unmasked and exposed, so that through that messianic activity we are afforded protection against these forces which take on themselves authority to which they are not entitled.

Walter Wink has sought to penetrate the essence of the "principalities and powers," describing them as "the inner and outer aspects of any given manifestation of power. As the inner aspect they are the spirituality of institutions, the 'within' of corporate structures and systems, the inner essence of outer organizations of power. As the outer aspect they are political systems, appointed officials, the 'chair' of an organization, laws—in short, all tangible manifestations which power takes" (Wink, 1978:5).[16] In this view, a power joins the inner or spiritual and the outer or material reality. The one cannot exist without the other. Whenever a power structure overreaches its proper role and demands absolute allegiance, it has become demonic. "Unsubmitted" power tends not to know its limits. It is in the nature of power to seek to enhance itself further.

The "Rationality" of Power

To one degree or another every power creates a "rationality" consistent with its character. This is its aura of authority—whether based on professional expertise, charisma, or technological prowess. Power, therefore, is self-justifying. The more it shields itself from criticism the more unable it is to accept criticism. The world continues to study with horror the Nazi episode in Germany that led to World War II because the overwhelming majority of the people of a nation that prided itself on being highly rational and enlightened was led down a path that history has judged to be totally morally offensive. Even the majority of church leaders were caught up in the "rationality" Adolf Hitler managed to create. Cults advocating a rationality based on violence and bizarre or deviant notions continue to attract followings by their promise of power. It is this prospect of empowerment—including protection and personal aggrandizement—that lures people to submit themselves to the powers.

The church—that body which claims its head to be the Lord of lords—has as its special task to proclaim the "manifold wisdom of God . . . to the principalities and powers" (Eph. 3:10), the more so when cloaked in the rationality of power. Such a proclamation can carry authority only to the extent it rises above the worldview of a particular culture and convincingly conveys the "mind of Christ."

The Messianic Response: Cross and Resurrection

The clue to history is the cross and resurrection precisely because this is the way God chose to bring the rebellious powers to heel. In the preceding paragraph, we have noted how the rationality of a particular power leads to self-justification. Everyone who submits to that rationality thereby reinforces it. Jesus refused to accept the Pharisees' "rationality" of Torah. He was convinced its ultimate effect was spiritual death. Similarly, Jesus did not accept the "rationality" of the Roman authorities, for it, too, meant oppression. These two rationalities cooperated in trying to force Jesus to conform to their respective demands. All they could do was to put him to death. But this proved to be an utter defeat for these powers/rationalities. Instead it exposed their moral bankruptcy and their actual impotence. The resurrection of Jesus in the power of God's Spirit was the beginning of the end for all these rebellious powers.

The Messianic Strategy and the Renewal of the Cosmos

In contrast to the varieties of rationalities of power considered in the previous section, the rationality of God's power is presented in hymnic form in Philippians 2:5-11. Jesus rejected all the conventional trappings of power. Instead he submitted himself to God, to humankind, and to death by crucifixion. This means he refused to acknowledge the claims of any other god, to exploit other humans, or to insist on his rights even on pain of death.

On this basis Jesus is recognized as God's Messiah, or anointed one, by whom the world will be redeemed. Paul follows this hymn with the comment: "Therefore, my beloved, as you have always obeyed, so now, not only as in my presence but much more in my absence, work out your own salvation with fear and trembling; for God is at work in you, both to will and work for his good pleasure" (Phil. 2:12-13). God's work of salvation can be accomplished only by the kind of power which was on full display in Jesus the Messiah. We can grasp the rationality of God's power only through the work of Jesus. Paul declares that this "is not a wisdom of this age or of the rulers of this age, who are doomed to pass away" (1 Cor. 2:6b). This is God's long-held secret. "None of the rulers of this age understood this; for if they had, they would not have crucified the Lord of glory" (2:8). So how is the impasse to be broken?

The New Creation

In continuity with God's election of Abraham to be the one by whom "all the families of the earth shall bless themselves" (Gen. 12:3; cf. Acts 3:25; Gal. 3:8), God had "prepared in the presence of all peoples, a light for revelation to the Gentiles, and for glory to thy people Israel" (Luke 2:31-32; cf. Acts 26:22-23). The old divisions could not be overcome by repairing or mending them. Only something entirely new would be capable of putting the cosmos right. Paul rejects, therefore, talk about circumcision on the part of some at Galatia, "For neither circumcision counts for anything, nor uncircumcision, but *a new creation*" (Gal. 6:15; italics mine). The time has come, according to Paul, to stop treating the malady based on a piecemeal diagnosis. The treatment must be adequate to the illness. The death and resurrection of Jesus Christ has opened the way to the fulfillment of that which had been promised in Abraham (Col. 2:8-15).

Paul asserts that "if any one is in Christ he is *a new creation*; the old has passed away, behold, the new has come" (2 Cor. 5:17; italics mine). Here Paul draws the contrast between "old" and "new" worlds. He now views the creation through the work of Jesus Christ and the way in which creation can be saved or made new (Minear, 1960: chap. 4). Paul develops further his idea of the "new creation" through his use of terms such as the new humanity, firstfruits, the last Adam, and the kingdom of God. The latter term was counterposed to the kingdom of this world, and the new creation was seen as forming a vanguard opposed to the forces of Satan (Eph. 5).

Conversion. The path to the new creation is by way of conversion. To be converted is to leave the old order and to join the new one. Breaking with the old and joining the new involves the double action of repentance and conversion (Heb. *sub*; Gr. *metanoia*). The basis for this conversion was the covenant, and the prophets took as their point of departure the failure of the people to honor the covenant with Yahweh. They reminded the people of what covenant obligations entailed: rejection of idolatry, authentic worship, and social righteousness. Jeremiah, for example, expected that the people would be able to enter fully into their covenant responsibilities only when they experienced a change of heart so that their wills inclined toward God (Jer. 24:4-7; 31:31-34; 32:37-41; 33:7-9; cf. Heb. 8:8-12; 10:16-17).

Jesus picks up the same note of repentance and call to covenant relationship in his message (Matt. 4:17, 23; Mark 1:14; John 3:3-6). Conversion signifies the complete change in personal orientation from bondage to the powers of this world by liberation into service in the kingdom of God. It is both a conscious turning to God and a continuing process of bearing the "fruits of repentance" (see Shank, 1980; Kasdorf, 1980: chaps. 2—3).

New community. The new creation takes concrete form in the new community. Jesus indicated that the new community was qualitatively different. He characterized it as being the source of salt and light for the world. He did not tell his disciples to seek these qualities, qualities which are inherent to the nature of the community (see Driver, 1983). Every time the church actualizes the joining together of "Jew and Gentile," it overrides the powers by extending the life-giving power of Jesus the Messiah (Eph. 2:11-22). Whenever the church acts in fidelity to the Messiah, it is asserting the messianic lordship over all other powers, be they the powers of racism, sexism, nationalism, or ideology. The church thus is refusing to allow that power to have the last word.

Sanctification. Proclamation of the lordship of Jesus Christ directly affects the position of the powers. In situations where the lordship of Christ has not been proclaimed or that lordship has already been widely acknowledged, the powers operate within known boundaries. As people begin turning from the powers to Jesus, or, conversely, as people turn away from Jesus, the powers become destabilized and a power vacuum emerges. It has been suggested that in the West where secularization has touched the very foundations of society, the result has been a loss of a center (Berkhof, 1977:51-63; 1979:507-09).[17]

Secularism and nihilism have been urged as answers to this vacuum, but they have failed to win a solid hold. In the process adherents have become angry anti-Christian belligerents. One recalls the warning Jesus gave about the risk of displacing the powers unless the power of God moves in and takes control (Matt. 12:43-45; Luke 11:24-26). Only the church is in a position to witness to one who can indeed hold all things together. The church can become a sanctifying presence in a situation where a multitude of "lordless" powers compete by proclaiming the lordship of Jesus the Messiah and calling the powers to their proper role in the economy of God (Eph. 3:10).

Intensification. In the coming of God's Messiah, the world has been given a sense of historical purpose and direction so that the human story is moving toward a goal or *telos*. As the lordship of Jesus

Messiah continues to be proclaimed as the fulfillment of that goal, the powers react in ever greater intensity. Pretender lords present themselves. Technology, a significant fruit of the biblical faith, was seized on by some as a sole and sufficient power by which human welfare might be assured.

This god has now been exposed as inadequate. Powerful ideologies have arisen in the nineteenth and twentieth centuries on the pretext they would liberate the human race. Each of these powers sought to make itself ultimate, only to be brought down by its own pretentiousness. The accelerated pace of change in all aspects of life coupled with the awareness that technology has produced the means of mass destruction intensifies the feeling that the denouement is unavoidable and near at hand (Berkhof, 1979:515-18; 1966: chaps. 5—6).

The Church in the World: Resident Aliens

The community that names Messiah as its leader can never find full acceptance in the world so long as these "lordless" powers continue to exert influence. The messianic view of the world is incongruent with all worldviews, each of which is limited by its particular time and space and the powers that control it. How then is the messianic community, concerned for missionary faithfulness, to relate to the world?

Although Abraham obeyed God's call to leave Haran and go to "the land that I will show you" (Gen. 12:1), when Sarah died at Hebron, Abraham had to petition his Hittite neighbors for a plot of ground on which to bury his wife. He said, "I am a stranger and a sojourner among you" (Gen. 23:4a). Thus did Abraham introduce a metaphor that continued to define the faithful community right through the Bible.[18] When Jacob met Pharoah in Egypt, he spoke of being a sojourner (Gen. 47:9). David pled before God: "For I am thy passing guest, a sojourner, like all my fathers" (Ps. 39:12). The epistle to the Hebrews describes the faithful in the same terms: "These all died in faith, not having received what was promised, but having seen it and greeted it from afar, and having acknowledged that they were strangers and exiles on earth" (Heb. 11:13).[19]

Jesus is linked with this line: "So Jesus also suffered outside the gate in order to sanctify the people through his own blood. Therefore let us go forth to him outside the camp, and bear the abuse he endured. For here we have no lasting city, but we seek the city which is to come" (Heb. 13:12-14; cf. Phil. 3:20). Peter appeals to the faithful as "aliens and exiles" to live a life of holiness and thus commend the world to God (1 Pet. 2:9, 12).

At no point in this litany of texts is there a call to withdraw from the world or to move. In fact, the community is never instructed to go elsewhere to seek its safety or well-being.[20] Rather the situation is one of critical engagement. The metaphor of "resident alien" does not focus on the inward life of the disciple or call for quietism. Rather it keeps clearly in view the tension between God and God's people in the world. It assumes the messianic community is the bearer of that tension and that it will allow its mission to be shaped by that tension: total loyalty to the Messiah and unbounded compassion for a world in bondage to the "lordless" powers.

Notes

1. The mission-world theme has been largely overlooked in missiological literature. The main study is Marc Spindler (1967).

2. Those situated in well-ordered societies may fail to appreciate what it means to live with the threat of chaos. Furthermore, even supposedly well-ordered societies mask incipient dis-order and anti-order. One has only to recall what happens when there is a sudden power failure in a city or when police service is interrupted. Repeatedly, we have seen an immediate outbreak of looting and violence. The human bent toward self-assertion and self-aggrandizement requires constant restraint in all societies.

3. "The New Testament shows very little interest in the tasks of civilisation and culture. How then can faith, which seems so indifferent to culture, be its basis? . . . First, it is true the main concern of the New Testament message is not culture or civilisation, not the temporal but the eternal, not the earthly but the heavenly life. The Gospel is not focused on culture, but on the world-to-come. 'This world passes away,' and with it civilisation. . . . The second point, however, which must be repeated, is that this perspective of the kingdom of God does not alienate men from their temporal life. Faith in the kingdom and in eternal life does not make men indifferent to the tasks which earthly existence lays upon them. On the contrary, the Christian is summoned to tackle them with special energy, and his faith gives him the power to solve these problems better than he could without faith. 'Seek ye first the kingdom of God . . . and these things shall be added unto you.' It is precisely the man whose first concern is not culture but the kingdom of God that has the necessary distance from cultural aims and the necessary perspective to serve them in freedom, and to grasp that order which prevents the various sections of civilisation from monopolising the totality of life. Only from beyond civilisation can its order and harmony come" (Brunner, 1949:130).

4. Scriptures quoted in this chapter are from the Revised Standard Version unless noted otherwise.

5. "The concept of judgment has more than one connotation in the Bible. . . . The relationships in the world are not at all in harmony with the intention of holy love. In the great leap of the world they will be radically set straight. In that context 'judgment' means as much as a revolution: the selfish mighty rulers will be dethroned and the oppressed, the 'poor,' the 'humble' will finally be allowed to breathe and be themselves. See e.g., Ps. 72; 75:8; Isa. 11:4; Luke 1:51ff.; 6:20-26; 16:19-31; James 5:1-11. With that connotation judgment is primarily glad tidings; the coming judge is the one who will set things straight, the savior who will bring about in the world the long-awaited structural righteousness" (Berkhof, 1979:520).

6. The only recent account of twentieth-century martyrdom is by James and Marti Heffly (1979). David B. Barrett continues to collect information on contemporary

martyrdoms which he summarizes in his statistical report on various aspects of the Christian mission published in the January issue each year of *International Bulletin of Missionary Research*.

7. For a review of the profusion of definitions of culture, see the study by Alfred Kroeber and Clyde Kluckhohn (1952).

8. See Charles H. Kraft (1979: chap. 5, "Human Commonality") for an overview of the universals which unite the human species.

9. This apparent omission is theologically significant. The distinction drawn in Scripture is that between the people of God and the peoples (*goyim*). Racial, national, cultural, and gender criteria are explicitly rejected as being of salvific significance. From the standpoint of the history of culture, it is important to keep in mind the observation of Charles R. Taber (1991: chaps. 1-2) that culture as an abstraction emerged only in the nineteenth century. This was a necessary intellectual step in order to be able to develop the tools for the formal study of culture and the comparative study of cultures.

10. This insight and some other clarifications in this chapter I owe to Charles R. Taber who kindly read a first draft and offered suggestions.

11. The lack of precision in definition is evident in the classic study by H. Richard Niebuhr (1951). For Niebuhr, "culture" refers to the total process and fruit of human effort "to which now the name *culture*, now the name *civilization*, is applied in common speech" (p. 32). See Charles Scriven (1988: especially pp. 37-48). Scriven notes that Niebuhr's question "has to do rather with two broad concerns. First, does Christ value cultural existence positively? And second, how does his authority relate to the way of life presently dominant in culture?" (p. 48).

12. See Charles H. Kraft (1979: chap. 3, "Human Beings in Culture") for a discussion of worldview. The suggestion to depict culture as a series of layers comes from Andrew Kirk (1990:24).

13. Alan Kreider has explored the importance of holiness for today's church, drawing on Old and New Testaments, church history, and contemporary challenges (1987).

14. The discovery of the theme of "the powers" by biblical scholars since 1950 is salutary. This line of development has been capped by Walter Wink's three-volume study of *The Powers*. Wink was drawn into the study initially by the writings of William Stringfellow and subsequent firsthand exposure to the terrors of totalitarianism in Latin America in the 1970s. Wink's painstaking reconstruction of the biblical and collateral material is impressive. It is important, however, to note that this is a highly culturally conditioned venture, for he and other scholars are trying to recover a part of the biblical witness that has been disallowed by the reigning worldview of the West by delving into what has gone wrong with Western culture in its refusal to come to terms with the powers. Christians in other parts of the world have not had these same hang-ups with the biblical testimony concerning the fact of the powers. One is reminded of an experience Lesslie Newbigin reports from the mid-1930s: "I recall my experience as a young missionary, struggling with the language, called upon to conduct the study of St. Mark's Gospel with a group of [Indian] village teachers. Before long I was deeply involved with the miracle stories, trying to put into Tamil the way of making sense of these which I had learned in an English theological college. My class watched me with visibly growing impatience until one of them said: 'Why are you making such heavy weather over a perfectly simple matter?' and proceeded to recount half a dozen examples of miraculous healings and exorcisms from the recent experience of his own village congregation" (Newbigin, 1978:99).

15. G. B. Caird (1956: chaps. 1—2) shows how the Jewish law and the state, both instituted by God, nonetheless became demonic. Note especially the conclusion (pp. 51ff.).

16. Karl Barth (1981: Part 78) includes in his exposition of the Lord's Prayer the ways the powers of Leviathan and Mammon gain control over people. Barth discusses these "lordless powers" in terms of such forces as technology, fashion, and sports which

exert so much influence over our lives. How can it be, he asks, that these things become *powerful?* It is obvious that this is possible because humans willingly cede power to them.

17. For a vivid illustration of Berkhof's point about the loss of a center, see Reginald W. Bibby (1987). For a probing of American cultural dynamics under the impact of modernity, see Robert Bellah, et al. (1985).

18. The history of the Jewish people over several millenia is relevant to this theme. Only since 1948 have Jews again had a "homeland" they could claim as their own. Jewish scholars have argued that Diaspora is necessary to Jewish identity. In those instances where Jews have become secular and assimilated into the mainstream of society, they have lost their identity. At critical points the Jewish experience poses important questions concerning the relationship between the community of faith and the larger environment. From the beginning of Abraham's sojourning, the point was that he and his descendents would be of value to the world only by being faithful to God. Assimilation always spelled the end to this faithfulness.

19. The usual interpretation of the epistle to the Hebrews is that it offers a theology of "pilgrimage." George Marchant terms much of this discussion a "muddle" and concludes "that Hebrews stands with the rest of the New Testament writers in depicting the present state of the Church and its individual Christian members by the model of the 'resident alien' " (1990:135).

20. See John H. Elliott (1981) for an elaborate development of the theme based on 1 Peter. He argues "that the fundamental contrast in 1 Peter is not a cosmological but a sociological one: the Christian community set apart from and in tension with its social neighbors" (p. 43), a line that counters much of the older interpretation of 1 Peter. Although Christopher Rowland (1985) cites Elliott's work, he adheres to the conventional line in his final chapter, "Coming to Terms with the Old Age," thereby emphasizing the temporizing and accommodationist moves in the early church—which Rowland suggests are necessary to being church rather than a messianic movement. An interesting counterpoint is "The Epistle to Diognetus" of the second or third century (Bettenson, 1956:73-79).

References Cited

Barrett, David B.
1985- Annual statistical table on Global Mission in the January issue of *International Bulletin of Missionary Research*.

Barth, Karl
1981 *The Christian Life: Church Dogmatics*, IV:4. Geoffrey W. Bromiley, trans.; Grand Rapids, Mich.: Eerdmans.

Bellah, Robert, et al.
1985 *Habits of the Heart: Individualism and Commitment in American Life*. Berkeley, Calif.: University of California Press.

Berkhof, Hendrikus
1966 *Christ, the Meaning of History*. London: SCM Press.
1977 *Christ and the Powers*. John H. Yoder, trans.; Scottdale, Pa.: Herald Press.
1979 *Christian Faith: An Introduction to the Study of the Faith*. Sierd Woudstra, trans.; Grand Rapids, Mich.: Eerdmans.

Bettenson, Henry, ed. and trans.
1956 "The Epistle to Diognetus," *The Early Christian Fathers: A Selection from the Writings of the Fathers from St. Clement of Rome to St. Athanasius*. London: Oxford University Press.

Bibby, Reginald W.
   1987   *Fragmented Gods: The Poverty and Potential of Religion in Canada.* Toronto: Irwin Publishing.
Brunner, Emil
   1949   *Christianity and Civilisation.* London: Nisbet and Co.
Caird, G. B.
   1956   "The Great Accuser," *Principalities and Powers: A Study in Pauline Theology.* Oxford: Clarendon Press.
Driver, John
   1983   "Mission: Salt, Light and Covenant Law," *Mission Focus* 11:3 (September).
Elliott, John H.
   1981   *A Home for the Homeless: A Sociological Exegesis of 1 Peter, Its Situation and Strategy.* London: SCM Press.
Gaster, T. H.
   1962   "Satan," *The Interpreter's Dictionary of the Bible,* vol. 4. George A. Buttrick, ed.; Nashville, Tenn.: Abingdon Press.
Heffly, James, and Marti Heffly
   1979   *By Their Blood: Christian Martyrs of the Twentieth Century.* Milford, Mich.: Mott Media.
Kasdorf, Hans
   1980   *Christian Conversion in Context.* Scottdale, Pa.: Herald Press.
Kirk, Andrew
   1990   "Theology for the Sake of Mission," *Anvil* 7:1.
Kraft, Charles H.
   1979   *Christianity in Culture: A Study in Dynamic Biblical Theologizing in Cross-cultural Perspective.* Maryknoll, N.Y.: Orbis Books.
Kroeber, Alfred L., and Clyde Kluckhohn
   1952   *Culture: A Critical Review of Concepts and Definitions.* New York: Vintage Books.
Kreider, Alan
   1987   *Journey Towards Holiness: A Way of Living for God's Nation.* Scottdale, Pa.: Herald Press.
Marchant, George
   1990   "Imagine the Church. . . ," *Anvil* 7:2.
Minear, Paul
   1960   *Images of the Church in the New Testament.* Philadelphia: Westminster Press.
Newbigin, Lesslie
   1978   "Christ and Cultures," *Scottish Journal of Theology* 31.
Niebuhr, H. Richard
   1951   *Christ and Culture.* New York: Harper & Row.
Rowland, Christopher
   1985   *Christian Origins—From Messianic Movement to Christian Religion.* Minneapolis: Augsburg.

Scriven, Charles
1988 *The Transformation of Culture: Christian Social Ethics after H. Richard Niebuhr.* Scottdale, Pa.: Herald Press.

Shank, David A.
1980 "Towards an Understanding of Christian Conversion," *Mission Focus: Current Issues.* Wilbert R. Shenk, ed.; Scottdale, Pa.: Herald Press.

Spindler, Marc
1967 *La Mission, combat pour le salut du mond.* Neuchatel, Switzerland: Delachaux et Niestle.

Taber, Charles R.
1991 *The World Is Too Much With Us: "Culture" in Modern Protestant Missions.* Macon, Ga.: Mercer University Press.

Williams, J. R.
1984 "Holiness," *Evangelical Dictionary of Theology.* Walter A. Elwell, ed.; Grand Rapids, Mich.: Baker Book House.

Wink, Walter
1978 *Naming the Powers: The Language of Power in the New Testament,* vol. 1. Basingstoke, Hants: Marshall Morgan and Scott.

CHAPTER 7

Messianic Mission and Ethics: Discipleship and the Good News

Neal Blough

EVER SINCE PAUL'S EPISTLES and the period of the New Testament, Christians have had to struggle with the relationship between faith and works, between justification and sanctification, between what one believes and what one does, between what God has accomplished once and for all in Christ and how Christians respond to that gracious act. In reaction to what was perceived as "works righteousness" in the Roman church, Martin Luther and the sixteenth-century Protestant Reformation demonstrated the continuing importance of that same question and formulated theological categories that continue to shape contemporary discussions on the subject.

At the same time, for sixteenth-century Protestants, this theological discussion was not directly related to mission. In the minds of Zwingli, Luther, and Calvin, European Christendom needed to be "reformed," but not "evangelized." Mission consciousness came later to Protestants and Evangelicals, and when that time came, mission was done in the Reformation heritage of *sola gratia* and *sola fide*. Mission and evangelization have essentially been understood to be a matter of "preaching the gospel."

Nevertheless, the basic question has not gone away. Presently there is much discussion about the relationship between word and deed, proclamation and presence, evangelism and sociopolitical involvement. The relationship between mission and ethics is an important question, but one that is most often dealt with on a pragmatic and strategic level rather than as a theological issue in and of its own right. My own experience has seen "liberal" Protestants, who place a great deal of emphasis on sociopolitical involvement (i.e., social ethics) as a part of missionary presence, characterize "conservative" evangelical concern for conversion and personal ethics as "synergistic" and a form of works-righteousness. On the other hand, the same evangelicals, who would probably reject a "theology of presence" as a basis for mission, sometimes have trouble understanding how their own "mission presence" closely tied with Western power and money ends up "proclaiming" a very different message than the gospel of Jesus Christ.

The basic thesis of this chapter is that ethics, or more precisely, discipleship (following Christ together in the power of the Spirit), should be considered integral part of the church's missionary relationship to the world. We contend that a messianic ethic of discipleship can provide a holistic framework which avoids many of the false dichotomies that have been set up in relation to word and deed. We hope this treatment can help bridge the gap between faith and works, proclamation and presence, personal ethics and social ethics.

It will soon become clear that our consideration of ethics is directly related to the other themes of this book. Ethics cannot be separated from the incarnation, God's sending of the Messiah. Its content is the kingdom reality manifested in Jesus. Neither can it be conceived of without the formation of the new covenant community, the body of Christ, which in turn is sent into the world as was the Messiah. And the very source of empowerment for following Christ depends on the sending of the Spirit by the Father and the Son. As we will attempt to show, a messianic mission ethic is fundamentally a trinitarian ethic.

The incarnational and trinitarian foundation for what we are trying to say is not first of all immediate in a simple (but, we hope, not simplistic) reading of the New Testament. These writings nevertheless show a direct relationship between the way disciples live and how the good news is made known to the world. Here are several examples:

1. The kingdom-living described in the Beatitudes is characterized as salt and light. This light (the lives of Messiah's disciples) is to shine forth so that people may "praise your Father in heaven" (Matt. 5:14-16).[1] Living as Jesus taught can lead people to see God.

2. The new commandment to love each other in John 13:34-35 has a missionary goal so that all "will know that you are my disciples."

Christians are known in the world by the way they love. This is even more clearly spelled out in John 17:23 where the unity of the disciples (their common life) is to "let the world know that you [God] sent me [Messiah]."

3. The book of Acts depicts the quality of community life as having missionary impact. "All the believers were together and had everything in common" (Acts 2:44). Jubilee living was part and parcel of the Jerusalem community's being. "And the Lord added to their number daily those who were being saved" (2:47).

4. Peter also talks about a way of life that witnesses to the reality of God in the world: "Live such good lives among the pagans that . . . they may see your good deeds and glorify God on the day he visits us" (1 Pet. 2:12).

If, as the main thesis of this book claims, the basic stance of disciples in the world is that of "missionary confrontation," this stance could be described ethically as living as Jesus lived, "because in this world we are like him" (1 John 4:17).

Mission can and should be seen as a continuation of that which God began in the incarnation. Disciples are sent as Jesus was sent. In the power of the Spirit and the context of the new community of the church, they are sent into the world to follow the Messiah in the way of the cross. As Jesus' mission included the preaching of good news to the poor, proclamation of freedom for prisoners, recovery of sight for the blind, and release for the prisoners (Luke 4:18), so will the mission of the disciples. As Messiah's mission consisted in following the way of the cross, so will the mission of the disciples (Mark 8:34). The Gospel of John presents Jesus as being sent into the world because of God's love for the world (John 3:16). This same notion of "being sent" characterizes all of Christian life and gives discipleship a fundamentally missionary basis and motivation (20:21).

This intuitive biblical approach needs further spelling out and development, and there are many valid ways to approach the question. Beginning with these New Testament examples, one could continue to develop a purely biblical and exegetical point of view. One could also engage in dialogue with current missiological literature dealing with the relationship between evangelism and social involvement, attempting to run the entire gamut from the church growth school all the way to liberation theology, lifting out the ethical and theological presuppositions of the various understandings. While both of these options would be helpful, the approach chosen here is somewhat different, being at the same time both historical and theological.

Ethics as Central to Anabaptist Theology

In order to elucidate the biblical foundation for the relationship between the way disciples live and their mission in the world, a sixteenth-century case study will be presented to develop a theological framework which is at the same time incarnational (that is, based on Messiah's life, death, and resurrection), trinitarian, ecclesiological, and missionary.

The case study comes from the life and writings of Pilgram Marpeck, an important sixteenth-century Anabaptist thinker. This example has been chosen for several reasons, one of the most important being that it is already an example of dialogue between several theological traditions. If this choice is seen only as a Mennonite referring to Anabaptist history to reinforce his own theological tradition (although there is probably some of that motivation present), the point will have been missed. Choosing Marpeck is a conscious way of trying to inject new elements into Mennonite theology and missiology as well as an attempt to be in dialogue with the larger Christian church on this important issue.

It is clear that ethics has always been an important part of Anabaptist theology, whether it be during the sixteenth century, in the following centuries of Mennonite experience, or with the recovery of the Anabaptist Vision which has taken place in the twentieth century.[2] Anabaptist ethics are usually qualified as a discipleship ethic: the teachings and the example of Jesus of Nazareth are taken to be normative in all settings. This is perhaps best exemplified in the Mennonite understanding of nonviolence and nonresistance. J. Denny Weaver's recent book, *Becoming Anabaptist* (1987), attempts to demonstrate the contemporary theological relevance of sixteenth-century Anabaptism. For Weaver, the present-day implications of sixteenth-century Anabaptism all have ethical overtones: community, discipleship, peace, and separation (1987:129-141).

Perhaps some will see the attempt to integrate discipleship ethics with mission as doomed to failure from the outset. After all, Anabaptism is typically seen to represent what H. Richard Niebuhr described as the "Christ against Culture" attitude (Niebuhr, 1951). According to this point of view, a strong discipleship ethic based on the Sermon on the Mount is exactly what pulls Anabaptists out of the world, rather than sending them into the world. Discipleship leads to separation and not to a missionary stance or positive and "responsible" participation in the world.

A detailed response to such a question is beyond the scope of this chapter.[3] Nevertheless, the relationship between "ethics" and "separation" from the world is a crucial issue that needs to be addressed. Is the only option for those who hold to an exclusively Christ-centered discipleship ethic to become separate and "sectarian"? It is exactly at this point that Marpeck's experience and thinking are useful.

Having said something about Anabaptism and ethics, what about mission? Contemporary research has shown that at its beginnings, sixteenth-century Anabaptism was marked by a strong mission consciousness (Schäufele, 1966) and by a strong mission impulse (Gingerich, 1980). But there was not necessarily an explicit theology or understanding of mission.

Wilbert Shenk notes the major shift from a strong Anabaptist missionary consciousness to the Mennonite experience of withdrawal from society (Shenk, 1989:4). This shift actually occurred early in the history of Anabaptism. A lot of the dynamism of the 1520s and 1530s lasted only that long. By the 1540s the Swiss Brethren were largely sectarian and legalistic, the Dutch Mennonites were going the same route, and even the mission-minded Hutterite communities were rather authoritarian.

Nevertheless, ethics remained a part of Anabaptist self-understanding at this point. *Nachfolge Christi* was still important, but it became an ethic of separation rather than an ethic of being sent into the world. Following Jesus meant leaving the world, not going into it.

The fourth article of the Schleitheim Confession (1527), a foundational document for sixteenth-century Swiss Anabaptist self-understanding, is illustrative of how much and how early the idea of being separate became part and parcel of Anabaptist self-understanding.[4] Those of us who live in the comfort of twentieth-century Western religious pluralism should not be overly critical, as Schleitheim was an understandable reaction to a context of severe persecution and rejection. The fourth article of this confession is in many ways a theological justification of the movement's social and political situation in 1527, that is, a situation of withdrawal.

> We have been united concerning the separation that shall take place from the evil and the wickedness which the devil has planted in the world, simply in this; that we have no fellowship with them. . . .
>
> [T]here is nothing else in the world and all creation than good or evil, believing and unbelieving, darkness and light, the world and those who are [come] out of the world. . . .
>
> From all this we shall be separated and have no part with such, for they are nothing but abominations (Yoder, 1973:37-38).

At a very early point in the movement's history, most Anabaptist leaders and theologians were either dead or on the run. Merely to survive, the movement had to go the "sectarian" route. This means that there are few sixteenth-century writings that are helpful in terms of thinking about the relation between mission and ethics.

One could possibly cite the Hutterites as an exception.[5] This group did have a strong missionary practice and theory. But they too were marked by the separation (*Absonderung*) motif. Mission meant asking people to leave their homes and to come to Moravia. The Hutterites lived in closed communities that had little to do with the surrounding culture. And as time went on, the Hutterites also became an ethnic, ingrown, and separate church with little consciousness of being sent into the world.

Pilgram Marpeck on Mission and Ethics: Incarnation, Body of Christ, Holy Spirit

As noted above, the concern for ethics remained strong in sixteenth-century Anabaptism, but increasingly it became an ethic of separation, of leaving Babylon. There is nevertheless at least one sixteenth-century Anabaptist theologian whose writings and theology are useful in thinking about the relationship between mission and ethics: Pilgram Marpeck.[6] Born around 1495, son of the the city's mayor, himself a city council member, engineer and civil servant by trade, Marpeck was not a university-trained theologian. He came to the Anabaptist movement in his home city of Rattenberg in the Austrian Tyrol around 1527-28. His refusal to denounce Anabaptist-minded employees under his direction cost him an important job and led to his expulsion from Rattenberg.

Marpeck found himself in Strasbourg between 1528-32 where he became an Anabaptist leader and municipal employee. Once again expelled for his theological convictions, Marpeck spent a dozen years more or less hidden from public view, traveling from place to place and contacting various Anabaptist groups. He finished his life in Augsburg (1544-56) where again he was leader of an Anabaptist community and a city employee. He left a literary legacy larger and theologically more sophisticated than that of Menno Simons. His writing was done basically in dialogue with other positions, be it against Caspar Schwenckfeld and other Spiritualists, the Strasbourg reformer Martin Bucer, or even other Anabaptists.

What is of special interest for us here is that Marpeck's writings develop an incarnational and trinitarian theology in which ethics are conceived as being integrally related to the church's presence and mission in the world while at the same time dealing head-on with the questions of separation and legalism that became so much a part of the Anabaptist-Mennonite experience.

Although some historians would disagree, it is possible to see Pilgram Marpeck as a legitimate theological heir to the early Swiss Brethren movement.[7] His theology, which is less "separatist," does not have to be considered atypical of sixteenth-century Anabaptism. Contrary to the experience of many other Anabaptist theologians, Marpeck had the time, the experience, and the intellectual ability to develop some of the early intuitions and impulses that almost disappeared with the death of the first-generation leaders.[8]

Based on the example of Pilgram Marpeck's experience and writings, the relationship between mission and ethics will be developed in three ways: (1) the sacramental and missionary foundation for ethics: the incarnation; (2) the communitarian nature of ethics: the body of Christ; and (3) the source of ethics: the Holy Spirit. We hope the contemporary relevance of this largely unknown sixteenth-century theologian will become obvious as we proceed.

The Sacramental and Missionary Foundation for Ethics: the Incarnation

The fundamental starting point and center of Marpeck's thinking can be found in the concept of the humanity of Christ. To avoid any ambiguity, it should be said that "humanity" of Christ refers to the incarnation, the Word become flesh, and not only to the human nature of Jesus.

How this notion of the humanity of Christ best relates to mission and ethics can be illustrated from Marpeck's experience with Spiritualist theologians while he was in Strasbourg (1528-32). At that time, alongside Bucer's and Capito's Reformation, there were several Anabaptist communities in the city. Marpeck, along with Wilhelm Reublin, one of the first and foremost Anabaptists in Zürich, was the leader of one of them. Because of its more tolerant stance toward religious dissidents, Strasbourg was also a haven for many Spiritualist thinkers, and their theology was becoming a tempting alternative to many Anabaptists. People such as Hans Bunderlin and Christian Entfelder were writing books and having them read and discussed in Anabaptist circles.

Spiritualism was one of the forms that Radical Reformation thinking took. For many historians, Spiritualist theologians such as Caspar Schwenckfeld can be seen as forerunners of Pietism, a movement which surfaced later in European church history. And since Pietism was and is an important source for the later evangelical and revival movements of the nineteenth and twentieth centuries, the dialogue between Marpeck and the Strasbourg Spiritualists on issues such as ethics is not without relevance for us today.

The Spiritualist position can be summarized rather easily in the following way: true Christianity is an inner and spiritual matter. Faith does not have to do primarily with visible or outward things. It is important to remember that at that time there was some rather serious squabbling going on about outward things such as baptism, the Lord's Supper (Luther versus Zwingli), church authority, ethics (nonviolence and separation). The Spiritualists were people who cared deeply about the church and were profoundly disappointed with fighting over "outward things." Thus, they began to say that true baptism is spiritual baptism, the true eucharist is spiritual, true authority comes from an inner call and not from official ordination, and church discipline is not important since the true church is invisible.

In the debate between Marpeck and the Spiritualists, these outward things were called "ceremonies." For many persecuted and harassed Anabaptists, it was tempting to be able to think that true baptism was "inner" and "spiritual." Is it really worth losing one's life over water?

This has much more relevance for ethics than it might appear, for it is in this context that Marpeck borrowed from Luther and then "Anabaptized" his borrowings.[9] In response to earlier Spiritualists such as Karlstadt, Müntzer, and Zwingli, Luther used traditional medieval sacramental logic to justify the use of outward ceremonies.

This logic was based on the incarnation and can be summarized as follows: since human beings are made of flesh and blood, since they have a visible, outward, and material side to them, God uses visible and outward things to make himself known. In Christ, God became visible and outward so that we may have access to spiritual and invisible reality. For Luther, the outer preceeds the inner: humans can know God and spiritual reality only through outward things such as preaching and the sacraments (justification by faith, *fides ex auditu*).

For Luther (and for Marpeck), these visible manifestations of the Christian faith were called the "humanity of Christ." In its outer life, the church extends and prolongs the incarnation. That which God began in Christ continues in time, space, and matter.

This was the logic that led Luther to an understanding of the "real presence," the corporal presence of Christ in the Lord's Supper. Jesus is really present in the bread because God continues to work and to offer grace materially as in the incarnation. For Luther, there where God reveals himself is the "humanity of Christ," the prolongation of the incarnation.

The context in Strasbourg of the debate between Marpeck and the Spiritualists was somewhat different from the Luther/Karlstadt-Müntzer confrontation. Nevertheless, as did Luther before him, using the logic of the incarnation, Marpeck argued against those who claimed that the outer manifestations of Christianity were of no intrinsic value, that true faith was inner and spiritual.

It is important to note here that Marpeck was developing a rationale for a discipleship ethic that went beyond a strict biblicist approach. Much of sixteenth-century Anabaptist theology consisted of citing biblical texts: the church baptizes with water because of Mark 16; Christians celebrate the Lord's Supper because of 1 Corinthians 11; enemies are to be loved because of Matthew 5.

Already in 1529-30 the Spiritualists were accusing the Anabaptists of having a merely literal or outward (and therefore legalistic) foundation for Christian life: "it is written." This is of course also what Luther and most of Protestantism have said against Anabaptism ever since the sixteenth century.

In such a context Marpeck could not just say, "This is what the Bible says." His approach was more "theological," using biblical texts, of course, but also drawing out the implications of the doctrines of the incarnation and the Trinity. As was already stated, for the Spiritualists, knowledge of God and salvation were inner matters, outward things having no intrinsic value. Marpeck himself summarized their thinking as follows: "Moreover, they say that at present, no longer does anyone have the power to employ the ceremonies of Christ, such as baptism, the Lord's Supper, teaching, the ban, and the laying on of hands, and that those who do employ these ceremonies do so apart from God's command" (Marpeck, 1531:71).

Marpeck was quite willing to concede that knowledge of God is spiritual. Instead, he asked a different question: How does one know that which is spiritual? The Spiritualists separated the inner and the outer, the spiritual and the material. Pilgram Marpeck's response, following Luther, was to bring them together, as God did in the incarnation. This is where the concept of the humanity of Christ fits in. Because God became flesh in Christ, he used and continues to use outward and material things to make himself known.

Just as Jesus revealed the true nature of God, so the ceremonies prolong this revelation. Marpeck saw them as the means that God continues to use in a material world (Marpeck, 1531).

> The Scriptures are also a witness to the true teaching of the humanity of Christ and the teaching of the apostles; *through Christ's humanity, the inward must be revealed and recognized* (p. 76; italics mine).
>
> This breath or Spirit of God would have remained an eternal secret without the humanity and the physical voice of Christ (p. 76).
>
> The secrets of God lie hidden under the outward speech, words, deeds, and ceremonies of the humanity of Christ (pp. 81-82).

This means quite simply that God continues to make himself known, that God is present in these outward things, through the ceremonies. Marpeck calls these ceremonies or outward manifestations the "humanity of Christ." We are thus in the presence of an incarnational and even sacramental logic. God is revealed and present in visible acts, gestures, and symbols just as in the incarnation. Through the words, acts, and life of Christians, Christ is "really" present.

For Marpeck, this sacramental logic was integrally related to the Anabaptist discipleship ethic. When Luther used this kind of reasoning, he was arguing against people such as Karlstadt and Zwingli, who rejected the bodily presence of Christ in the eucharist, or against Müntzer, who gave priority to the inner Word over against the outer Word. Marpeck used this same concept of the humanity of Christ when talking about the ceremonies but extended its meaning beyond a Lutheran understanding, where God was primarily present in the preached word and in the sacraments of baptism and the eucharist.

Marpeck extended the definition and scope of the ceremonies. For him, a ceremony was not only baptism or the Lord's Supper but rather anything that Jesus or the New Testament apostles taught. All of Christ's teachings become ceremonies. The New Testament texts on baptism or the Lord's Supper have no intrinsic superiority over other teachings. This clearly means that all of Christian outward life takes on a sacramental character. Preaching, baptism, and the Lord's Supper can be considered as the humanity of Christ, but so can church discipline, teaching, loving one's neighbor, and loving one's enemy. In other words, following Christ becomes a sacrament; it extends or prolongs God's presence; the incarnation goes on in time and space. Real presence happens not just in certain rituals or sacraments but in the daily life of discipleship, in being faithful to New Testament teaching.

As is the case with Luther, the biblical basis for Marpeck's thinking is found primarily in the Gospel of John: "The Word became flesh and dwelt among us" (1:14, RSV). "For God so loved the world, that he gave his one and only Son" (3:16). "Anyone who has seen me has seen the Father" (14:9).

This language is sacramental (God's presence in a physical way). That which began in the incarnation continues in the lives of the disciples. But it is also missionary language because of the use of the verb "to send" in John's Gospel: "whoever accepts anyone I *send* accepts me; and whoever accepts me accepts the one who *sent* me" (13:20; italics mine). "As the Father has *sent* me, so, I am *sending* you" (20:21; italics mine).

Marpeck's incarnational theology makes no sense without the notion of "sentness." In the incarnation Jesus is sent into the world. Now it is the disciples who are sent, sent to live as Jesus lived—"As the Father sent me, *so* I am sending you" (John 20:21; italics mine). Incarnation and following Christ are closely related. Living as Jesus taught and lived is part of what it means to be sent into the world; it is an integral part of mission. The model of this mission is what God himself did in the sending of the Messiah. Now the Messiah sends his followers in the same way—to go into the world, to be salt and light—in order that the good news be proclaimed. Being sent means being obedient, just as Jesus was obedient: "If you obey my commands, you will remain in my love, just as I have obeyed my Father's commands and remain in his love" (John 15:10).

The Communitarian Nature of Ethics: the Body of Christ

If Marpeck's "sacramental/incarnational" logic comes from the Gospel of John, it also draws heavily on the Pauline concept of the "body of Christ." The humanity of Christ becomes the body of Christ, the church, the place where Christ is present, the place, the space for discipleship.

There is an interesting point to be made here. If the ceremonies—anything Jesus or the apostles commanded—are equated with the humanity of Christ, it becomes necessary also to claim that the very lives of those who practice these ceremonies also become Christ's humanity or the body of Christ. The words, actions, and life of the body of Christ keep God's action visible in the world. The humanity of Christ is the binding and loosing community which corporately follows the head. This corporate following is sacramental (mediating God's presence) and missionary (because the disciples are sent as was the Son). A few quotes from Marpeck (1531) illustrate this point:

> Therefore, even today the physical Christ serves us in His members (p. 84).
>
> Oh, it annoys the fleshly to the highest degree that the Son of Man, in a physical way, should act and walk upon earth by means of His members (1 Cor. 6:9-20; Acts 13:2-47; 1 Cor. 12:4-31; Eph. 4:3-16, His body (Eph. 5:30), His flesh and bone. It annoys them that those who are regarded by the world as humble, insignificant, simple, and foolish (1 Cor. 1:18-25), who preach the crucified Christ and follow Him in the cross should have the keys to the kingdom of heaven, to bind and to loose, to forgive and to retain sin upon earth (p. 81).
>
> When speaking of the church, Marpeck wrote that these "despised people . . . embody the physical Christ or the humanity of Christ" (p. 81).

Following Christ is a ceremony, a visible and outward way of making God's presence known. However, by associating the humanity of Christ (prolongation of the incarnation) with the body of Christ (church), Marpeck makes another important point. This means that discipleship is essentially communitarian; it is in the body of Christ that Christ's humanity most fully expresses itself, not in the life of the individual disciple.[10]

> In these united members, God is all in all (1 Cor. 15:28). For God the Father is not completely in any one member of Christ's body (which body endures until the end of the world) or in the single member alone; rather, He is all in all when the members are knit together under the Head and united through his Spirit, which compensates for all failure and deficiency in them. If the foot does not have an eye, in this union it receives an eye, just as the eye receives a foot, hand, ears, and all corporal members (Marpeck, 1531:74).

Saying that the body of Christ is sent into the world to follow Jesus corporately gives Marpeck's theology an ethical bent not present in Luther. The body of Christ sent into the world needs to look like Jesus, that is, to take the same outward, visible, and material form. In other words, the church, the community that lives like Jesus, is God's missionary presence in the world.

To illustrate this better, another writing from later in the career of Marpeck can be cited. In the 1540s Marpeck engaged in a rather long and verbose debate with the Silesian Spiritualist Caspar Schwenck-feld. The focal point of their debate was Christology, but of course ecclesiology and ethics were also directly involved. Schwenckfeld's theology was one of following Christ, just as Marpeck's, but it is clear that theirs were two rather different Christologies.

Schwenckfeld had developed a theory claiming that Jesus' flesh was not of human but rather of heavenly origin. This "celestial flesh" was not tainted by the sin of Adam. In such a perspective, the incarnation took place so that humanity could also take on this sinless new flesh. Salvation meant that human flesh was to be transformed into celestial flesh, and for this reason the eucharist, feeding on the flesh of Christ, was very important. But, according to Schwenckfeld, what happened to Jesus was that because of his "celestial flesh" he became more and more "spiritual."

Therefore, following Jesus means becoming more spiritual and less material, less "visible." Salvation means leaving the human material condition. In following Jesus, one becomes more and more like the glorified (invisible and spiritual) Christ seated at the right hand of the Father. Salvation and ethics, in this perspective, lead us away from the world into the spiritual and the invisible.

This was, of course, totally unacceptable for Marpeck. The task of the disciples on earth is not to follow the "glorified" invisible Jesus, that is, ascend into the spiritual realm; their task is to be the "unglorified body of Christ," the church.

Yes, Jesus has ascended into heaven. But as long as he has not returned, he works on earth through what Marpeck called the "unglorified body." Christ the Lord reigns today through this unglorified body. And how does this "unglorified body" operate?

> Through every commandment, word, and teaching concerning outward acts for the common good—teaching, baptism, Lord's Supper, exhortation, excommunication, discipline, love, laying on of hands, betterment. The glorified or reigning Christ acts in and through these means through the Holy Spirit which proceeds from him and the Father.[11]

God continues to act on earth through this body of Christ, and this body can only look like Jesus of Nazareth.

> When Paul exhorts us to be of the same mind as Christ, he is not talking about Christ as he is now (that is in heavenly glory) but about Christ as he was on earth . . . . He first humbled himself and only afterward did

God raise him to the heights (Phil. 2) (Loserth, 1929:156; my translation).

"To look like Jesus" has a specific significance: it is the self-giving, self-abandoning death of Jesus on the cross that exemplifies discipleship for Marpeck. We are to "take up the cross of Christ himself and follow him according to the example that he gave in his self-abandonment ("Gelassenheit") unto death" (Loserth, 1929:154; my translation).

Salvation is not a matter of fleeing the body or the world. In the incarnation God loved the world, came into the world, was involved in the world. Through the presence of the body of Christ sent into the world, God continues to be involved in the creation. This body takes the same path the Messiah took, and if necessary, it is willing to die at the hands of a hostile world to fulfill God's plan.

The Source of Ethics: the Holy Spirit

The central point of this third section can be summarized as follows: the church's conformity to the example of Christ's self-giving love is possible only through the presence and the work of the Holy Spirit. Ethics and spirituality are integrally related.

This point is also related to one of the weaknesses of Anabaptist ethics. In the minds of the sixteenth-century Reformers and Spiritualists, the Anabaptist emphasis on following Jesus was seen as legalism, as a return to the works-righteousness that the Reformation wanted to leave behind. Although these criticisms were not always entirely justified, there is a certain truth in them. Anabaptist communities were certainly prone to legalism, and that has also been one of the main problems of their Mennonite descendants. But the danger of legalism is no reason to jettison the discipleship ethic.

Marpeck was aware of these criticisms and took them seriously when formulating his theology. One could claim that the humanity of Christ is the central category of Marpeck's thinking. It could be equally claimed that his theology is one of the Holy Spirit. This will be illustrated in three ways: the difference between the Old and the New Testaments, sanctification, and the Spirit's transformation of the body of Christ into the image of Jesus.

The Old and the New Testaments. In the introduction to *The Priestly Kingdom*, John H. Yoder speaks of the marks of the Anabaptist or believers church heritage. One of these marks is an insistence that the historical-political humanity of Jesus is compatible with the classic confession of the true humanity of Christ (Yoder, 1984:9). That is exactly what we have been talking about up until this point: "the political pertinence of the humanity of Jesus." Another mark, according to Yoder, is that the believers church heritage sees movement within the canonical story and therefore a difference between the Testaments (1984:9). This is also true for Marpeck's theology and helps us to clarify what we are saying about the Holy Spirit and ethics.

In this theology the difference between the Testaments has its origin in the incarnation and the ensuing sending of the Spirit by the Father and the Son. The trinitarian basis becomes clearer at this point. Against sixteenth-century Anabaptists, the Reformed theology of Zwingli and Martin Bucer posited a unity between the Testaments. This allowed them to justify infant baptism and Christian participation in state-sponsored acts of violence. In such a perspective, infant baptism was compared to circumcision, and since King David was essentially a good Christian, European (Christian) princes needed not to worry about theological objections to waging war or applying the death penalty to heretics.

Marpeck's answer (first written in a confession of faith presented to Martin Bucer at Strasbourg) was that the incarnation (humanity of Christ) brought about a new reality, a new Spirit, and the possibility of a new Christocentric ethic in history. What was promised to the patriarchs is now accomplished in Christ. What was not possible before (accomplishing God's law) is now possible through faith and the reception of the new Holy Spirit. An important part of Christ's work is the sending of the Spirit, which brings this newness into time and space.

Sanctification. This newness is related both to the incarnation and the Spirit. What is special about Christ's humanity is not only the fact that he was human, but that in this human body God was fully present. This divine presence allowed Jesus to be fully obedient unto death. Marpeck wanted to take seriously the Reformation doctrine of justification by faith. His insistence on the two natures of Christ avoids a purely adoptionist Christology and being overly optimistic about human capacity to be good in and of its own nature.

But there is still an important difference with the Lutheran understanding of justification by faith. Because of his (over)reaction to Roman works-righteousness, Luther's theology separates justification and sanctification. Faith saves, but it doesn't sanctify. Works should follow, but they are not intrinsically related to justification.

As did all sixteenth-century Anabaptists, Marpeck reacted to the Lutheran formulation of justification by insisting that faith saves and sanctifies. It is one and the same movement, not two unrelated processes.

The Holy Spirit is integrally related to and involved in this process. The believer, through faith, receives the Spirit, and the Spirit transforms the person, giving power to live a new life. The person who believes is justified but is also made or rendered obedient.

Justification by faith means receiving the transforming Spirit into one's life. Ethics (new life) is the result of the Spirit's presence. John's Gospel also helps us see the relationship between ethics and divine indwelling: "If anyone loves me, he will obey my teaching. My Father will love him, and we will come to him and make our home with him" (John 14:23).

The body of Christ transformed into the image of Jesus. Marpeck took seriously the credal affirmation that the Spirit proceeds from the Father and the Son. For him this meant that the Spirit works to transform the body of Christ into the image of Christ.

> For God knows his own before ever they were, and also ordained that they should be shaped to the likeness of his Son (Rom. 8:29).
> The Holy Spirit proceeds from the Father and Son, and He witnesses to the Father and Son in the hearts of all the faithful; He copies and repeats the perfect law of the liberty of Christ. The faithful look into this law of liberty in order that they may fervently do what Christ spoke and commanded (Marpeck, 1547:458).

Two things are important here. First, the Spirit teaches only what Christ taught. There is complete conformity (the Spirit proceeds from the Father but also from the Son). In other words, human actions having their origin in the Spirit will not contradict the way God acted in Christ. "Only what Christ Himself has said and taught, and no other word, does the Spirit of wisdom bring to remembrance in His own" (Marpeck, 1547:451).

The body of Christ takes the same form as Jesus, this form being characerized always as self-renunciation, refusal to dominate, and the way of the cross (nonviolence). "Whoever does not grasp that he must be condemned with and in Christ in the depths can never understand nor achieve the height of Christ" (Marpeck, 1547:434).

Second, this Christ-like behavior (ethics) is a result of the Spirit's transforming work. It is not from the disciple's own capacities, nor is it a form of works-righteousness. Marpeck's concern for justification and the dangers of legalism are found in his doctrine of the Holy Spirit. "Without this copier of the law of Christ, I mean the Holy Spirit, the apostles could neither understand nor bear the teaching of their Master" (Marpeck, 1547:459).

The emphasis on the Holy Spirit also guards Marpeck's theology from a kind of "automaticity" that lurks in certain sacramental theologies. Because of Luther's influence on Marpeck, his thinking has a sacramental character that is not found in other sixteenth-century Anabaptists theologies. The church, the body of Christ, prolongs the incarnation; it is God's presence in the world. This sacramental overtone comes close, in some ways, to Roman Catholic theology, which especially since Vatican II speaks of the church as a sacrament for the world. But of what church are we speaking?

Yes, the church, body of Christ, is a "sacrament"; it is where God is present in the world.[12] But Marpeck's is a different understanding of the church. It is not the church conceived of as an institution whose ritual actions automatically channel God's grace and presence. God's action in the world cannot be controlled or manipulated. Only the church which looks like Jesus is the prolongation of the incarnation. Only the church which is transformed by the Holy Spirit can look like Jesus.

There is a kind of dialectical relationship between inner and outer, spiritual and material, church and Holy Spirit. The church mediates God's presence, but just going through the motions doesn't means that the Spirit is present. Only if the body looks like the Messiah can we say that the Spirit is there.

Marpeck fought against two positions. First of all, the Spiritualists claimed that faith was an essentially inward matter. The outer doesn't matter. But this position allows for many deviations. The incarnation means that the Spirit's work continues to be visible in the world and also continues to "look like" the Messiah. "Certainly, a spirit who teaches contrary to the Son of Man . . . is a deceiving spirit" (Marpeck, 1547:455).

Second, there is a more formalist theology of the validity of the sacraments and the institution. But for Marpeck, such a theology is no proof of the Spirit's presence.

> Again, they deceive themselves to think that, when they serve, teach, and baptize, simply because the apostolic service is performed, it follows that the Holy Spirit also moves and teaches. Nor is the church of Christ merely where the external service is properly done. *Not so!* If the inner, through the Holy Spirit, does not witness to the external, through faith, everything is in vain (Marpeck, 1547:455).

Inner without outer (Spiritualism) denies the incarnation. Outer without inner denies the continued need for the transforming Spirit's presence in the world.

Messianic Mission:
Following the Christ of the Incarnation and Trinity

In all of this, Christology, ecclesiology, pneumatology, and ethics have been closely related. At this point, in closing, it is important to recapitulate what has been said about mission and ethics.

Marpeck's incarnational/trinitarian theology helps to see ethics as integrally related to mission. The Johannine emphasis on the Word become flesh cannot be understood without the concept of "sentness." The church is seen as being sent into the world as Christ was sent. Mission is foundational, the *raison d'etre* of the body of Christ. Even if Marpeck did not explicitly state this conclusion, his logic leads us to this point. The church is not to retreat from the world, but is fully present in a missionary way. Instead of leading to the conclusion that a strong discipleship ethic means that Christians are against culture, this theology shows that ethics is part of the good news that the church proclaims and lives in the midst of the world.

Doing what Christ commanded is the reason for being sent. How disciples live becomes sacramental; it is a vehicle of God's presence. In the body of Christ, people are sent into the world to love each other and to love their enemies, just as much as they are sent to preach the gospel. Ethics becomes part, an integral part, of the good news.

Ethics means being part of a new community, the body of Christ. Mission implies a communitarian ethic; it means being salt and light.

Ethics is the result of the transforming work of the Holy Spirit, who recreates the body into the image of the Son. The Spirit allows the church to look like Jesus, to go the way of the cross.

It is essential to underline the importance of interpreting the Anabaptist concern for following Christ and discipleship in this larger biblical and theological context of the incarnation and the Trinity.

The incarnation reminds us of God's saving work, of his love for the world, and of the sending of the disciples into the world. Following Jesus does not lead to separation as has sometimes been the case in radical tradition and experience. At the same time, in this perspective, the incarnation is not merely a speculative or intellectual concept that keeps God's action in the past or far from the practical realm of everyday Christian living. Neither does it dissolve into a "theology of the world" or a "death of God" theology as have some more modern uses of the incarnation theme. The world is taken seriously, but an eschatological tension remains so that the world is not just uncritically accepted. Incarnation means being sent into the world, but it does not mean becoming like the world. If there is no difference, there is no mission. In fact, being sent into the world will sometimes mean being rejected by the world: "He came to that which was his own, but his own did not receive him" (John 1:11). In this understanding of the incarnation, the necessary tension between being in the world but not of the world is maintained.

Just as important as the incarnation is the Trinitarian aspect of Marpeck's theology. God's mission of sending the Messiah into the world also includes the sending of the Spirit. Pentecost is also fundamental for missiology and for messianic ethics. The Spirit is present at the beginning of the Messiah's mission, whether we think of his baptism (Matt. 3:16) or the episode at Nazareth where he reads from Isaiah, "The Spirit of the Lord is on me" (Luke 4:18). The Johannine account of the sending of the disciples also includes the resurrected Christ's giving of the Spirit: "As the Father has sent me, I am sending you . . . . Receive the Holy Spirit" (John 20:21-22).

This recognition of the Spirit's role in mission is important for ethics. Radical ethics can be freed from legalism and become integrally related to spiritual life. Marpeck's trinitarian framework reminds us that the transforming work of the Holy Spirit is an integral part of ethics. The charge of legalism against a discipleship ethic needs to be taken seriously. Worship and openness to God's Spirit are the only source of discipleship. And when God's Spirit is present in our lives, our ethics become a sacrament, as Jürgen Moltmann has suggested in a way quite similar to Marpeck:

> In the sacrament of Christian ethics, we experience the *real* history, for the ethic is the element of the kingdom of God coming into the material of our history. Christian praxis—in its suffering, struggle, and hope—celebrates and completes then the presence of God in history (Moltmann, 1983:78).

Notes

1. Biblical references in this chapter are taken from the New International Version unless noted otherwise.

2. Harold S. Bender's 1944 *The Anabaptist Vision* played a key role in this process. See Guy F. Hershberger (1957).

3. Such a response would go in the same direction as seen in John H. Yoder (1984) and Stanley Hauerwas and William H. Willimon (1989).

4. The text of the Confession of Schleitheim can be found in John H. Yoder (1973:34-43).

5. See "Hutterian Mission: Encounter with the World" (Gross, 1980).

6. In relation to Marpeck, see William Klassen (1968), William Klassen and Walter Klaassen (1978), Neal Blough (1984), and Stephen Boyd (1991).

7. It is striking how close Marpeck's theology is to that of the Swiss Brethren as described by John H. Yoder (1968). See also Neal Blough (1989:147-64).

8. It would be an interesting historical debate to determine the motivations for sixteenth-century Anabaptist separation. Was separation fundamental to their theology, or was it forced on them by circumstances? Hauerwas and Willimon argue for the second point of view: "The early Anabaptists had no desire to withdraw from the world. . . . Their withdrawal came in an attempt to prevent people opposed to them . . . from killing their children. The Anabaptists did not withdraw. They were driven out" (1989:42).

9. A more detailed presentation of Marpeck's and Luther's thinking in this regard can be found in Neal Blough (1987:203-12).

10. Hauerwas and Willimon make exactly the same point: "The Sermon [on the Mount] is not primarily addressed to individuals, because it is as individuals that we are most apt to fail as Christians. Only through membership in a nonviolent community can violent individuals do better" (1989:77).

11. This is my translation from Marpeck's response to Schwenckfeld's criticisms (Loserth, 1929:135).

12. This is not meant to claim that the church is the only means of God's presence in the world.

References Cited

Bender, Harold S.
1944   *The Anabaptist Vision*. Scottdale, Pa.: Herald Press.

Blough, Neal
1984   *Christologie Anabaptiste: Pilgram Marpeck et l'humanite du Christ*. Geneva: Labor et Fides.
1987   "Pilgram Marpeck, Martin Luther and the Humanity of Christ," *Mennonite Quarterly Review* LXI:2 (April).
1989   "Pilgram Marpeck et les freres suisses vers 1540," ". . . *Lebenn Nach der Ler Jhesu . . .*" "*Das Sind Aber Wir!*": *Berner Taufer und Prädikanten im Gesprach*. Bern: Schweizerischen Verein fur Taufergeschichte.

Boyd, Stephen
1991   *Pilgram Marpeck: His Life and Social Theology*. Durham, S.C.: Duke University Press.

Gingerich, Ray
1980   "The Mission Impulse of Early Swiss and South German-Austrian Anabaptism" (Ph.D. dissertation). Nashville: Vanderbilt University.

Gross, Leonard
1980   *The Golden Years of the Hutterites: The Witness and Thought of the Communal Moravian Anabaptists During the Wolpot Era, 1565-1578*. Scottdale, Pa.: Herald Press.

Hauerwas, Stanley, and William H. Willimon
1989   *Resident Aliens: A Provocative Christian Assessment of Culture and Ministry for People Who Know That Something Is Wrong*. Nashville: Abingdon.

Hershberger, Guy F. (ed.)
   1957   *The Recovery of the Anabaptist Vision: A Sixtieth-Anniversary Tribute to Harold S. Bender*. Scottdale, Pa.: Herald Press.
Klassen, William
   1968   *Covenant and Community: The Life, Writings, and Hermeneutics of Pilgram Marpeck*. Grand Rapids: Eerdmans.
Klassen, William, and Walter Klaassen (trans. and eds.)
   1978   *The Writings of Pilgram Marpeck*. Scottdale, Pa.: Herald Press.
Loserth, Johann, ed.
   1929   *Pilgram Marbecks Antwort auf Kaspar Schwenckfelds Beurteilung des Buches der Bundesbezeugung von 1542*. Vienna: Carl Fromme.
Marpeck, Pilgram
   1531   "A Clear and Useful Instruction," *The Writings of Pilgram Marpeck*. William Klassen and Walter Klaassen, trans. and eds., 1978; Scottdale, Pa.: Herald Press.
   1547   "Concerning the Lowliness of Christ," *The Writings of Pilgram Marpeck*. William Klassen and Walter Klaassen, trans. and eds., 1978; Scottdale, Pa.: Herald Press.
Moltmann, Jürgen
   1983   *Following Jesus Christ in the World Today: Responsibility for the World and Christian Discipleship*. Elkhart, Ind.: Institute of Mennonite Studies.
Niebuhr, H. Richard
   1951   *Christ and Culture*. New York: Harper and Brothers.
Schäufele, Wolfgang
   1966   *Das missionarische Bewusstsein und Wirken der Taufer*. Hamburg: Neukirchener Verlag des Erziehungsvereins.
Shenk, Wilbert R.
   1989   *A Developing Missiological Vision: Mennonite Writing on Mission, 1970-1989*. Elkhart, Ind.: Mennonite Board of Missions. Reproduced in Calvin E. Shenk, ed., *A Relevant Anabaptist Missiology for the 1990s*. Elkhart, Ind.: Council of International Ministries, 1990, pp. 43-61.
Weaver, J. Denny
   1987   *Becoming Anabaptist: The Origin and Significance of Sixteenth-Century Anabaptism*. Scottdale, Pa.: Herald Press.
Yoder, John H.
   1968   *Taufertum und Reformation im Gesprach: Dogmengeschichtliche Untersuching der fruhen Gesprache zwischen Schweizerischen Taufern und Reformatoren*. Zürich: EVZ-Verlag.
   1984   *The Priestly Kingdom: Social Ethics as Gospel*. Notre Dame, Ind.: University of Notre Dame Press.
Yoder, John H., trans. and ed.
   1973   *The Legacy of Michael Sattler*. Scottdale, Pa.: Herald Press.

CHAPTER 8

Messianic Evangelization[1]

John Driver

THE GREAT COMMISSION has traditionally served as a rallying cry
for mobilizing the church in its evangelizing mission. However, the
church's social stance has tended to color its interpretation of this text.
Accompanying the long tradition of Western imperial conquest, as it
has since the days of Constantine to the present, this missionary "going" has been interpreted almost entirely as a geographical impera-
tive. This has contributed to a spirit of paternalism and, what has been
even more noxious, of triumphalism, which has characterized much
of the church's evangelistic mission.[2] In the process the meaning of the
gospel and its power to save have been seriously compromised.

As the church moved farther and farther from its roots in Jesus of
Nazareth, the content and the methods of its evangelization have concentrated less on the forming of disciples of Jesus and more on communicating the church's teachings about Jesus. In this process the goal
of evangelization has moved from the creation of Jesus' likeness in his
followers to the formation of orthodox believers who receive the appropriate sacraments and assent to correct doctrines. The fact that this
process has been gradual and has happened in the context of changing historical realities has made this development all the more difficult
to critique and to correct.

Of even more serious consequence, we note the tendency to pri-
vatize salvation, accompanied by an almost exclusively individualistic
evangelistic practice. This has often led to an evangelization largely
bereft of the universal scope which characterizes the biblical vision.
The ultimate reconciliation of all things to God through the Messiah is

the goal toward which authentic evangelization points. Therefore, in light of the scope of God's salvific intention, no aspect of life within the created order lies outside our evangelizing concern.

Occasionally, in the course of its history, parts of the church have recaptured the radical New Testament content and methods of evangelization. More often than not these have been minority movements caught in situations socially and politically similar to those which characterized the primitive messianic movement. These include movements of radical renewal, beginning with the Montanists and Donatists of the second and fourth centuries and extending all the way to a variety of radical communities in our own time, including Christian base communities which have emerged in the context of third-world Catholicism.

The content of the evangel and the methods of evangelization take on surprisingly new and powerful dimensions when they are perceived and focused in radical perspective.

Subversive Evangelization[3]

In the New Testament the saving gospel comes to us from a position of socioeconomic and political weakness, humanly speaking, rather than from a position characterized by human power. In this sense, the saving power of the gospel comes to us from below, rather than from above, as has been generally taken for granted by the church throughout most of its history. The messianic movement described in the New Testament was a minority movement which originated on the periphery of Judaism.[4]

The great commission is prefaced by references to Galilee. "Galilee of the Gentiles," located as it was on the geographical, sociological, and religious periphery of Judaism, is clearly identified in the Gospels as the point of departure for God's eschatological initiative of messianic salvation. The Gospels are really quite emphatic about the Galilean provenance of the messianic movement and its evangel.[5] This fact is all the more surprising when we realize that the pressures on the early church to make it more socially and religiously acceptable would have led it to downplay its humble origins.

This is the note on which the evangelization of Israel began. "In those days Jesus came from Nazareth of Galilee. . . . Jesus came into Galilee, preaching the gospel of God, and saying, 'The time is fulfilled, and the kingdom of God is at hand; repent, and believe in the gospel'" (Mark 1:9a, 14b-15; cf. Matt. 4:12-17; Luke 4:14-21).

The evangelization of the Gentiles, begun by Peter in the household of the Roman centurion, Cornelius, also took the Galilean origins of the messianic movement as its point of departure.

> You know the word which he sent to Israel, preaching good news of peace by Jesus Christ (he is Lord of all), the word which was proclaimed throughout all Judea, beginning from Galilee after the baptism which John preached: how God anointed Jesus of Nazareth with the Holy Spirit and with power; how he went about doing good and healing all that were oppressed by the devil, for God was with him (Acts 10:36-38).

The ultimate insult which the Jewish religious establishment cast in the teeth of those who dared to express dissent was, "Are you from Galilee too?" (John 7:52). That the Messiah could possibly come from Galilee was, for respectable Jews, highly doubtful (7:41). And those who insisted that it was impossible for a true prophet to arise out of Galilee claimed scriptural support for their view (7:52). This official disdain of all things Galilean makes the early New Testament emphasis on the Galilean provenance of the messianic evangel all the more remarkable.[6]

The implications of a gospel which is mediated from below and by outsiders have rarely been grasped by a church allied, in one way or another, with power. That Jesus has come as prophet, priest, and king means, since the incarnation, that Jesus of Nazareth is the definitive model for prophetic witness, for priestly intercession, and for the exercise of kingship. They are not mere theoretical images by means of which we can grasp the purely spiritual dimensions of Jesus' messiahship.

The Galilean provenance of the messianic movement is not just an isolated element of merely geographic importance in the gospel story. It is a part of a larger picture in which God's saving initiative arises from the bottom side of the social and religious structures and from the periphery of the political sphere. In Luke and John especially we find a seemingly disproportionate emphasis on the Samaritans, for example, in spite of a very strong Jewish prejudice to the contrary. The disenfranchised within Israel—the poor, the "little ones," the prostitutes, the publicans, those afflicted with leprosy, and the foreigners—not only appear in the Gospel narratives as special objects of God's grace, but they are also active protagonists in God's project of evangelization. These examples all point toward a salvific economy which is subversive. God's kingdom initiative emerges from below.

The New Testament is full of evidence which points to the lowly beginnings of the messianic movement. Among the earliest self-designations which the primitive community applied to itself are "the way," "strangers and sojourners," "exiles" or "pilgrims," "the meek," and "the poor." These images reflect the early church's understanding of its nature and evangelizing mission. These values, so diametrically contrary to those which predominated in both Jewish and Greek culture, can most certainly be traced to Jesus himself. And the fact that the early church retained these images, in spite of all the social pressures to the contrary, witnesses to their importance for the identity of the primitive community and its understanding of its evangelizing mission. The Gospels contain abundant references to Jesus' lowly estate. He was poor. In earliest childhood he is presented as a political refugee. All of the women named in his genealogy would have been considered social outcasts.[7]

This movement from the bottom and from the outside is continued in the evangelizing activity of the early church. Hellenists, considered outsiders by Jewish contemporaries, occupied a prominent place in the evangelizing mission which carried the messianic movement into Asia Minor to the north and east, into Africa on the south, and into the Greco-Roman world to the north and west.

Paul, whose evangelizing work occupies a prominent place in the New Testament, is probably representative of many more who evangelized from the outside and from below. Although it has generally not been given the emphasis which the New Testament places upon it, "weakness" or vulnerability is a hallmark of apostolic evangelization.

Paul's Damascus-road experience convinced him that Jesus of Nazareth was indeed God's Messiah. This meant that suffering servanthood was to characterize God's evangelizing strategy. It was therefore understandable that Paul's evangelization would be marked by weakness and vicarious suffering.

First Corinthians 1:17—2:5 is a fundamental passage for grasping Paul's understanding of his evangelizing stance as one of "weakness." The power of God is found in the cross of his Messiah (1:17). This crucified Messiah is concretely the power and the wisdom of God (1:24), in contrast to the exercise of power and intellectual clout on the part of the Jews and the Greeks of the first century. Paul understood that in the incarnation God had restored the values which characterize his kingdom.

First Corinthians 9:19-23 is sometimes interpreted as a model for sociological accommodation and psychological adaptation in the interests of effective evangelization. Actually, it is a remarkable example of Paul's stance of "weakness" in evangelization. Although Paul enjoyed the status of a free man, he voluntarily made himself a slave of all (9:19). Although Paul had been freed from the narrowness of nationalistic legalistic Judaism, he was willing to submit to legalistic Jewish requirements (9:20). Although Paul by birth belonged to the covenant community, he voluntarily became a Gentile (9:21). Although Paul was of a strong conscience, he willingly accommodated himself to others with weak consciences (9:22).

The actions described here were not aspects of a mere strategy of evangelistic accommodation nor of a methodology of psychological identification. He did it "for the sake of the gospel that [he might] share in its blessings" (1 Cor. 9:23). He did these things because it is the nature of the gospel to live this way. Jesus himself had set the precedent for Paul: "though he was rich, yet for your sake he became poor, so that by his poverty you might become rich" (2 Cor. 8:9); "who, though he was in the form of God, . . . emptied himself, taking the form of a servant" (Phil. 2:6-7).

The messianic community understood that Jesus, "who, though he was in the form of God, . . . emptied himself, taking upon himself the form of a servant," was its model for a "manner of life . . . worthy of the gospel of Christ" (Phil. 2:6-7; 1:27). The same evangelizing strategy with which Jesus had so powerfully manifested God's love to humankind was now commended to the messianic community by the apostles (Phil. 2:5-8).

When we note the radically outsider provenance of the messianic movement in the New Testament, we will be better able to understand the truly radical character of Jesus' message. There was a profound difference between the approach of Jesus and that of all the other political, social, and religious groups of the period. Sadducees and Pharisees, Zealots, and Essenes all had in common their willingness to accept, in one way or another, the Jewish social system: the monarchy, the temple, the priesthood, and the right of the Jewish people to a place of divine favor among the family of nations. For his part, Jesus rejected all of this.

Jesus was not a reformist. He was radical in that he did not accept the validity of the system. He called for radical change. In this Jesus stood in the prophetic tradition of the Old Testament. But he went beyond the prophets of the Old Testament. They called for justice in the context of what they seem to have believed to be essentially valid social institutions. Jesus did not simply call for justice on behalf of the oppressed. His was a movement of even more radical renewal. He announced a kingdom characterized by "blessedness" (Matt. 5:3-10). Under the rule of God humans are offered freedom from the idols of wealth (the desire to possess), prestige (the drive to be somebody), and power (the will to dominate). According to the messianic evangel, there is sharing instead of accumulation, there is compassionate service instead of seizing selfish superiority, and there is love in a context of peoplehood instead of rivalry and violence.

It has been suggested that a truly radical critique of the system is possible only when the prophet, in some sense, stands outside of the system. This may help us to understand why there is such a strong emphasis in the New Testament on the "differentness" of the messianic movement. God's Messiah could not arise in Jerusalem. He needed to come from Galilee, from the periphery and from below, in order truly to evangelize. Jerusalem killed him because of his evangel, a fate which he shared with the authentic prophets before him.[8]

If it is true that radical evangelization can be done best from outside the system, then there are unexpected and important lessons for the church of our time to be learned from the Galilean provenance of the messianic evangel. This would free us, for example, to hear in the message of the authentic prophets of our time a salvific gospel word. We might be able to recognize the evangelizing function of prophets as well as the prophetic impact of true evangelists in our midst. It should also alert us to the possibility that hope for truly evangelical renewal may continue to be found in the witness of some of those radical groups on the fringes of our religious establishments.

Kingdom-Oriented Evangelization

In the New Testament the prime element in the messianic evangel is the reality of the kingdom of God being made present in human history. This is the clear implication of Jesus' words in the Matthean version of the great commission: "All authority in heaven and on earth has been given to me" (Matt. 28:18). According to the Lukan version in Acts 1:6-8, teaching about the kingdom of God forms the context for the commission to evangelize with which Jesus charged the messianic community (Acts 1:3). In the Markan version, the commission to evangelize is accompanied by the same kind of kingdom activity which had characterized Jesus' evangelizing mission and that of the messianic community in the synoptic Gospels (Mark 16:17-18). It is clear that the presence of the kingdom is a fundamental element in messianic evangelization, for Jesus, as well as for his community.

The church, in the way in which it has traditionally approached its evangelistic task, has all too rarely taken note of the primacy of the kingdom of God in the Gospel accounts of messianic evangelization. Therefore, kingdom agenda has not been an essential part of its evangelistic message and practice. This has contributed to a serious deformation in both the content and the strategy of the church's evangelistic activity. This becomes especially clear when it is measured against the New Testament paradigm of messianic evangelization.

According to the synoptic Gospels, Jesus began his messianic mission with an announcement of the kingdom of God. "Jesus came into Galilee, preaching the gospel of God, and saying, 'The time is fulfilled, and the kingdom of God is at hand; repent, and believe in the gospel' " (Mark 1:14-15; cf. Matt. 4:17; Luke 1:33; 4:43). Not only did Jesus begin with the call to kingdom repentance, the reality of the reign of God underlies the entire Gospel narrative from beginning to end. This theme is especially dominant in Matthew, but it is also prominent in Mark and Luke. Even in John, where the term "kingdom" appears on the lips of Jesus only five times, the concept is present in the frequent use of a Johannine equivalent, "eternal life."

Although Jesus nowhere gave a detailed definition of the term, his life and teachings are full of clues for understanding the meaning of the kingdom. It is apparent that Jesus' hearers were familiar with the concept of the kingdom. The reality of Yahweh's kingship permeated all of life in ancient Israel. And the messianic expectations held by the wide gamut of contemporary Jewish movements all had in common their hope that God's reign would be restored in one way or another among his people.

Jesus' understanding of the kingdom was rooted in the Old Testament. In ancient Israel God's reign had to do with the concrete forms which life takes among his people. God's rule took the form of his saving activity. It was in the relationships among God's people that his righteous rule manifested itself.

Psalms 145 and 146 reflect this view of the kingdom expressed in concrete relationships of covenant justice. Here the elements of God's reign include an unflagging covenant faithfulness, bringing justice to the oppressed, providing food for the hungry, setting prisoners free, opening the eyes of the blind, lifting up the bowed down, watching over the sojourners, and sustaining the widows and orphans.

The Old Testament story contains many indications of the concrete social shape which God's rule was intended to take among his people. The Decalogue is undoubtedly the clearest and most concise description of God's intention for social relationships under his rule.

The sabbatical and Jubilee provisions offer another example of the concrete forms which relationships take under God's rule. Allowing the land to remain fallow, forgiving indebtedness, freeing slaves, and returning lost inheritances were all ways for restoring social relationships to the covenant wholeness which God intended.

God's kingdom embraces concrete political and social events. According to the prophetic vision, warfare as a solution to differences would cease, weapons could be converted into implements for the production of food, and the fear and deprivation, so common under evil rulers, would be superseded under God's righteous rule (Mic. 4:1-4).

This prophetic kingdom vision was primarily historical. It was not simply a utopian dream for the future. This kingdom which has no end is present in God's just and compassionate ordering of human relationships. God's rule is characterized by the wholeness of life as he has always intended it to be, in marked contrast to the social injustices and the suffering of which Egypt was a paradigm in Israel's experience. It was expected that with the coming of the Messiah, God's rule would not only be renewed but would be experienced in a way which would surpass all that Israel had known previously. An authentic salvation of covenant love, justice, and peace would become reality because God would dwell in the midst of his people, shepherding them as a good king should.

The kingdom context of messianic evangelization sheds light on the meaning of the New Testament call to repentance and conversion. The call to repentance is basically an invitation to return to the foundational relationship of God's gracious covenant with his people. It is an appeal to submit once more to God's rule of justice and peace. To be converted is to turn away from those "other gods" who compete for human loyalties and to return to covenant relationships of faithfulness to God and to one another, to justice in interpersonal dealings, and to the wholeness of shalom.

The meaning of conversion is illustrated in John's response to queries about the meaning of repentance (Luke 3:10-14). The alternative to selfish accumulation of possessions is generous sharing; to the oppressiveness of economic greed, transparent dealings within the covenant community; to violence, the solidarity of genuine compassion. John's answers to the multitudes, the tax collectors, and the soldiers[9] are all appeals for a radical return to faithfulness, compassion, justice, and peace, all characteristics of the social relationships practiced within the covenanted community under the gracious reign of God.

The conviction that the kingdom of God has come into their midst provides the essential context in which to understand all of Jesus' messianic evangelizing activity. Matthew's concern was to show that God's reign was being made present in the person of the Messiah. This accounts for the remarkable parallels between the Exodus-Sinai restoration of God's people and the messianic salvation which Jesus brought.

Matthew 4:17-23 is, in a sense, a microcosm of the message of Matthew's Gospel. There is a call to repentance, a radical return to covenant faithfulness in the light of God's rule which is again becoming operative in their midst. This means a new exodus and the reconstitution of a people among whom God's sovereign rule is effective. It also means preaching and teaching with kingdom authority and restoring people to wholeness in the conflict with all the powers of evil. These are sure signs of the kingdom's arrival.

The salvific content of kingdom-oriented evangelization is far richer than the salvation generally offered in typical Protestant evangelistic offers. The Gospels are unanimous in their conviction that Jesus' messianic mission is salvific. And when the Gospels indicate that Jesus began his saving mission by announcing the kingdom, they clearly imply that salvation is to be found under the rule of God. We see in the values which characterized relationships within the messianic community, described in Matthew 5—7 and Luke 6, a picture of the concrete social forms which messianic salvation takes.

The prophetic vision of God's reign found in Isaiah 61:1-2 furnishes Jesus with his point of departure for understanding messianic salvation in Luke's Gospel (Luke 4:16-22). Here salvation is understood in terms of the restoration of God's gracious covenant relationships and, concretely, in terms of sabbatical and Jubilee renewal. This provides a key for grasping the rich dimensions of Jesus' evangelizing mission. A few examples taken from Luke's Gospel will serve to illustrate this.

The "blessings" and the "woes" found in the Sermon on the Plain are perfectly comprehensible in light of the Jubilee paradigm (Luke 6:20-26). Those who are poor, hungry, afflicted, and persecuted will find salvation in the new era of messianic salvation. But for the rich, the powerful, the uncompassionate, and the oppressors who are unrepentant the message of messianic restoration spells judgment.

Under God's beneficent rule, goods are shared with those in need (Luke 6:30, 35). Love is shown without discrimination, simply because this best reflects God's character (6:27-28, 35). People are merciful and forgiving and share with one another because this is the way in which God acts (6:36-38). In the restored messianic community, forgiveness is freely given and freely received, since the community owes its very existence to God's forgiveness (11:4).

The stories of the rich young ruler and Zacchaeus become clearer when understood in the kingdom context and viewed in light of the sabbatical and Jubilee paradigms. To take the Decalogue seriously is not to fall into legalism, but to experience salvation under God's rule. Jubilee restoration and participation in the messianic community as a follower of Jesus would have been a truly salvific experience for the rich young ruler, as it was for Zacchaeus (Luke 18:18-30; 19:1-10).

The kingdom context of Jesus' messianic evangelization, with its appeal to the jubilee paradigm, provides a concrete foundation for both the content and the strategy of the early church's evangelistic mission. It is not merely a matter of reestablishing God's old covenant reign. It offers a salvation which is far richer than that experienced under the old covenant. The Messiah has come and his Spirit dwells among his people. Kingdom evangelization announces a salvation which is both messianic and charismatic.

The traditional tendency to distinguish clearly between Christians as evangelizers and pagans as objects of evangelization is not fully sustainable from the biblical perspective. Evangelizers are also evangelized in their evangelizing activity. In this process Messiah is really the Evangelizer who evangelizes both those who are near as well as those who are far off. The people of God are effectively evangelized in the reconciliation of the outsiders (Eph. 2:13-18). Peter offers a prime example of this reality in the evangelization of Cornelius. Peter's confession, "Truly I perceive that God shows no partiality" (Acts 10:34), shows that the gospel had gripped him in a new and powerful way. Peter had, in fact, been evangelized anew. Although we do not generally use the term in this sense, "conversion" is probably the best word to describe how Peter was changed by the new encounter with the messianic evangel.

Evangelization Which Makes Disciples of Jesus

"Go therefore and make disciples of all nations, . . . teaching them to observe all that I have commanded you" (Matt. 28:19a, 20a). The call to follow Jesus as a disciple is foundational for authentic evangelization. In Mark 16:15-16 evangelization leads to believing commitment. In Luke 24:47-49 and Acts 1:6-8, the commission to evangelize is accompanied by the promise of the presence and the power of the community-creating Spirit of the Messiah. The same is true in the Johannine version of the commission (John 20:19-23).

But not all of Jesus' evangelizing activity effectively led to authentic discipleship on the part of his hearers. When it became evident that to follow Jesus was literally a matter of death and life, "many of his disciples drew back and no longer went about with him" (John 6:66). Not all who heard the evangel had counted the cost of following the Messiah who had evangelized them (Luke 9:57-62). And Jesus warned his disciples that their proclamation of the kingdom would be received by some and rejected by others (Matt. 10:13-14; Luke 10:6-11). In fact, the messianic evangel of the kingdom proved to be the occasion for conflict which resulted in divided families and brought suffering to the messianic community (Matt. 10:34-39).

In every one of the Gospels, we note that Jesus began his evangelizing mission by forming a disciple community (Matt. 4:18-22; Mark 1:16-20; Luke 5:1-11; John 1:35-51). The messianic evangel did not consist merely of a saving ideology or a utopian social vision. Essential to truly saving evangelization was the formation of a concrete social group in which God's reign is experienced. Apart from the existence of this community, salvation would remain an illusion in the minds of the seekers and Jesus' evangelistic message would turn out to be another ideology. This is the reason why the call to evangelize is a call to form disciple communities which incarnate faithfully the messianic evangel.

In recent years programs for discipling have become common among evangelical groups. In church-growth circles, to make disciples is to incorporate new members into a congregation. In other cases the term is applied to a kind of spiritual apprenticeship in which new converts commit themselves to receive instruction from older members. In still other cases, to be a disciple means mainly to receive training in methods of evangelism. And in some cases, training in discipleship is a term applied to denominational programs of Christian education. However, these programs sometimes have relatively little in common with the practice of making disciples which is depicted in the New Testament, or with the Anabaptist insistence on *Nachfolge Christi*, or with those third-world spiritualities oriented in a radical *seguimiento de Jesús*.

In first-century Judaism the practice of making disciples was not limited to Jesus. Other forms included the proselytizing practices of the Pharisees, the rabbinic schools, and the Hellenic academies scattered throughout the Greco-Roman world, including Palestine, dedicated to the pursuance of knowledge. The fundamental epistemological presupposition in these circles was that intellectual theory leads to practice, that rational knowledge will lead to the desired actions. The rabbinic schools probably furnish the closest parallel to Jesus' concern for making disciples. But even here there were differences.

Jesus' followers were called to discipleship by their Lord. In the case of the rabbinic schools, disciples learned from the teacher of their choice. To be able to follow Jesus was a gift of grace. On the other hand, to follow Jesus was costly. He required the absolute commitment of his followers. For their part, rabbis were not in a position to make this kind of demand of their disciples. And for Jesus' disciples, to know God was clearly a matter of doing his will (John 7:17).

While the earliest followers of Jesus were called disciples in the Gospels, the term naturally came to be applied to the larger messianic community which emerged and continued to grow after the death and resurrection of Jesus. The term "disciples" appears in the Gospels and Acts some 250 times. Its use in the New Testament, as a motif to designate the messianic community, witnesses to the power of the experience of following Jesus in the lives of the earliest disciples.

Since, as the early church confessed, God had revealed himself most fully and most clearly in Jesus, the best way to know God was to follow Jesus in discipleship (Heb. 1:1-3). It appears that the early disciples of Jesus found this difficult to grasp (John 14:6-11). And it has escaped large portions of the church, especially since the Hellenizing period of the early centuries. Hans Denck, the early Anabaptist, perceived this reality in a truly remarkable way: "No one can truly know Christ unless one follows Him in life" (Bauman, 1991:viii). Discipleship is not merely a result of evangelization. The New Testament and the subsequent experience of the church lead us to recognize that discipleship is an essential part of authentic evangelization.

In our time, Christians who are living under the difficult conditions which characterize the third world seem to be grasping this vital relationship between evangelization and discipleship. "The originality and the authenticity of a Christian spirituality consists in our following a God who has taken upon himself the human condition. A God who has shared our history; who has lived our experiences; who has made hard choices; who has given himself for a cause for which he suffered dearly; who experienced successes, joys and failures; who gave himself unto death. This man, Jesus of Nazareth, just like us, except without sin, in whom 'all the fullness of God was pleased to dwell," is the only model for our life as humans and as Christians" (Galilea, 1982:59; translation mine).

According to the New Testament vision, the words and deeds, the ideals, and the teachings of Jesus of Nazareth are the only way truly to know God (John 14:4-11). Jesus is the way, not in some strangely abstract and spiritualized sense, but concretely in his life and in his death. Jesus reveals the true God to us, powerful in his suffering love and compassion. In Jesus we discover the values of the kingdom as well as our model for kingdom living.

It is not merely a question of evangelizing in such a way that disciples are made. Nor is it only a matter of evangelizing and being evangelized in the context of discipleship. It is also essential that we follow Jesus in our evangelization—evangelizing as Jesus did.

The call to be a disciple of Jesus is also a call to participate in God's evangelizing mission in the world. Traditionally, we have tended to understand the call to discipleship as a call to personal salvation or as a call to ethical commitment. Only rarely, if ever, do we perceive in the call to discipleship a call to participate in God's evangelizing mission, that is, to evangelize just as Jesus has done.

This is the context in which Jesus' call to discipleship appear in the Gospels. In Matthew 4:17-24 Jesus' call to discipleship (4:18-22) is set in the context of Jesus' kingdom proclamation (4:17) and his kingdom activity (4:23-24). The calls to follow Jesus, narrated in Matthew 8:18-23 and 9:9, are set in a section which treats Jesus' kingdom teaching and activity, including healings, exorcisms, and stilling the storm (5:2—9:31). Then, following another summary statement of Jesus' own kingdom proclamation, teaching, and healing activity (Matt. 9:35-36), Jesus called the twelve to follow him in his evangelizing mission (9:37—10:4). The evangelization of the disciples consisted of precisely the same elements which characterized the messianic mission of Jesus: kingdom proclamation (10:7); kingdom teaching (10:11, 14); and kingdom signs (10:8).

The instructions which Jesus gave his followers for carrying out their evangelizing mission reflect the evangelizing posture of Jesus himself (Matt. 10:5—11:1). Their participation in the evangelizing mission was to be freely assumed (10:8). It was to be carried out without any power to coerce, from a position of weakness rather than from one of imposition (10:9). Its power to convince lies in its capacity to serve, and the key to success in effecting change lies in the heart of the hearers (10:8, 14).

The context of evangelization is conflict. Jesus' disciples are likened to "sheep in the midst of wolves" (Matt. 10:16). The success of the mission is measured in terms of capacity to endure persecution, to be steadfast in resisting evil while refusing to respond to evildoers with their own violent means. This was the *patientia* of which the early Latin church fathers wrote. As Augustine defined the term, it "prefers to endure evil so as not to commit it rather than to commit evil so as not to endure it" (Hornus, 1980:220). Nonviolence is not merely a "counsel of perfection," an option taken only by Christians who are particularly serious about their faith. It is not simply a matter of Christian ethics. It is essential to the evangelizing mission of God in the world. Just as God's Messiah has evangelized most powerfully by assuming the innocent and vicarious suffering of the cross, so Jesus' disciples must evangelize as their Lord has done (Matt. 10:24-25).

Jesus' compassionate solidarity with the "harassed and the helpless," bereft of the benefits of God's righteous rule, provides the model for the evangelizing mission of his followers (Matt. 9:36-38). For Jesus this meant rejection and persecution at the hands of the Jewish establishment. It is precisely this innocent and vicarious suffering which became the focal point of Jesus' evangelizing mission. It is also the point at which the evangelizing activity of the messianic community comes most sharply into focus.

> A disciple is not above his teacher, nor a servant above his master; it is enough for the disciple to be like his teacher, and the servant like his master. . . . And he who does not take his cross and follow me is not worthy of me. He who finds his life will lose it, and he who loses his life for my sake will find it (Matt. 10:24-25a, 38-39).

To judge by their recurrence in the synoptic Gospels, these words must have made a deep impression on Jesus' followers. In one form or another, they occur five or six times in the Gospels. A community which proclaims with integrity the message of the cross must itself be marked by the reality of the cross. The posture evoked by lambs in the midst of wolves is absolutely essential for authentic evangelization. In our evangelizing we are not simply called to make disciples of Jesus. We are also called to be followers of Jesus in our evangelization.[10]

The Spirit of the Living Christ
Empowers His Body for Evangelizing

The fundamental role of the Spirit in the evangelizing mission of the messianic community is underscored in each of the Gospel versions of the great commission. In Matthew, the evangelizing mission of the community is carried out in the presence of the Spirit of Christ: "I am with you always, to the close of the age" (Matt. 28:20). In Mark, evangelization is done in the "name" (authority) of the risen Lord (Mark 16:17). In John, Jesus imparted the Holy Spirit to the disciples on the occasion of their being sent (John 20:21-23). And in Luke-Acts, the commission is accompanied by "the promise of my [the] Father" (Luke 24:49; Acts 1:4). They will be "baptized with the Holy Spirit" (Acts 1:5) and receive "power" (Acts 1:8).

Luke-Acts contains the fullest treatment of the Spirit's role in the ongoing evangelizing mission of the messianic community. In a sense, the Spirit fills Jesus' place in the community following the ascension. This accounts for the prominent role assigned to the Spirit in Acts (54 occurrences) as compared to the Gospel of Luke (16 occurrences). The story in Acts of the community's evangelizing mission is a continuation of the mission of Jesus narrated in the Gospel. Just as Jesus was anointed by the Spirit for the messianic mission, so his body is empowered by the Spirit for evangelization. In reality, the work of the Spirit can be best understood in relation to God's evangelizing mission—through his Messiah and then through his Spirit.

The activity of the Spirit in Acts appears to be concentrated in three areas of the church's life and evangelizing mission: the fundamentally communitarian character of the church, the universality of the evangelizing mission, and the role of suffering in its evangelization.

The Communitarian Character of the Church

In Acts 1 and 2 we find ten direct references to the activity of the Spirit. Here the emphasis falls on the preparation of the disciple group as the community of the Spirit charged with continuing the messianic mission "to the end of the earth." The interpretative summaries found in Acts 2:42-47 and 4:32-37 show that the primary result of this Pentecostal experience was the creation of a witnessing community.

In chapters 6 to 8 the activity of the Spirit is specifically mentioned eleven times. Here the emphasis falls on the development of the common life of the community and the incorporation of new cultural, geographic, and ethnic groups into its communion. These include Hellenists, nonresident Jews, and an Ethiopian proselyte. In this process the Spirit is instrumental in the consolidation and extension of community.

In chapters 10 and 11 there are ten more specific references to the work of the Spirit. Here again the emphasis falls on the incorporation into the community of the Spirit still another sector of society—the Gentiles. The Holy Spirit is the principal protagonist in this process. First, he prepared Cornelius, the Roman centurion, for what was about to happen. (Of all of the possible candidates to break the racial barrier which still separated the Gentiles from the messianic community, Cornelius must have certainly been the most unlikely.) Then the Spirit prepared Peter for something unimaginable: table-fellowship with Gentiles (10:48). And finally, the Gentiles who heard Peter's message "received the Holy Spirit" independently of the imposition of Peter's hands.

Although the struggle to assimilate into the conscience and practice of the early church that which the Holy Spirit had created—community without racial barriers—continued for some time, the outcome would never again be in doubt. Even though Judaizing elements in the early church tried to limit the community of the Spirit to the social parameters which characterized contemporary Judaism, the response of the church, under the guidance of the Holy Spirit, was clear (Acts 15:8-9, 28).

There is one overarching theme which unites these seven chapters in the first part of the book which contain 60 percent of the references to the Spirit which appear in Acts. It is the Spirit's role in the creation of a new evangelizing community whose dimensions surpassed by far the wildest dreams of its members. The community of the Spirit embraces all aspects of life—spiritual, social, liturgical, and economic. The communion of the kingdom of God, anticipated under the old covenant in the Sabbatical and Jubilee provisions, had become reality through the powerful impulse of the Spirit of the living Christ. The meaning of Pentecost is, first and foremost, the creation of the community of the Spirit.

The Universality of the Evangelizing Mission

Through the intervention of the Spirit, the evangelizing activity of the church soon took on universal dimensions. Under the impulse of the Spirit, Jesus had been obedient to the Father's commission. This meant, among other things, moving from Galilee to Jerusalem where he evangelized at the cost of his life. The same Spirit inspired the primitive community to continue the messianic mission to "the end of the earth."

The Pentecostal gift of tongues made it possible for the disciple community to communicate "the mighty works of God" among the peoples of the diaspora who found themselves in Jerusalem for the Harvest Feast (Acts 2:5-12). The book of Acts documents the ever-widening circles in which evangelization took place. Stephen and Philip, men "full of faith and the Holy Spirit," evangelized in Jerusalem and Judea among Hellenists and proselytes and, finally, in Samaria as well (6:8-10; 8:26-40). In the power of the Spirit, Peter evangelized Cornelius and his family, who were incorporated into the primitive community because "the Holy Spirit had been poured out even on the Gentiles" (10:45).

Pauline evangelization was initiated and carried out under the impulse of the same Spirit. The Spirit moved the church to send Paul and Barnabas forth (Acts 13:2, 4). The Spirit led, even in the decisions affecting travel routes, so that they eventually reached Greece (16:6-10), Subsequent travel to Jerusalem and then to Rome was also under the impulse of the Spirit (19:21; 20:22-23; 21:4, 11).

According to Acts, a second major role of the Spirit in evangelization is the realization of the biblical vision of the universal scope of God's salvific rule, envisioned by the prophets, anticipated in the ministry of Jesus, and fulfilled in the apostolic community of witness.

The Role of Suffering

In their evangelization the apostles courageously confronted the hostile powers of their time (Acts 4:8-12, 19-20, 23-31; 5:29-32). For the cause of Christ, they joyfully bore imprisonments, torture, and even death (5:17, 40-41; 12:3). As Jesus had warned, Jerusalem was known for "killing the prophets" (Matt. 23:37). From the very beginning, as in the case of Jesus, evangelization was carried out under the sign of the cross. Acts tells the story of a community of witness sustained by the Spirit of Christ as they joyfully bore the birth pangs which accompanied the dawning of the new era of the kingdom.

The courage with which the disciple community bore witness to Christ and the kingdom came from the Spirit. The Spirit had sustained Jesus in his struggle against the powers of evil (Luke 4:1-13). And Jesus had promised his disciples that his Spirit would sustain them, too, in their hour of trial (Luke 12:11-12; cf. Matt. 10:9-10; Mark 13:11).

Apostolic evangelization in the book of Acts is characterized by the Spirit's empowerment in the face of adversity. "Filled with the

Holy Spirit," Peter defended himself before the Sanhedrin (Acts 4:8). And faced with the opposition of the religious and civil authorities, the entire community dared to speak "the word of God with boldness," thanks to the Spirit's empowering (4:23-31). Stephen's prophetic denunciation of Judaism's prostitution of Israel's institutions was uttered in the power of the Spirit (6:5, 10; 7:55). Paul was filled with the Spirit in order to suffer for the name of Jesus (9:16-17). In the power of the Spirit, persecution became the occasion for the experience of deep joy in the community (13:50-52).

The same Spirit who had inspired and sustained Jesus in messianic evangelization also filled the primitive community with courage for faithful witness. Like Jesus, the evangelists of the messianic community also suffered from all sorts of rejection, persecution, imprisonments, tortures, and even death. The call to discipleship is a call to an evangelization which is cruciform, inspired and sustained by the same Spirit. God's saving activity, which had been remarkably clear in Jesus' life and death and resurrection, continued to be manifest in the sufferings of Messiah's body.

A People Restored to Wholeness

The evangel is the good news of God's loving intention to restore all of creation to wholeness. This means that there is nothing in the universe which lies outside God's saving concern. The life, death, and resurrection of Jesus the Messiah furnish us with the keys we need to begin to understand the character of this restoration. However, it is in Jesus' suffering, death, and resurrection that we perceive most clearly God's saving presence in the world.

Evangelization is the joyous participation of God's restored people in this design to bring all things to their pristine fullness. Therefore, an essential ingredient of this salvific project is the creation of a new humanity born of God's life-giving Spirit, a charismatic community charged with God's ongoing mission of evangelization.

The universal scope, which characterizes the biblical vision of God's intention to restore all of creation, will save us from those strategies which lead to privatized forms of salvation, those which create the senseless dichotomy of words and deeds and the empty activism which are so common in much of the evangelism of our time.

Our evangelization must be marked by the evangel. Only that life and mission and those words and deeds which grow out of the evangel will be effective in authentic evangelization. This calls for the restoration of the messianic community to gospel wholeness, in order to "make known the whole Gospel to the whole man throughout the whole world" (Response, 1975:251).

Notes

1. I have chosen to use the term "evangelization" rather than "evangelism" in this chapter for several reasons. First, "evangelism" has another technical meaning. In church history it refers to a movement of renewal which flourished principally in Spain and Italy from about 1500 until 1542 when it was crushed effectively by the Papal Inquisition. Catholic Evangelism, as it has been called, was an undogmatic and ethically serious movement with roots in medieval piety and Christian humanism marked largely by a recovery of the relevance of the Gospels to the life of the church (see Williams, 1962:2, 8-16). Second, in the English language "evangelization" conveys the idea of action and participation in a dynamic process more clearly than does the more static term, "evangelism." Third, "evangelism" carries implicitly, and often explicitly, the idea of the methodology by which the gospel is proclaimed, by such means as preaching, teaching, and personal or family visitation programs. In the church's search for effective methods, strategies, and techniques for evangelizing, it has sometimes compromised the radical substance of the evangel. Modern practices of evangelism have at times become alarmingly similar to the proselytizing practices of first-century Judaism which Jesus denounced with such vigor. In my concern for recovering a more biblical vision of God's saving evangel, both in terms of its substance and the ways in which God has communicated it, I have used the term "evangelization." Fourth, although in English "evangelism"—and "evangelization"—refers to the communication of the gospel, other languages (Spanish, French, and German) employ the equivalent of "evangelization."

2. Within evangelical circles there has been a marked tendency to distinguish rather sharply between evangelization and mission. Evangelization is seen essentially as reaching people with a verbal proclamation of the gospel or calling them to a personal acceptance of Christ as their Savior. On the other hand, mission is viewed as a more comprehensive concept. It refers to all of God's saving activity in behalf of the world and to the church's ongoing participation in this task. While both evangelization and mission refer to God's saving intention in the world, they are clearly distinguished.

Although this urge to distinguish between evangelization and mission for purposes of logical analysis is understandable, these neat distinctions may owe more to our modern need for precise categories than to the biblical vision.

It is true that Jesus understood that the Father had sent him. It is also true that he came evangelizing. Furthermore, he sent his disciples just as he had been sent. They, in turn, continued to evangelize. But to insist on distinguishing sharply between the sending (mission), as if this were a broader more inclusive category, and evangelization, as if this were a narrower category limited to preaching, is to open the door to unbiblical dichotomies such as presence and proclamation, service and evangelism, deed and word, being and doing. As long as we cling to the "and" in these dichotomies the holistic character of biblical salvation and evangelization will continue to escape us. In the biblical view, evangelization is not separated from deeds of authentic righteousness. Nor is God's salvific intention somehow more inclusive and richer than his evangel incarnated fully in Messiah. Just as Jesus was the bearer of God's evangel, so the messianic community evangelizes with integrity through all that it is and says and does in the Spirit of Messiah himself.

For an excellent statement of a more holistic understanding of evangelization, see David J. Bosch (1981:65-74). For a fuller discussion of Bosch's understanding of the concepts of "mission" and "evangelism" and the relationship between them, see David J. Bosch, "Mission and Evangelism: Clarifying the Concepts" (1984). He observes that "*mission* is a much wider concept than *evangelism*. It is the total task which God has set the church for the salvation of the world. Mission therefore has to do with the crossing of frontiers between Church and world, frontiers of all kinds: geographical, sociological, political, ethnic, cultural, economic, religious, ideological. . . . Mission means being sent by God to love, to serve, to preach, to heal. . . . *Evangelism* is, in the words of Emilio Castro, 'our opening up the mystery of God's love to all people inside that mission, the linking of all human lives with the purpose of God manifested in Jesus Christ.' As such evangelism is the heart of mission. . . . *Evangelism is calling people to mission.* Evangelism serves the wider mission of the Church. All evangelism is mission, but not all mission is evangelism. Nonetheless, all mission must have its focus in evangelism as its core dimension" (Bosch, 1984:169-170, 173).

The tendency to define these terms either too narrowly or too broadly has often led to serious deformations in their understanding and practice. In an effort to correct these problems and to find a way out of the impasse characterized by theological confrontation and marked differences in practice, the author calls for the understanding and practice of "mission and evangelism as separate yet deeply integrated mandates" (Bosch, 1984:187).

3. I use the term "subversive" here in a literal sense. It reflects the conviction that evangelization in the biblical story brings change without recourse to human social, economic, or political power. In fact, the power of God manifests itself through human weakness. In the Old Testament a weak and obscure people, Israel, was called in its radical differentness to bring God's salvific good news to the nations. In the New Testament the same dynamic characterizes the Messiah as well as the messianic community in their communication of God's salvation. Truly salvific change occurs, not through the exercise of coercive power in any of its forms, but rather through the noncoercive activity of God who works from below, subverting the deformed and rebellious structures of human disobedience, both personal and collective.

4. The Gospels offer remarkable examples of the evangel coming from unexpected sources. Persons without status bear witness to realities of ultimate consequence. From the Samaritan woman we have occasion to learn that "Jesus is Messiah" and that "God is Truth" (John 4). From Mary Magdalene we learn that "Jesus is risen" (John 20). From a hated foreigner, the Roman centurion, we learn that Jesus is "Son of God" (Mark 15). What seems "remarkable" to us, who read the Scriptures from a Constantinian perspective, is normal from the standpoint of the Bible's upside-down world.

5. Several references display this emphasis (Matt. 21:11; 26:32; 27:55; 28:7, 10, 16; Mark 1:9, 14; 14:28; 15:41; 16:7; Luke 23:5, 49, 55; 24:6; John 7:41, 52; Acts 10:36-38). Bible references are from the Revised Standard Version unless indicated otherwise.

6. "The narratives of Jesus the Galilean that have been left to us in the gospel portraits of his career are an eloquent testimony of just how radical and transforming that experience had, after all, proved to be" (Freyne, 1988:268).

7. In the genealogy given in Matthew's Gospel, all five women mentioned (Tamar, Rahab, Ruth, the wife of Uriah, and Mary) would have been considered outcasts.

8. "Insofar as all those narratives use Galilee as a symbol of the periphery becoming the new non-localised centre of divine presence, and portray a Galilean charismatic and his retinue replacing the established religious leaders of Judaism, there is a highly paradoxical, even comic, character to the story. The pilgrim from Galilee subverts the place of pilgrimage even as he goes there; his journey becomes the new way that replaces the torah-symbol for those who follow him; their journey is to lead them, not to the centre where their Jewish faith has told them God can be encountered, but to bear witness to a new mode of encounter outside the land. Thus, the religious implications of the narratives of Jesus' career bear a striking resemblance to the paradoxical, comic kerygma of the folly of the cross confounding the wisdom of this world. The two statements, the one in narrative form, the other a kerygmatic proclamation, have a similar pattern and intent" (Freyne, 1988:271-72).

9. "These men did not belong to the regular troops of Herod Antipas or the Ro-

man Procurator; they rather provided armed support for the tax collectors . . . 'rob no one'; lit., 'shake no one violently,' in order to extort money from them" (Stuhlmueller, 1968:44:49).

10. In a profound sense, God becomes most visible in our time in the twisted, disfigured faces of those followers of Jesus persecuted and tortured for the kingdom.

References Cited

Bauman, Clarence, ed.
1991   *The Spiritual Legacy of Hans Denck: Interpretations and Translations of Key Texts*. New York: E. J. Brill.

Bosch, David J.
1981   "Evangelism," *Mission Focus* 9:4 (December).
1984   "Mission and Evangelism: Clarifying the Concepts," *Zeitschrift fur Missionswissenschaft und Religionwissenschaft* 68:3 (July).

Freyne, Sean
1988   *Galilee, Jesus and the Gospels: Literary Approaches and Historical Investigations*. Philadelphia: Fortress.

Galilea, Segundo
1982   *El camino de la espiritualidad*. Buenos Aires: Ediciones Paulinas.

Hornus, Jean-Michel
1980   *It Is Not Lawful for Me to Fight: Early Christian Attitudes Toward War, Violence, and the State*. Alan Kreider and Oliver Coburn, trans.; Scottdale, Pa.: Herald Press.

"A Response to Lausanne"
1975   "Theological Implications of Radical Discipleship," a response to "The Lausanne Covenant" from The International Congress on World Evangelization, 1974. Printed in *Mission Trends No. 2: Evangelization*. Gerald H. Anderson and Thomas A. Stransky, eds.; Grand Rapids: Eerdmans.

Stuhlmueller, Carroll
1968   "The Gospel According to Luke," *The Jerome Biblical Commentary*. Raymond S. Brown, Joseph A. Fitzmyer, and Roland E. Murphy, eds.; Englewood Cliffs, N.J.: Prentice-Hall.

Williams, George H.
1962   *The Radical Reformation*. Philadelphia: The Westminster Press.

CHAPTER 9

Consummation of Messiah's Mission

David A. Shank

W HAT IS THE SIGNIFICANCE of the "last (*eschatos*) days" (Acts 2:17 from Joel 2:28; 2 Tim. 3:1; Heb. 1:2; James 5:3; 2 Pet. 3:3), "the end of the times" (1 Pet. 1:20), "the last hour" (1 John 2:18), or "the last time" (Jude 18) for the dynamics of the messianic mission of Jesus and his people?[1] This is the concern and preoccupation of eschatology as it relates to the essential mission and calling of the messianic community.

Here we recall the importance of such in the first apostolic epistle to the Thessalonians, the earliest missionary document.

> The "coming of Messiah" for the final ingathering has now become the focal point of orientation for the time since Jesus' death and resurrection. . . . The fourfold messianic understanding portrays a picture of human history under the reign of God with culminating events fulfilled and articulated by the life, death, resurrection, present ministry, and coming of the Messiah Jesus as he gathers together God's people . . . in view of the salvation of humanity into the service of God. There is the event of Jesus' life, teaching, sufferings, and death; there is the event of the resurrection; there is the event of exaltation lived in fellowship with the apostolic gathering sent out on the mission of assembling disciples; there is the eschatological event-to-come of the full ingathering of the people of God with the appearing of Messiah (Shank, 1993:49f.).

The "day of the Lord" (1 Thess. 5:2) was an old expression of Israel's hope, which the writing prophets took up with fuller content

(Amos 8:9; Isa. 2; Mic. 1:2ff.; Zeph. 1; *et al.*), including coming historical, political, and cosmic changes involving both salvation and judgment. It came to signify the ultimate fulfillment of the saving purposes
and reign of God as sovereign over humanity—both in Israel and in
the nations. In Jesus' language in the Gospels it has become the "day
of judgment" (Matt. 10:15; 11:22; 12:36), the "day of the Son of man"
(Luke 17:24, 30; John 8:27-56), the "last day" (John 6:39-54; 11:24;
12:48). Finally, in the apostolic language, as in the Thessalonian letter,
that day is totally identified with the exalted Jesus Christ and his return in glory. Hence "the day of our Lord Jesus Christ" (1 Cor. 1:8),
"the day of the Lord Jesus" (1 Cor. 5:5; 2 Cor. 1:14), or "the day of Jesus Christ" (Phil. 1:6).

Basic New Testament Understanding

But this apostolic accent on the coming of Messiah as that which is yet
to come (1 Cor. 11:26) dare not remove from our minds the more fundamental idea that the "day of the Lord" has already come in the life
and work of Jesus (John 8:56; Luke 4:21); salvation with its inherent
judgment has come in Jesus of Nazareth (cf. John 3:16-21). In Scripture this *eschaton* or final fulfillment must be seen from the perspective
of the prophets of Israel looking forward to it (1 Pet. 1:10-12), from
that of Jesus incarnating it (Matt. 12:28; Luke 9:10f.), and from that of
the apostles who experienced and lived it (2 Cor. 6:1f.) and looked
forward to its culmination with Jesus' universal manifestation
(*epiphaneia*) or coming/appearing (parousia) in glory.

The nearly 2,000 calendar years that have passed since the death,
resurrection, and exaltation of Jesus do not change that latter perspective which we share with the apostles, even though the chronological
time span tends to distort the reality of the time of our Lord in the ongoing Christ-event by giving an impression of distance from the death
and resurrection and/or rapprochement to the parousia. One biblical
critic has stated it well:

> The clue to the meaning of the nearness of the End is the realisation of
> the essential unity of God's Saving acts in Christ—the realization that the
> Events of the Incarnation, Crucifixion, Resurrection, Ascension and
> Parousia are in a real sense one Event. The foreshortening, by which the
> Old Testament sees as one divine intervention in the future that which
> from the viewpoint of the New Testament writers is both past and future,
> is not only a visual illusion; for the distance actually brings out an essen-

tial unity, which is not so apparent from a position in between the Ascension and the Parousia (Cranfield, 1954:287/1974:323).

With the coming of Messiah, the endtimes have come; we are in that position—in the year of our Lord 1991 as I write—and we live in the hope and expectation of its ultimate fulfillment, as announced by the prophets, incarnated and taught by Jesus, and interpreted by the apostles with a rich variety of understandings.

New Testament Eschatological Understandings

When the New Testament writers wrote of the "last things"—the *eschaton*—a wide variety of expressions was used to portray its meaning. The following summary indicates the universality, totality, and comprehensiveness of that reality, the outcome of the *missio dei*:

> "The time is fulfilled, and the kingdom of God is at hand" (Mark 1:14: Jesus);
> "to restore [*apokathistanein*] all things" (Matt. 17:11; Mark 9:12: Jesus, referring to the Malachi endtimes promise re: Elijah redivivus);
> "the renewal [*palingenesia*] of all things" (Matt. 19:28, NIV: Jesus, in reference to the glorious reign of the Son of Man);
> "Everything must be fulfilled [*plarothanai*] that is written about me in the Law of Moses, the Prophets and the Psalms" (Luke 24:44, NIV: the resurrected Jesus);
> "the . . . restitution [*apokatastasis*] of all things" (Acts 3:21, KJV: Peter);
> "to bring [*anakephalaioumai*] all things in heaven and on earth together under one head" (Eph. 1:10, NIV: Paul);
> "to reconcile [*apokatallassein*] to himself all things, whether on earth or in heaven, making peace [*eiranopoein*] by the blood of his cross" (Col. 1:20: Paul);
> " 'For God has put all things in subjection [*upotassein*] under his feet.' . . . that God may be everything to every one" (1 Cor. 15:25ff.: Paul);
> "and every tongue confess [*exomologasatai*] that Jesus Christ is Lord" (Phil. 2:11; pre-Pauline hymn?);
> "a salvation [*soterion*] ready to be revealed in the last time" (1 Pet. 1:3-5; cf. Rev. 12:10; 19:1);
> "The end [completion/consummation/*telos*] of all things" (1 Pet. 4:7);
> "a new heaven and a new earth [*kaina poio*]" (Rev. 21:1, 6: John; cf. 2 Pet. 3:13);
> "The kingdom of the world has become the kingdom of our Lord and of his Christ, and he shall reign for ever and ever" (Rev. 11:15).

When Jesus spoke of the kingdom of God, regeneration, restoration, or fulfillment of all things, he was clearly referring to the end-times promises in the prophetic writings, of which John the Baptist was the harbinger. Jesus himself was the inaugural manifestation, whose full actualization he expectantly anticipated. Whether it was the promise of the messianic banquet (Isa. 25:6ff.) or the restored kingdom (Jer. 23:5ff.; Ezek. 37:20-28; Dan. 7:13ff.; Isa. 11; 49:8ff.; 60) with its promises of peace and justice and prosperity (Isa. 65:17ff.; Joel 2; Mal. 4), in Jesus' perception their fulfillment had begun definitively since the Spirit of God had begun to break into Israel's life in his life and service.

Peter, John, and Paul used the language of restitution, recapitulation, reconciliation, making peace, subjection, consummation, renewal of all things, or the kingdom of God in the light of the same promises; but they had the new perspective of Jesus' life of service, crucifixion, resurrection, and messianic exaltation as well as their own Spirit-anointing by the anointed. Their mission anticipated, participated in, and contributed to those immediate and long-range consequences. They knew for a certainty that the endtime fulfillment promised by the prophets had begun in Jesus; sent by Christ/Messiah, their mission was a participation in that free Spirit-movement of love and grace within Israel and the nations which manifests God's ultimate purpose.

They were to expose and declare it to the world as they shared in that apocalyptic inbreaking. The end was near, they knew, for they were participants in it already; the reconciliation of all things was nigh, for they experienced it; the submission of all things could not tarry, since they lived out daily their own obedience to Messiah, who had already united them under his headship. Indeed, the resurrection of Jesus was the firstfruits of the coming harvest (1 Cor. 15:20), and the gift of the Spirit was down payment of that which was yet to come (Eph. 1:13f.).

This diversity of language should not, however, overshadow the one reality that is expressed: that Jesus, God's Messiah, reveals and fulfills God's purposes in and for creation. That one reality is a certainty that clearly orients life in the midst of all of the present uncertainties. It is a vision that takes on actuality in the present. But it is above all an experience of participation "in God the Father and the Lord Jesus Christ" (1 Thess. 1:1)—the personal, vital dynamic power who is bringing it to pass, who gives the certainty and assures the vision.

Thus it is not strange that the personal faith-within-community appropriation of that ultimate prophetic hope is itself also expressed in terms of regeneration (John 3:3-6; 1 Pet. 1:3, 23), reconciliation

(2 Cor. 5:18-19), peace or peacemaking (Rom. 5:1; Eph. 2:14; Matt. 5:9), renewal (2 Cor. 5:17f.), perfecting (Matt. 5:48; Phil. 3:12ff.; 1 Cor. 13:9ff.), subjection (Eph. 5:21-24), salvation (Eph. 2:5-8), confession (Rom. 10:9f.), or kingdom (Col. 1:13). That future which is promised by God through Israel's prophets is already really, truly, and effectively known in Christ, even if only in part (1 Cor. 13:8-13). Thus, for example, Paul wrote to the Colossians of God's purposes through Christ "to reconcile to himself all things. . . . And you, . . . he has now reconciled" (Col. 1:20-22). It is that "now," used so consistently in the apostolic writings (see Stählin, 1967:1112-23), which emphasizes strongly what George Ladd has characterized as the "presence of the future."[2]

The ultimate ending-out, completion, or perfecting of God's purposes is—to use Paul's expression in relation to "subjection"—when "God [is] everything to every one" (1 Cor. 15:28). John's Revelation uses similar language to say the same thing about this ultimate end: "Behold, the dwelling of God is with men. He will dwell with them, and they shall be his people" (Rev. 21:3). What is significant is that this is not new language, but that of Moses and the prophets (Exod. 6:7; 25:8; 29:45; Lev. 26:12; Jer. 31:1, 33; Ezek. 37:27) expressing God's intention and purpose. The apostles are simply expressing what has already become true in Jesus (John 1:14) and now in the churches (2 Cor. 6:16ff.; Heb. 8:10—9:28). There is a continuity of intention but an ever greater fulfillment of that purpose, with its ultimate completion yet coming; that is nothing more nor less than God fully present in humankind, and humankind fully in the service of God (Exod. 8:1, 20; et al.; Lev. 25:42, 55; Deut. 6:13; Matt. 4:10; Rev. 22:3).

To speak of God's intention for humankind in this way is to speak most certainly of spiritual reality; the intention is also certainly social (interpersonal) and political (ordered/governed)—a reign, the kingdom of God, "on earth as it is in heaven" (Matt. 6:10). Whether in heaven or on earth, within history or beyond history, it is an eminently social and political spiritual reality. Hence the *ecclesia*/church "in God the Father and the Lord Jesus [the Messiah]" (1 Thess. 1:1) is the gathering of those now/already called together "into his own kingdom and glory" (1 Thess. 2:12).[3] The church of the Messiah is a manifestation of the "last times," of the kingdom of God come and coming. It is eschatological, an endtimes reality; its collective interpersonal life is ordered by the Holy Spirit (1 Thess. 4:8) of Messiah in view of his coming (1 Thess. 3:11f.) when he brings all things to fulfillment.

The Content and Character of the Eschaton in the New Testament

The unanimous consensus of the writers of the New Testament is that in Jesus the Messiah, God is revealed as active love (*agape*) and grace (*charis*). We recall that in the oldest apostolic and missionary document—to the Thessalonians—Paul can speak of this young church that they "have been taught by God to love one another" (1 Thess. 4:9). It is not teaching as precept, but the teaching given through God's self-revelation in the life, death, and resurrection of Jesus the Messiah, who, when trusted and obeyed, reproduces such love in the life of whomever thus participates in his Spirit (Rom. 5:5-8). John saw the full manifestation of that love of the Father for the Son (John 17:24-26) and of the only begotten Son (John 3:16) for the Father (John 17:4) in his obedient service for humankind, even unto death, and for the expiation of sin. The endtime (1 John 2:18) revelation is that "God is love (*agape*)" (1 John 4:8).

In the last times, the righteousness/justice (*tsedek/dikaiosune*) of God, so fundamental to Israel's existence and understanding, is revealed in the Messiah Jesus to be an expression of the one true God of love which the gospel proclaims (Rom. 1:16f.; 3:21-26). The peace of God (*shalom/eirene*), so dominant a theme in Israel's life and hope (see Yoder, 1987), is revealed in Jesus the Messiah to be an expression of the one true God of love (Eph. 2:14; Phil. 4:7) who takes upon himself the injustice and strife of sinful humanity in order to restore it. The joy of the Lord and rejoicing in God, so spontaneous in Israel's worship of God, in response to God's acts of mercy and compassion, are revealed in the Messiah Jesus to be expressions from the presence of the one true God of love (John 15:11) and which are intrinsic to life in the Spirit in his service (1 John 1:4; Matt. 25:21-23; John 16:22-24).[4]

Within the context of Messiah Jesus' ultimate revelation of love, its full, complete, endtime manifestation is expressed necessarily in the eschatological dimensions of covenant justice, peace, and joy. The classic Pauline text and locus of the Protestant Reformation's *sola fide* reports this eschatological appropriation of covenant justice, peace, and joy (Rom. 5:1-2) as a consequence of God's love (*agape*) in the Messiah Jesus "while we were yet sinners . . . [or] enemies" (5:8-10). Toward the end of that same letter Paul insists that the endtime (13:11f.) understanding of the kingdom of God is precisely "righteousness and peace and joy in the Holy Spirit" (14:17). These are fundamentally categories of personal relationships and of ordering of human life (social and political) which now become functional within the church of the kingdom of God (Rom. 14:19; Col. 3:15; 1 Thess. 5:13; Rom. 6:17-19; Phil. 4:4) at whatever cost (1 Pet. 2:20ff.) as it is scattered within human society (Matt. 13:37f.; 2 Tim. 2:22; Heb. 12:14; Phil. 2:15f.; Rom. 12:17-18). The Messiah is the example, even as he taught those who confessed his Messiahship (Matt. 16:24ff.).

The content of the eschaton, when "God [will] be everything to everyone" (1 Cor. 15:28), will be divine love within the gathering of God's people in the Messiah Jesus "from every nation, from all tribes and peoples and tongues" (Rev. 5:9); it will be expressed in that reign as justice, peace, and joy over and among this new humanity with and under God. But most significantly, it is already to be found in the communities of the Messiah and in societies where disciples of Messiah Jesus discern their true calling and freely live it out. It recalls Jesus' parable of the kingdom of God: "It is like leaven which a woman took and hid in three measures of meal, till it was all leavened" (Luke 13:21).

The Itineraries of the Messianic Community (ies) in the Endtimes

There is a certain paradox in the juxtaposition of Jesus' parable of the leaven with the early one (Mark 4:3-20) of the sower whose seeds fell along the path, on rocky ground, among thorns, or into good soil where it "brought forth grain, growing up and increasing and yielding thirtyfold and sixtyfold and a hundredfold" (Mark 4:8). The first speaks figuratively of an action that is totally fulfilling: "till it was all leavened" (Luke 13:21). The second speaks figuratively about receptivity to the messianic word of the kingdom of God; in contrast to the first, only a part—apparently a minority—of those who hear become fruitful. Indeed an apparent majority are not fruitful for the kingdom.

The mystery of the satanic taking away of the word clearly leaves some hearers outside the pale of receptivity; Jesus appears to have been conscious of their loss. But he is also conscious and concerned about those who, like young plants in rocky ground that wither in the heat of the sun, receive the word and fall away "when tribulation or persecution arises on account of the word" (Mark 4:17). He is no less conscious of those who, like plants choked out by thorns, are unfruitful because of the choking effect of the "cares of the world, and the delight in riches, and the desire for other things" (Mark 4:19). The hearers of the good news of the kingdom of God in the last days go their four ways. Those who receive the word of the kingdom and are clearly under its influence nevertheless go three separate ways. The ones who bear fruit are those who hear and accept or "understand" (Matt. 13:13, 19, 23) or "hold . . . fast in an honest and good heart" (Luke 8:15) the word of the kingdom; they are the ones who are oriented to and by the kingdom of God as they walk the "way of Messiah."[5]

Near the beginning of his ministry Jesus interpreted the parable of the sower and the soils for the twelve that he had called together to form the new Israel, the new messianic community where the end-times' content was to take social and political shape. Thus, he openly informed them of the possible sidetracks that their community—and others called together through and after them—could take. And he clearly accented the eschatological path of the coming kingdom of love ordered in justice, peace, and joy. On another early occasion he had insisted: "Seek first [God's] kingdom and his righteousness, and all these things shall be yours as well" (Matt. 6:33). And during the last week of his passion, in the Olivet discourse, he continued to insist: "Take heed that no one leads you astray" (Mark 13:5).

Insofar as Jesus the exalted Messiah is himself the mediator between the times of the apostles and the future fulfillment of the kingdom, with historical hindsight we may become more and more aware that these potential itineraries have indeed been played out. Much has depended upon how the communities that have borne his name have understood or misunderstood him and his mission in relation to the kingdom and his church.

The Itinerary of Faithfulness
From the Olivet discourse (Mark 13) we grasp Jesus' understanding of the itinerary of the fruitful church of the kingdom of God;[6] it is along a way where:

- false messiahs will indeed lead many astray (13:5f.);
- wars and rumors of wars are part of the agenda before the end (*telos*), with nation rising against nation and kingdom against kingdom (13:7);
- earthquakes will occur in various places (13:8);
- there will be famines (13:8);
- the disciples will be delivered up to councils and beaten in synagogues (13:9);
- the disciples will bear witness for the sake of Messiah before governors and kings, the Holy Spirit giving them what to speak (13:11);
- the gospel must be preached to all nations (13:10);
- family members will deliver disciple-members of the family up to death—brother against brother, father against chidren, children against parents (13:12);

- disciples will be hated for the sake of Jesus' name, but salvation is in endurance (13:13);
- a desolating sacrilege will be set up, no doubt in the temple at Jerusalem, leading to a time of terrible unequalled tribulation (13:14-20);
- false messiahs and false prophets showing signs and wonders will seek to lead disciples astray (13:21ff.);
- "powers in the heavens will be shaken" in a context of cosmic disturbances affecting sun, moon, and stars (13:24f.);
- finally, the powers will see the Son of man coming in the clouds with great power and glory, as he sends his messengers to complete the gathering of his people from out of all the earth and heaven (13:24-27).

All of these things are to be seen as signs of the nearness of the Son of Man, the mediator of the end and the eschatological savior and judge of humankind (Mark 13:29).[7] Watchfulness (13:33-37) is the order of the times, because of the uncertainty of the day and the hour of the end which are known only by the Father (13:32-37).

The prophetic "I have told you all things beforehand" (Mark 13:23) is fully in harmony with the prophetic "Take heed" (13:5, 9, 23, 33) clearly given in the context of a perceived ongoing history. The apocalyptic dimensions of cosmic shaking of the heavenly powers— who see the glory of the Son of man in his calling together a humanity from the four corners of the earth and heaven—portray, as it were, a telescoped history fully consonant with the prophetic proclamation of Daniel 7:14: "To him was given dominion and glory and kingdom, that all peoples, nations, and languages should serve him; his dominion is an everlasting dominion, which shall not pass away."

Today we find the telescoping at least partially undone and opened, with a continuing projection of the signs of the nearness of the Son of man on the screen of human history. Here Messiah's call in view of the end of the endtimes is to watch, to take heed, to endure or persevere unto the end, to witness to authorities under the leading of the Holy Spirit, to suffer in the face of the opposition from the religious, political, and ethnic powers.

This is in a context of earthquakes and famines, nationalistic wars and uprisings, false messiahs and prophets with their signs and wonders, where the necessity of proclaiming the good news of the kingdom to all nations thus remains as a messianic priority. This, from Messiah Jesus, is the way of fruitfulness and salvation for the community he calls, and which is ordered by God's love in justice, peace, and joy in the Holy Spirit, as we have seen.

The Deviated Itineraries[8]

How striking is Jesus' awareness of those who in the midst of opposition and difficulty—or preoccupied with cares of the world—would not persevere in the way of the word of the kingdom of God. That is also Paul's major preoccupation with the young assembly at Thessalonica (1 Thess. 3:1-5ff.); he tries to prepare the church there for suffering from opposition as an inherent dimension of life in the Messiah. He is concerned that they not abandon the faith. What he probably does not (yet) anticipate is the way a faith community bearing the name of Jesus the Messiah could maintain the name yet lose both its meaning and the faith/life of the kingdom he reveals. Yet he does later discover this to be true in Galatia, Corinth, and Colossae; and before the end of the century "Christian" churches addressed in Revelation 2—3 are maintaining the name but are also being called to repent. In the epistle to the Hebrews it is clear that zeal is cooled, and "the Day drawing near" (Heb. 10:25) is the appeal for stimulation. Second Peter makes it clear that the not-yet-fulfillment of the eschatological hope is bringing the scoffers with their reference to non-fulfillment: "all things have continued as they were" (2 Pet. 3:4); it is necessary to restore assurance in the prophetic vision of the "new heavens and a new earth" (3:13) beyond the judgment of the worldly system and those involved in it (3:1-13).

The "last days" have come; the new age has broken into the old, with a real salvation yet to be totally fulfilled with judgment of the old (cf. 2 Cor. 5:17). Yet the power of the old age continues to impinge upon the communities of Messiah, either through direct opposition and persecution or through seduction, in its various and devious forms. In the former case, the lines are often clearly drawn, as becomes clearer with those of Israel who reject Jesus' messiahship and with Rome's Caesar which cannot bear the "Messiah is Lord" claims as over against its own lordship (cf. Eph. 1:21). More difficult is the maintenance of clarity in the midst of seductive pressures, often heightened, paradoxically, through the leavening effect of the gospel of Messiah and his church upon surrounding society, where the lines become fuzzy.

Moreover, since the gospel of Messiah is a proclamation of God's saving truth for all peoples, it must first be interpreted from Aramaic, the popular Hebrew of Jesus and his circles, and appropriated in popular (*koine*) Greek, which is already such a dominant influence in non-Palestinian Judaism. The same is true for Latin, Syriac, Armenian, Coptic, Gothic, and Ethiopic as the circle of mission expands and the need for translation of the Scriptures arises. But it becomes necessary also to attempt to "save" that truth from competing understandings, perceptions, and systems of thought which function as truth for many peoples. Hence, the truth of the simple confession, "Jesus the Christ is Lord," is perceived to be "saved" by the successive confessional councils and their creeds.

However, we have already noted that the intent of the Messiah is to save and restore humanity, to gather a people whose life together bears the sociopolitical signs of the eschatological "God being everything to everyone": loving service, ordered in justice, peace and joy, as incarnate in the Servant-Messiah, at any cost. The perseverance given to preserving the truth of the confession of faith is not always paralleled with perseverance in the itinerary of community (i.e., sociopolitical) fidelity traced by Jesus, the Servant; yet endurance in the obedience of faith in love, as a sign of the last days, is also essential truth (Eph. 4:14-15; 1 John 2:4-6; 3:18). "The love of most will grow cold, but he who stands firm to the end will be saved" (Matt. 24:12-13, NIV). Such a community is what Origen, in the times of imperial persecution more than two centuries later, could call "another sort of country created by the Logos of God," (*Contra Celsum*, VIII, 2). But within another century and a half things changed rapidly.

"The glorious City of God pursues its pilgrimage through the times and impiety [of the earthly city], living here below by faith," writes Augustine of Hippo in 413 as he begins *The City of God*; "with patience she awaits the eternal sojourn where its justice in its turn will be judge, and its holiness will be in possession of the last victory and of inalterable peace" (Augustine: Book I, 1; p. 1). Like Paul sixteen generations before him, Augustine also states his eschatological hope of justice and peace, but in different terms. From within the perspective of a couple of generations of Rome's imperial tolerance and cooptation of the messianic movement, he also adds at the end of Book 1, given the difficulty of knowing who is or is not a Christian: "the two cities are entwined and intermingled in this age until the last judgment separates them. It is [only] on their origins, their progress, and the end which awaits them that I wish to develop my thoughts" (Augustine: Book I, xxxv; p. 20). Indeed, between the two statements is found his classic word on divinely authoritative exceptions to the interdiction of killing:

Sometimes God orders murder either by a general law or by a temporary and special command. He is not morally homicidal who owes his
ministry to the authority; he is only an instrument, like the sword with
which he strikes. Thus they have not transgressed the precept, those
who by order of God have made war; or in the exercise of public power
have, following its laws, that is to say following the will of the most just
reason, punished criminals with death" (Augustine: Book I, xxi; p. 14).

Here the social and political orientation is based not upon the
Servant Messiah, but on the "just reason" of Roman public power and
its laws, and is illustrated by Abraham, Jephtha, and Samson from the
Old Testament.

This is not the place to trace the churches' generations of experience or to offer a critique of their various sociopolitical stances. But it
is important to illustrate an endtimes itinerary other than that which
Jesus and the early apostolic church lived and taught. For now, imperial reason with its legal system and legion-imposed *Pax Romana* orders the life of the church bearing the name of Messiah Jesus, while
his justice, holiness, and peace will come only at the last judgment. In
such a perception, the full force of the eschatological "now" in the
messianic community is gone; the future is not yet present but is
wholly future; old things have not passed away, for it is the old era (illustrated by the Old Testament) that has overtaken the new that is
come in Jesus the Messiah.

Yet in fact the church sees itself as over and above the rest of society, consciously ordering it with Roman and Old Testament ways as a
theocratic millennial reign of Christ. But the illustration of Augustine
is intentional, for there can be no doubt that this eschatological perception has dominated the Western Christian mission in ways that are
parallel to that indicated for Christology (see Shank, 1993:), following
Andrew Walls' cultural history of Christianity (Walls, 1985:58-73).[9]

This dominant but deviant itinerary makes it considerably easier
to explain the ever-recurring alternatives in the so-called sectarian reactions to this so-called mainstream. One recalls the Waldensian
movement, the Wycliffe influence through the Lollard mission and its
social impact, the early Hussite movement with the Moravian Brethren spin-offs in missionary pioneering, the Anabaptist Mennonites
with their nonresistant, free church alternative with its missionary impact, the Pietist *ecclesiolae in ecclesia* with its strong social mission, the
Quaker mission with its creative peace and social thrust, the Method-
ist awakening, the Adventists with their holistic gospel, the nine-

teenth-century Blumhardt revival, or the Pentecostals with their accent on the Spirit of the last times.

A common thread of perseverance—at whatever cost—appears in
the beginnings of these various efforts to take the spirit of the New
Testament and the Christ of the Gospels as the last and definitive
word. That thread is the rediscovered messianic mission of Jesus
Christ, Spirit-Anointed and Anointer, as the one who transforms, restores, recreates, and regenerates humanity into a new spiritual/social
community with its new life as a challenge and alternative to the old.
In it there is an implicit—and sometimes explicit and apocalyptic—eschatological orientation which seeks to bring about now in the
present the promises of the endtime.[10]

From such a perspective we must observe that the reappearance
of such movements of mission within Christendom points out clearly
a line of continuity in these last times, from which the Augustinian eschatology and its sociopolitical shaping is itself a deviation.[11] Indeed
the great evangelical missionary movement of the nineteenth and
twentieth centuries emerges from such movements often in the face of
opposition from the mainstream churches. The eschatological dynamic is a most important dimension in that movement, although the motif was later shifted to "while there is yet time"/"before it's too late."
More recently the major holistic and biblical eschatological motif of
the kingdom of God is there again coming to the fore.

Also in recent years, messianic dynamics as sociopolitical phenomena are being studied by scholars, precisely because of their social and political creativity. Particularly helpful is the work of Henri
Desroche indicating the sociological directions taken within so-called
messianic movements when the holistic restoration of the promised
kingdom does not intervene as or when expected.[12]

In the midst of oppression, domination, injustice, and alienation a
personality appears as God's instrument for bringing about a new humanity, interpreted as a coming new creation/ kingdom/order and vi-
sualized as the promise of a holistic reality encompassing religious,
social, economic, and political aspects of life. Those who break with
the old order to follow the leader form new communities which become a critique of the old order and a foreshadowing of the new when
it will be wholly fullfilled.

When the promised order fails to appear in the world, the initial
impetus wanes and the movement undergoes a fission, one part veer-
ing in a religious direction and the other taking on a political shaping.
The breakup thus denatures the original holistic thrust; each deviation

from the initial intent becomes itself a movement which reinterprets the hope-event from a reductionist perspective, downplaying the other accents found in the original vision, and reacting to their shape in the sidetracked itineraries.

Under new conditions the initial event may be newly appropriated by either or both of these. The original holistic thrust is rediscovered, thus provoking a messianic resurgence which picks up and draws upon the original eschatological vision and dynamic, with re-creation of holistic alternative communities.

One cannot but be struck with the manner in which the cycle discerned by Desroche has been played out not only in so-called sectarian movements, but within Western Christianity as a whole, during this continuing age of our Lord; the Augustinian synthesis is now being fully critiqued by renewal in the midst of its demise, and eschatology has been a major dimension in that renewal. One has only to recall the Evanston meeting of the General Assembly of the World Council of Churches. But Latin Europe was also impacted. Vatican II itself was a call for a more eschatologically oriented church.[13] Indeed, one of the leading French Catholic theologians influential in Vatican II, Yves Congar, later wrote a volume on the church as "a messianic people" (1975), where he fully exploits the expression *populus messianicus* (with the intentional Latinization of the Hebrew this time) which is found inserted twice in the text of *Lumen Gentia* No.9 at his insistence.[14] One of the leading European Protestant theologians, Jürgen Moltmann, wrote his volume on ecclesiology as "a contribution to messianic ecclesiology" (Moltmann, 1977). A leading theologian/ethicist published a significant volume defending the "possibility of messianic ethics" (cf. Yoder, 1973:chap.1).

It would appear that an important part of that corrective—messianic resurgence—is also a spin-off of the worldwide mission of the nineteenth and twentieth centuries already referred to. The World Council of Churches is itself a direct outgrowth of that movement. The insertion of *populus messianicus* in Vatican II documents is due to the earlier influence of theologian M. D. Chenu, who is particularly sensitive to the religious messianic dynamics developing in the third world where the missionary movement is carrier of a new worldview with an ending-out of history.[15] Moltmann indicates clearly that his own volume does not grow out of his study or the lecture rooms at Tübingen University:

> The experiences of Christians in Korea, their missionary zeal and their suffering in political resistance, the charismatic experiences of the inde-

pendent churches in Kenya and Ghana, their prayers and exuberant dances; the work of Christian communes in the slums of Manila, and the villages of the campesinos in Mexico, their life among their people and their persecution by the police—all these things impressed me more vividly than I probably realized myself. They have at least shown me the limitations of the church in Germany (Moltmann, 1977:xv).

This incursion from the third world into the West is also a recall to Western Christianity, where the kingdom of Christ is either generally interiorized, spiritualized, or privatized, if not put simply into a millennial future in the plan of God. And it is a recall to the Western theocratic hangovers from Augustine, which easily can reject Jesus Christ's sociopolitical significance as an irrelevant model since he is indeed presented only as personal, religious, inner, and private. Indeed the new messianic community where Jesus is followed takes its sociopolitical cues from the Servant-Messiah often more spontaneously than self-consciously and deliberately. The latter becomes necessary where Christianity has become a cultural given.

In a colloquium of Catholic scholars studying the possible current understandings of the "Return of Christ," sociologist Jean Séguy observed that theologians, exegetes, and philosophers presented it as being quite problematical, as a part of the human "imaginative"; instead of the return being a real historical future, they re-presented it quite flatly as being strictly a question of here and now. How, he asked the intellectual elite, does that relate to the traditional affirmations—"stupidly traditional, foolishly traditional"—of the creeds where it is clearly a question of the real return of Christ?

> There is a whole density of history in which one sees the Christian people in its diverse forms await that return (with a realism which is very moving in the failure—each time renewed—of the expectation), love that return, fear that return. [Where others in the colloquium saw these as "aberrations," "temptations," or "mirrors of temptations," he responded:] I observe very simply that thousands, hundreds of thousands of Christians across the centuries, even today in numerous countries await the return of Christ; and this helps them to read things, to situate themselves in the world where they live, to get a real hold on the world. Then, they will not transform it perhaps in the manner that certain others speak of transforming the world, but in their own particular way, and around them they will certainly transform it in a certain manner. . . . I am certainly much more moved by the expectation of a Brazilian tribe seeking for the earth without evil and the return of Christ; by the waiting of an Adventist, of a Darbyist, by the expectation of a Joachim de Fiore

watching for the opening of the Third Age; or even by the expectation of
Newman (to cite a cardinal of the Holy Roman Church) in his two famous sermons on, precisely, "Waiting"; much more moved by that attitude than by that which consists in relativising that value of expectant
waiting. . . . In speaking of the imaginative one should observe that it is
what permits man to go beyond himself. It is that which permits him to
consider himself other than what he is, that is to say to conceive another
reality, and eventually to start moving to bring it to pass. . . . There are
several ways of conceiving the expectation. But it is always active, either
by prayer and holiness in the type of church which wishes to be renewed
according to the old, or else peacefully but already in a concrete way in a
messianic community, or else by taking up arms (Séguy, 1983:181-88;
translation mine).

The sixteenth century, which has so much conditioned the shape
of Western Christianity, experiences the same resurgence and the
same fission. In response to the oppressive sacral *corpus Christianum*
due to Augustine's synthesis, the Reformation reaction appears, moving in several directions: the Lutheran religious orientation, with certain Spiritualists (such as Franck or Schwenckfeld) pushing it even
further; the theocratic/political direction of the Calvinists as earlier on
a smaller scale with Thomas Müntzer or the infamous Münster kingdom; or the direction of free communities of witness and suffering
and mission (see Shenk, 1984), with Jesus the Messiah as sovereign
Prince of peace and example, as over against the ruling prince of the
times.[16]

In these last times then, directions do clearly differ in relation to
the eschatological mission and itinerary shaped and taught by Jesus
the Messiah and his early apostles as they lived out the foolishness of
the cross in the light of the experienced coming and future fulfillment
of the kingdom of God.

The Different Eschatological Scenarios

If we have observed different itineraries, we must also observe that
they are due partly at least to differently perceived scenarios of the
penultimate endtimes. The different apostles with their different influences, emphases, and accents write of Jesus' resurrection being the
firstfruits of an end-time resurrection of humanity. Or they may refer
to that resurrection as the presence of and struggle with the antichrist
(anti-Messiah); deliverances from divine wrath—a final judgment of
the nations, of individuals, of death and Hades; the binding of Satan

during a thousand-year reign of Christ with his martyrs; the salvation of all Israel; the new Jerusalem; hell and the lake of fire; Christ's victorious combat; his coming with the saints, or the so-called rapture.

There appears to be no end of image, symbol, analogy, or metaphor used to portray and represent the necessary changes, threats, surprises, crises, outcomes, conflicts, interventions, tribulations, transformations, testings, judgments, deliverances which must inevitably be effected in time, in history, in the church, in the world, in Israel, among the nations, in the universe before the complete fulfillment of the kingdom of God, when "God will be everything to everyone." All of the resources of language of the prophets of Israel, of Judaism's apocalyptic writers, and of then current reality is used by the Spirit to prepare, to save, to proclaim, to exhort, to win, to forewarn, to strengthen, and to console the churches and the disciples in their perseverance and faithfulness in mission under the rule and in the service of Messiah.[17]

It is in the interpretative arrangements of those descriptions and events that the greatest divergences have been found in countless scenarios purporting to portray a precise history of the endtimes. We have only alluded to Augustine's, where, following the influential Origen, the "thousand years" was interpreted symbolically (a-millennial) as the time of Christ's dominion over the world through the church. This was in contrast to clear, future, earthly expectations of some earlier writers such as Justin and Irenaeus. But later millennial scenarios did not agree as to whether Christ would return before or after an earthly millennial reign. It was indeed the latter post-millennial view which predominated during the great missionary century after 1800.

Among those who agree that Christ's return would be before (the pre-millennial scenario), there is not agreement on whether it will be before or after great tribulation to which Jesus and John's Apocalypse refer. Since the historicizing eschatological writings of the Chilean Jesuit Lacunza at the end of the eighteenth century, much disagreement about the role, restoration, and timing of the salvation and mission of Israel is reflected in the scenarios of Irvingites, Darbyists, Adventists, and other so-called dispensationalists.

These scenarios grow out of the following situations and states: the natural desire to know ahead of time; the new lenses provided by political changes and opposition to the gospel in a given time span; the literal, predictive character imposed on all prophetic and apocalyptic writings in Scripture; the cultural distance from the scriptural texts; and the imaginative and speculative character of human understandings. These and others may combine with the great diversity already mentioned to accentuate unduly the importance of penultimate scenarios and debate about them, to the detriment of the basic eschatological thrust of Scripture. That thrust is the shaping now through the gospel, in and through the Holy Spirit in the churches, God's ultimate saving purpose as revealed through Israel in Jesus the Messiah's life, death, resurrection, magistracy, and coming. And that purpose features divine, *agape* love ordering human life, existence, and service in justice, peace, and joy on earth as it is in heaven.[18]

The present on-the-earth, in-the-world faith participation in that salvation in the Spirit of Christ is already the service-of-God of the endtimes. It is out of love for the Servant Lord, Jesus the Messiah; and "whether we live or whether we die, we are the Lord's" (Rom. 14:8). Being gathered in, by and for him, and gathering with him others in such mission is sufficient personal eschatological knowledge beyond the hope that his own resurrection is the "first fruits of those who have fallen asleep" (1 Cor. 15:20ff.), and that he "will change our lowly body to be like his glorious body" (Phil. 3:21).

Proclaiming the Fulfillment of Time

This brief study has not addressed the precise nature of the relationship of the church to and in society where the old order protests the call of the new. Both in history and geography the temporal, cultural, political, and socioeconomic contexts in which the churches find themselves vary considerably, and thus we cannot here venture into such developments. But it is essential that the church as human community express concretely in its existence that the last days of God's fulfilled purpose for humanity in the Messiah Jesus are taking shape in temporal, cultural, political, and socioeconomic patterns. And wherever in the world that is not to be found, the church is called to an apostolate of teams—cells of salt and light—which proclaim, "The times are fulfilled, the kingdom of God is at hand; repent and believe the good news of the king, the Messiah Jesus." This is indeed the meaning of the so-called great commission found in the four Gospels and the Acts of the Apostles, the very heart of the churches' calling between the ascension and the parousia.[19]

Notes

1. Scripture references in this chapter are from the Revised Standard Version unless noted otherwise.

2. See Ladd (1974). This is well spelled out by John Driver, (1993: chapter 2, this volume).

3. Jürgen Moltmann portrays this correctly and effectively with the expression "the church of the Kingdom of God" (Moltmann, 1977:chap. 4).

4. "The new life under his [Messiah's] influence cannot be understood merely as new obedience, as a reversal of life's direction and as an endeavor to change the world until it visibly becomes God's creation. It is also, and with equal emphasis, celebrated as the feast of freedom, as joy in existence and as the ecstasy of bliss" (Moltmann, 1977:109).

5. This is particularly well developed in Mark, as has been shown by Willard M. Swartley in his helpful analysis of Mark's use of *"hodos*/the way" (1979).

6. Hendrikus Berkhof has pointed this out so well (1966); see especially pages 70ff. where he deals with the *Fernerwartung* (distant expectation) in Jesus' eschatological thought.

7. See the "Son of Man" section in Shank (1993).

8. Throughout this section I will use the present tense, writing of what is past and history as present in these last days of Christ. Perhaps the best discussion of the shift from messianic movement to Christian religion is by Christopher Rowland (1985).

9. "Augustine's influence on the course of subsequent theology has been immense. He moulded the whole of that of the Middle Ages down to the 13th century, and even the reaction against Augustinianism with the rediscovery of Aristotle in the 13th century . . . was less complete than has widely been supposed. The Reformers also appealed to elements of Augustine's teaching in their attack on the Schoolmen. . . . Without Augustine's massive intellect and deep spiritual perception Western theology would never have taken the shape in which it is familiar to us" (Cross 1958:107).

See particularly Walter Klaassen (1981:218-30). A brief critique from a modern Anabaptist perspective is offered by Harold S. Bender (Goshen College Biblical Seminary): "In fact the church is equated with the Kingdom of God in which Christ reigns. (It should be noted that Augustine was the first to make this identification.) . . . . The contrast between the splendor of the church and the fast-decaying Roman empire is such that Augustine was convinced that the millenium [sic] forecast in the Revelation of John was already in effect; it had begun with the first coming of Christ upon the earth and would continue until his second coming. (Augustine was the one who put the death knell to the millenialism [sic] of the Ante-Nicene age.)" (Bender, 1955:48). A more thorough critique is given by John H. Yoder (1983). The fullest analysis from this perspective is Reformed scholar Leonard Verduin, *The Anatomy of a Hybrid,* Grand Rapids: Eerdmans, 1976.

10. See particularly Christopher Rowland (1988). Reinhold Niebuhr also indicates how in his judgment the doctrine of the second coming of Christ has been particularly fruitful of error (which he attributes to a chronological illusion making it a "point in history" rather than a trans-historical reality symbolized by time): "It has led to fantastic sectarian illusions of every type. Yet it is significant that the dispossessed and disinherited have been particularly prone to these illusions, because they were anxious to express the Christian hope of fulfilment in social as well as in individual terms. Sectarian apocalypticism is closely related to modern proletarian radicalism, which is a secularized form of the [former]. In both, the individualism of Christian orthodoxy is opposed with conceptions which place the corporate enterprises of mankind, as well as individuals, under an ultimate judgment and under ultimate possibilities of fulfilment. In these secular and apocalyptic illusions the end of time is a point in time beyond which there will be an unconditioned society. But there is truth in the illusions" (Niebuhr, 1937:22-23). Is the truth not also in Niebuhr's own underestimation of the biblical witness to the way in which history's consummation comes by way of the peaceful kingdom of Christ "on earth as it is in heaven" and of which the messianic community is the visible sign?

11. In the language of the French sociologist Gurvitch, as used by Roger Bastide,

"the history of Christianity is that of a discontinued continuity or a continued discontinuity" (Bastide, 1972:8).

12. See Desroche (1969). The interpretative introduction has been expanded into a volume translated into English (1979). The work grew out of the author's concern to understand how so often the Christian faith expressed in alternative movements was not Marx's "opium of the people" but a renewing ferment. Indeed, the role of persecuted Christians in Eastern Europe must surely be seen in this perspective along with the demise of the communist system in 1989-90, itself functioning as a veritable opium.

13. The eschatological dimension of this shift in Latin Europe has been well described by Etienne Fouilloux (1971).

14. E.g., *Lumen Gentium* II, No. 9, 2. Congar also attempted to insert it into a passage of *Gaudium et Spes* and in No. 5 of *Ad Gentes divinitus*, but it was erased during corrections and editing (Congar, 1975:93, n. 50).

15. See Chenu (1962; 1967). His conversation with Desroche is reported in Desroche (1969:5).

16. This fourfold direction, so parallel to that of Desroche's findings, has been pointed out effectively by John H. Yoder (1969:250ff.).

17. A balanced examination of these materials is found in David Ewert (1980).

18. An excellent accent on the major thrust of Scripture in the face of different scenarios is found in Paul Erb (1955).

19. The exaggerated use of "obedience to the great commission," as a motivation for modern Western missions under the imperialism of European colonialism, has caused some contemporary missiologists, starting with Roland Allen's reaction, to downplay its importance. For example, Lesslie Newbigin—often quoted—goes so far as to say that after Christ had given the mandate, it is no longer cited in the apostolic writings. This, of course, completely ignores the command and empowered obedience to it as confirmed by the exalted Lord's messenger (Acts 5:20) to Peter and the latter's "We must obey God rather than men" as related to that command. It obviously overlooks the command's central place in Peter's Caesarean summary of the christological event (Acts 10:42—an early, important Anabaptist text), and its most significant reiteration by the exalted Christ (Acts 26:17-20) to Paul, who most significantly ties it to the Servant Messiah of Isaiah 42:6 and 49:6, as at Antioch in Pisidia. Its structured significance for the ending-out of history within the freedom of the Christ-event was fully grasped by the sixteenth-century free churches of the Anabaptists, precisely in the context of an imperial Christendom. Franklin H. Littell has spelled that out in "The Anabaptist Theology of Mission" (1946; see Shenk, 1984) and pointed out its implications for mission and history in "A Response" to the pivotal Roman Catholic Vatican II "Religious Freedom in the Light of Revelation" (1966). It is true that this foundational dimension of the mission of the messianic community becomes functional only after Pentecost, as Harry Boer insists (1961). But, contrary to Newbigin, et al., as the above references indicate for three important turning points in the apostolic period, the relationship in the messianic movement between mandate and Spirit-anointing after Pentecost is one of ongoing interdependence. Within the *missio dei*, Lamin Sanneh has insisted, for the planting of Christian faith in West Africa, the nineteenth-century missionary transmission of the message (i.e., obedience to the great commission) was both *marginal* and *crucial* "even if in practice it may have been prosecuted by uncouth means" (Sanneh, 1983:247).

References Cited

Augustine of Hippo
413   *The City of God*. English translation by David A. Shank from the French found in *La Cité de Dieu* annotee par le Chanoine G. Bardy (1949), Paris: Bordas.

Bastide, Roger
    1972   "Preface," *Les messianismes congolais*. Martial Sinda, Paris: Payot.

Bender, Harold S.
    1955   "Augustine's Doctrine of the Church and Its Influence on the Re-
            formers," *Conference on Augustinian Thought*. Wheaton, Ill.: Wheaton
            College Department of Bible and Philosophy.

Berkhof, Hendrikus
    1966   *Christ, the Meaning of History*. London: SCM.

Boer, Harry
    1961   *Pentecost and Missions*. Grand Rapids, Mich.: Eerdmans.

Chenu, M. D.
    1962   "Libération politique et messianisme religieux," *Parole et Mission* 19.
    1967   "Un peuple messianique; Constitution de l'Eglise," *Nouvelle Revue
            Théologique* 89:9.

Congar, Yves
    1975   *Un peuple messianique*. Paris: Cerf.

Cranfield, C. E. B.
    1954   "St. Mark 13," *Scottish Journal of Theology* VII; cited in *The Presence of
            the Future: The Eschatology of Biblical Realism*. G. E. Ladd, Grand Rap-
            ids, Mich.: Eerdmans (1974).

Cross, F. L., ed.
    1958   "Augustine, St. of Hippo," *The Oxford Dictionary of the Christian
            Church*. New York: Oxford University Press.

Desroche, Henri
    1969   *Dieux d'Hommes. Dictionnaire des Messianismes et Millénarismes de l'Ere
            Chrétienne*. Paris: Mouton.
    1979   *The Sociology of Hope*. Carol Martin-Sperry, trans.; Boston: Routledge
            and Kegan Paul.

Driver, John
    1993   "The Kingdom of God: Goal of Messianic Mission," *The Transfigura-
            tion of Mission*. Wilbert R. Shenk, ed.; Scottdale, Pa.: Herald Press.

Erb, Paul
    1955   *The Alpha and the Omega: A Restatement of the Christian Hope in Christ's
            Coming*. Scottdale, Pa.: Herald Press.

Ewert, David
    1980   *And Then Comes the End*. Scottdale, Pa.: Herald Press.

Fouilloux, Etienne
    1971   "Une vision eschatologique du christianisme: *Dieu Vivant* 1945-
            1955," *Revue de l'Histoire de l'Eglise de France* (January-June).

Klaassen, Walter
    1981   "The Anabaptist Critique of Constantinian Christendom," *Mennonite
            Quarterly Review* LV:3 (July).

Ladd, George Eldon
    1974   *The Presence of the Future: The Eschatology of Biblical Realism*. Grand
            Rapids, Mich.: Eerdmans.

Littell, Franklin H.
  1946 "The Anabaptist Theology of Mission," reprinted in *Anabaptism and Mission*. Wilbert R. Shenk, ed.; 1984, Scottdale, Pa.: Herald Press.
  1966 "A Response," *The Documents of Vatican II*. Walter M. Abbott, ed.; New York: Association Press.

Moltmann, Jürgen
  1977 *The Church in the Power of the Spirit: A Contribution to Messianic Ecclesiology*. New York: Harper.

Niebuhr, Reinhold
  1937 "As Deceivers, Yet True," *Beyond Tragedy: Essays on the Christian Interpretation of History*. New York: Charles Scribner's Sons.

Origen
  1965 *Contra Celsum*. Henry Chadwick, trans.; Cambridge, England: Cambridge University Press.

Rowland, Christopher
  1985 *Christian Origins*. Minneapolis: Augsburg.
  1988 *Radical Christianity: A Reading of Recovery*. Maryknoll, N.Y.: Orbis Books.

Sanneh, Lamin
  1983 *West African Christianity: The Religious Impact*. Maryknoll, N.Y., Orbis Books.

Séguy, Jean
  1983 "(Title Unknown)," *Le Retour de Christ*. Charles Perrot, et al., eds.; Bruxelles: Facultés Universitaires St. Louis.

Shank, David A.
  1993 "Jesus the Messiah: Messianic Foundation of Mission," *The Transfiguration of Mission*. Wilbert R. Shenk, ed.; Scottdale, Pa.: Herald Press.

Shenk, Wilbert R.
  1984 *Anabaptism and Mission*. Scottdale, Pa.: Herald Press.

Stählin, G.
  1967 "The NT Now," *Theological Dictionary of the New Testament* Vol. IV. Gerhard Kittel, ed.; Geoffrey W. Bromiley, trans.; Grand Rapids, Mich.: Eerdmans.

Swartley, Willard M.
  1979 *Mark: The Way for All Nations*. Scottdale, Pa.: Herald Press.

Walls, Andrew
  1985 "Christianity," *A Handbook of Living Religions*. John R. Hinnells, ed.; Harmondsworth, Middlesex: Pelican Books.

Yoder, John H.
  1973 *The Politics of Jesus*. Grand Rapids, Mich.: Eerdmans.
  1983 "The Meaning of the Constantinian Shift," *Christian Attitudes to War, Peace, and Revolution*. Elkhart, Ind.: Goshen Biblical Seminary.

Yoder, Perry B.
  1987 *Shalom: The Bible's Word for Salvation, Justice, and Peace*. North Newton, Kans.: Faith and Life Press.

Scripture Index

Subject Index

Author Index

About the Authors

Neal Blough has served with Mennonite Board of Missions and Mission Mennonite Francais in Paris, France, since 1975 where he currently directs the Mennonite Study Center. He is author of *Christologie Anabaptiste: Pilgram Marpeck et l'humanite du Christ.*

John Driver served in Puerto Rico (1951-1965), Uruguay (1966-1974; 1985-1989), Central Argentina (1981-1982), and Spain (1977-1980; 1983-1984) as pastor and teacher. He has written *Community and Commitment, Understanding the Atonement for the Mission of the Church*, and *How Christians Made Peace with War*, among other books.

Roelf S. Kuitse taught in Indonesia (1952-1961), then was an advisor of the Islam in Africa Project (1962-1969). After nine years as pastor of the Mennonite congregation at Texel, Netherlands, he joined the faculty of the Associated Mennonite Biblical Seminaries as director of the Mission Training Center and professor of mission. He retired from this position in 1990. He has written articles on a variety of missiological topics, especially in relation to Islam.

Larry Miller was on the staff of Mennonite Board of Missions, 1975-1990. He directed the Student Centre in Paris, then was administrative director for Mennonite Board of Missions in Europe, 1984-1990. He is now executive secretary of Mennonite World Conference located in Strasbourg, France.

David A. Shank has been a missionary with Mennonite Board of Missions in Belgium (1950-1973) and Ivory Coast (1976-1990). He is author of *Who Will Answer, His Spirit First, William Wade Harris: A Prophet of Modern Times* (Aberdeen University, Ph.D. thesis), and many articles.

Wilbert R. Shenk has been director of the Mission Training Center, Associated Mennonite Biblical Seminaries (Elkhart, Indiana) since 1990. From 1965-1990 he was on the staff of Mennonite Board of Missions. He has edited *Mission Focus*, a quarterly journal, since 1972 and is a contributing editor of *International Bulletin of Missionary Research*.